PRAISE FOR *COMM*
IN A CRISIS

"I've specialized in crisis management for more than 20 years and the principles which underpin a successful crisis response haven't changed in that time. However, the external context which drives and escalates a crisis has been transformed. Kate Hartley's book provides a timely analysis of the environment in which crises emerge and must be managed. Her insights and advice on navigating this new world are essential reading for anyone wishing to emerge from a 21st-century crisis with their reputation intact."
Jonathan Hemus, Managing Director, Insignia

"Kate Hartley and the team at Polpeo have consistently delivered world-class training to hundreds of people for the PRCA, and her passion and commitment to equipping professionals to deal with crises is unparalleled. Communicate in a Crisis is an outpouring of her decades of experience in the industry: filled to the brim with anecdotes, tips and strategies that will be invaluable to anyone wanting to maximize brand impact."
Souha Khairallah MPRCA, Talent and Professional Development Director, PRCA

"Few people know as much about crisis management as Kate Hartley and she knows how to handle digital crisis communications better than anyone. This book has it all: practical advice based on years of experience, shrewd observation of well-known brands mangling their crisis responses, tips and recommendations on how to get the communications team and the spokespeople crisis-ready – and above all a sane and sympathetic approach to the people embroiled in a crisis at the sharp end. Buy this book, read it, follow Kate Hartley's advice and breathe more easily."
Adrian Wheeler, author of *Crisis Communications Management* and *Writing for the Media*

"This is a powerful companion to any how-to crisis management textbook. It's as relevant for the seasoned professional as it is to a student learning the communications craft. Whilst the principles of crisis communications haven't changed the environment has – beyond recognition. Understanding what that means to the corporation under fire and how best they should engage with all stakeholder audiences is the essence of this book. The author guides us through what it takes to achieve meaningful and authentic dialogue and gives grounded and practical advice on how to cope as a fast moving and intense scenario plays out. The importance of 'Think human' comes through loud and clear. Supported by interviews with some of the industry's luminaries and referencing plenty of memorable case studies, this is a great read for anyone interested in the business of reputation."
Alison Clarke FPRCA FCIPR, Alison Clarke Consulting

"*Communicate in a Crisis* comes at the subject from a fresh perspective. Engaging and accessible, it tackles how to respond to the new threats to brands posed by social media."
Tamara Littleton, CEO, The Social Element

"Social media has changed the way both consumers and brands behave during a crisis. This is a vital point of reference to give crisis communicators practical advice and tips on how to adapt their crisis planning and be effective in minimizing the damage limitation."
Lisa Barnett, Communications and Crisis Director, Polpeo

Communicate in a Crisis

Understand, engage and influence customer behaviour to maximize brand trust

Kate Hartley

KoganPage

Publisher's note
Every possible effort has been made to ensure that the information contained in this book is accurate at the time of going to press, and the publishers and authors cannot accept responsibility for any errors or omissions, however caused. No responsibility for loss or damage occasioned to any person acting, or refraining from action, as a result of the material in this publication can be accepted by the publisher or the author.

First published in Great Britain and the United States in 2019 by Kogan Page Limited

2nd Floor, 45 Gee Street
London
EC1V 3RS
United Kingdom

122 W 27th St, 10th Floor
New York, NY 10001
USA

4737/23 Ansari Road
Daryaganj
New Delhi 110002
India

www.koganpage.com

ISBNs

Hardback 978 0 7494 9892 4
Paperback 978 0 7494 8650 1
Ebook 978 0 7494 8682 2

British Library Cataloguing-in-Publication Data

A CIP record for this book is available from the British Library.

Library of Congress Cataloging-in-Publication Data

A CIP record is available from the Library of Congress.

Typeset by Integra Software Services, Pondicherry
Print production managed by
Printed and bound by

CONTENTS

FIGURES AND TABLES

Figures

Table

FOREWORD

When Kate asked me to write the foreword for a book she was working on, I immediately had one simple question: does the world really need another book on crisis communication?

Having read *Communicate in a Crisis*, there is a simple answer: yes, if it's this book. Because by turning the normal process-led approach on its head, Kate has produced exactly the right work at precisely the right time.

In thinking about crisis communication, it's worth quickly going back to the original, literal meaning of the word 'crisis'. Invariably, the term conjures up catastrophic images of Munch's *Scream*. It actually comes from the Greek word *krisis* meaning the turning point in a disease that indicates recovery or death. In other words, a true crisis *can* bring with it as much opportunity as it does risk, if – and only if – the response is right.

Communicate in a Crisis certainly provides a long-overdue alternative take on getting it right. But it also comes at a point in our history when few words better sum up today's almost global sense of uncertainty and unease than *crisis*.

The march of populist nationalism is inverting the traditional spectrum of left and right. As protectionism rears its head for the first time in decades, serious concerns are emerging about the Chinese slowdown and the prospect of a 2008-style global recession.

Opinion and debate on pretty much every topic has becomes polarized and bitter. Consumers are hyper-attuned to the slightest whiff of political or corporate obfuscation and demand authentic transparency. And with traditional bureaucratic approaches often failing to respond, trust in institutions of all kinds is its lowest ebb.

Our approach as business leaders and professional communicators simply has to adapt to this new normal, and this is where *Communicate in a Crisis* comes into its own. I say this mainly because approaches to crisis communication have often been too obsessed with system, process, protocol and infrastructure. To be clear, it is not that these are unimportant – quite the opposite! They are utterly critical, and Kate covers them with real panache.

But this excessive focus on the process realm ignores the essence of true crises – that they are invariably human catastrophes that require truly human responses. Responses which – beyond the all-important crisis infrastructure – ultimately come down to very human decision-making by individuals or small groups.

That decision-making isn't driven by the escalation process and contacts log in your crisis manual – no matter how crucial. Instead the best crisis communication is founded on fundamental questions of corporate values, culture and purpose, driven by an acute understanding of how consumers operate in our fast-moving social age.

In short, the key to success lies in operationalizing empathy: acknowledging that no two crises are ever quite the same and marrying operations with humanity.

Our confused and complex times present a huge opportunity for professional communicators willing to think differently. But they also represent an enormous responsibility. So as we go about safeguarding and enhancing the standing of our client or organization, it is also worth asking a simple question: *Am I adding to (or helping ease) today's collective sense of a world in crisis?*

In answering that question, I cannot imagine a better place to start than this book, and I know you will enjoy it as much as I did.

Rod Cartwright
Crisis communication counsellor

PART ONE
Understanding how consumer behaviour has changed

Introduction

There are some fantastic books available to corporate communicators that give advice on the best ways to manage communications through a crisis (Adrian Wheeler's *Crisis Communications Management Practice Book* for the PRCA, for example). I wanted to write a book that focused on the way that ordinary people behave in a crisis, how they respond to brands and organizations and how that has changed with the rise of social media and digital communications.

Organizations today face an unprecedented level of scrutiny by consumers, and are judged – rightly or wrongly – for every action they take. The balance of power is shifting. Ordinary people are putting pressure on companies and institutions at a level we have never seen before, holding them to new ethical standards and demanding complete transparency in communications.

This is changing how organizations behave. We're seeing the rise of 'purpose-driven' marketing – no longer the domain of a few, niche companies, but seen as a competitive differentiator, a way to attract consumers who want to know that the companies they buy from meet their own values. But the businesses that fail to meet these new standards have far to fall in a crisis. Those same consumers who demand more from organizations are swift to judge, and to condemn. Social and digital media give them the tools to express their outrage, organize boycotts, join campaigns and influence others at scale.

So, while the principles of crisis communications may not have changed, the environment in which a crisis plays out has changed beyond recognition.

I have spent the last 25-plus years working in public relations, reputation management and crisis communications. I co-founded Polpeo with Tamara Littleton in 2014, to train and rehearse companies in how to manage a crisis, by simulating a crisis as it unfolds on social and digital media. We've worked with some of the biggest brands in the world across Europe, the United States, the Middle East, Asia and Africa in handling a crisis. I have learned that the organizations that understand not just how consumers behave, but why – the motivations and imperatives that drive them – are better equipped to navigate and manage a crisis successfully.

Kick a brand when it's down 01

Why we love to hate our favourite brands

It's like we're breaking up. We can either be friends or hate each other. Maybe we'll even get back together, but not right now.

(ASHLEY SCARPA, FLORIDA RESTAURATEUR)[1]

Anyone who has been through a break-up will recognize the feeling. You thought you knew the person you'd committed to. And then they did something that made you question everything – who they are, what they believe in, what they stand for. You've been betrayed and your judgement is in question.

But Scarpa wasn't going through a relationship break-up. She'd bought a Volkswagen, just before news broke that the car firm had falsified information on emissions – a scandal that cost the firm at least €30 billion (the equivalent of more than two years' worth of operating profit for the firm), and from which it took two years for its share price to recover.[2] Scarpa is an environmental campaigner, so the car she drives is a statement. She felt let down: Volkswagen had broken her trust. So she hit back, by talking publicly about the betrayal.

Passion brands and betrayal

The idea of having a relationship with a brand seems strange. But some brands inspire passion. We want to be associated with them – it gives us social currency. They become part of our social identity.

Mostly, we're indifferent to brands. Our loyalty to everyday brands is declining. But some really get to us. Passion brands are those for which we feel 'loyalty beyond reason' (a phrase coined by Kevin Roberts, former Chief

Executive Officer (CEO) of Saatchi & Saatchi and author of *LoveMarks*[3]). Try to persuade a Mac user to switch to a PC, or a Harley Davidson owner to trade for a Honda, and see how that goes.

Passion brands are the ones that create real connections with people: Apple, Coca-Cola, Google, Netflix, Nike, Harley-Davidson, Ben & Jerry's. The kind of brands that stand for something. The kind you might have tattooed on your arm. But when those brands betray us, that passion turns to anger.

Gill Green is a clinical psychologist and lead consultant at business psychology firm OR Consulting. She works with businesses on areas such as conflict resolution and the effects of trauma. 'We don't just have a written contract with brands we use. We have a psychological contract with them,' she says. 'We believe we have a deal with them, that they stand for something. It might be something that we infer from the brand, rather than something it outright claims.'

This was certainly the case with Facebook, which in 2018 found itself the subject of intense scrutiny after personal data was shared with Cambridge Analytica without users' permission. It was alleged that, at worst, the data could have been used to influence political election outcomes; at best it was a breach of trust. Most people – or at least most adults – know that by using Facebook you are giving it permission to use your data to target advertising to you. When you know, more or less, where that data is going, and you see advertising for brands you've indicated you like, that seems like an ok deal.

We trust Facebook to look after some of our most personal and precious things: private conversations, relationship information, memories, photos of our children. When it broke that trust, it broke a psychological contract with its users. The backlash was swift. Facebook fell out of favour with many: an Axios/SurveyMonkey poll in March 2018 showed that its favourability among Americans had plunged, and in the United Kingdom a reported one in five people deleted their Facebook account after the scandal.[4]

Facebook knew it had messed up. Just look at Mark Zuckerberg's change in tone from this statement when he was speaking at the Crunchie Awards in San Francisco, 2007, a decade before the Cambridge Analytica scandal: 'People have really gotten comfortable not only sharing more information and different kinds, but more openly and with more people… That social norm is just something that has evolved over time'[5] to this public statement on Facebook on 21 March 2018, after the scandal had broken: 'We have a responsibility to protect your data, and if we can't then we don't deserve to serve you.'[6]

Another stark example of betrayal of trust by a brand came from Boohoo.com, an online fashion retailer that prides itself on its animal welfare policy, and is endorsed by the animal rights campaign group PETA. Boohoo.com opposes the fur trade, and sells faux fur clothes and accessories. But in December 2017 it emerged that Boohoo.com was one of a handful of British companies that were selling animal fur as faux fur (as reported by *Drapers Record* in 2018).[7] 'That led to a huge sense of betrayal,' says Gill Green.

The issue was in Boohoo.com's supply chain, and the retailer quickly discontinued trading with the offending supplier. It's a great example of how a company can have strong principles, but if its supply chain doesn't adhere to those same principles, they can backfire spectacularly. 'Provenance is so important,' says Green. 'People who care about these things are into the detail. They will track back anything in the supply chain. There are some things that are so emotive – the environment, animal welfare, children's rights – that they go right to people's core belief systems. Betray those things at your peril.'

Emotional ownership

I talk to Gemma Storey, a creative copywriter with whom I have worked for many years, creating scenarios for brands to rehearse how to manage a breaking crisis. In order to create those scenarios and make them realistic, she meticulously researches how people behave towards brands in crisis. 'As a brand, you want people to be a fan of your product, but some people get so attached to it, they feel ownership,' she tells me. She points to an example in the literary world. In 2015, Harper Lee's *Go Set a Watchman* was published, the sequel to *To Kill a Mockingbird*, which had been published in 1960, fifty-five years earlier. In it, the lawyer and hero of *Mockingbird*, Atticus Finch, is portrayed as a racist. Lee was publicly condemned by fans of *Mockingbird* and her mental health called into question; others claimed *Watchman* portrayed a far more realistic version of Atticus, the inspiration for whom came from Lee's own father. (Interestingly, *Go Set a Watchman* was actually written before *Mockingbird*. Reportedly, Lee's publishers were so intrigued by the flashbacks of Scout in the book that they suggested she write a novel based on those passages.) To many, it felt like betrayal: *Mockingbird* has traditionally been viewed as such a symbol of the fight for civil rights that to find out its hero is so fundamentally flawed feels, as the *Guardian* put it in 2015, 'as if the Statue of Liberty had been discovered to have cloven hooves'.[8]

'People have a clear image in their heads, and when it's challenged, they don't like it,' Storey tells me. 'They feel ownership of it. When that's challenged, it steals something from you.' She tells me that when *Star Wars: Episode VIII – The Last Jedi* was released, some diehard fans objected to the role women played in it. There was a crowdfunding campaign to remake the film, with the 'mistakes corrected'. 'Never mind that this is a story of intergalactic warfare,' says Storey. 'Women are perceived as taking over this male-owned space, and some male fans feel the loss.'

Storey is a gamer, as well as a writer. Nowhere is emotional ownership more prevalent than in gaming – just look at the backlash against games developers when they release something fans object to. It's brutal. I ask her why. 'Take *Dragon Age: Origins* (a BioWare game). You inhabit and identify with a character and you have different experiences based on it. Imagine you play a character whose life is turned upside down by others. You're abducted and abused by them. When you decide to play another character, you remember that experience – you take it with you. It colours your view of them and it carries through to future games in the series. This creates tensions between groups of players who've had different experiences within the same game.'

Those tensions are made very public: according to Sprout Social, YouTube's dedicated gaming section had nearly 80 million subscribers in September 2018, and represented some of YouTube's most-viewed content.[9]

From passion to hate

Love and hate are terrifyingly close to each other. There's a neuroscientific reason for that: research shows that we deal with love and hate in the same regions of our brain, the putamen and insula.[10]

There is a difference, though, in the way we deal with love and hate. Love deactivates large parts of the cerebral cortex, which is associated with reasoning. But hate only deactivates a small part. That means when we're in love, we lose the ability to reason, or think logically. We'll look past mistakes. But when we hate, our judgement is much clearer. We see all those flaws and we judge them. We may not make good decisions (hate leaves little room for compassion), but we see the world with crystal clarity. Hate is calculating.

So, if we love a brand, we'll probably overlook its minor flaws. If one product is a bit dodgy, well, that's ok. We don't stop drinking a brand of coffee just because the chain doesn't pay what we consider to be fair tax, for example. I have friends who will march on the street in protest against companies who don't pay their taxes, but still buy from Amazon (which pays what's legally required of it, but – like many companies – pays less than what many people consider to be fair in the United Kingdom). I totally relate to this. I want Amazon to pay its way, because I want to love it. I live by Amazon Prime, I watch TV via an Amazon Firestick and I read from an Amazon Kindle. It makes my life so much easier. But I also believe in paying taxes. So I feel vaguely guilty about using it, but I find my moral vacuum and carry on.

This isn't unusual, according to Green. 'You can turn against a corporate's principles, but still support it on the ground. Uber is a great example. I use Uber whenever I'm in a city that allows it. I love the service. Like many people, I've been through a couple of transitions with it. I started off not trusting the checks and balances, and then I learned more about it. Then it went through the scandal of the zero hours contracts. I don't like what it stands for as a corporate, but I completely support the drivers on the ground, so I carry on using it.'

The key, she says, is in relationships. 'With Uber, for example, you can strike up a relationship with the drivers. They represent the brand on the ground.' So while the corporate entity might not meet our standards of fairness, we can still have a relationship with it, through the people we meet every day who work for the company.

This raises another interesting issue: who actually represents the brand? In Uber's case, it's not a spokesperson in Silicon Valley. It's the driver from Ukraine who picks you up and delivers you home safely after a night out. If they support the brand, that will ultimately do more to influence your decision than any far-flung corporate scandal. That goes for the person on the checkout at your local supermarket, or the plumber who comes to fix your washing machine. They are the people directly delivering the brand experience, not a branding agency in a far away city. They're who we have the relationship with.

Imagine you've gone a step further. More people are getting corporate logos tattooed on their body (Harley, VW, Apple). Say you're one of those people. You might collect branded memorabilia and put it on display in your house. The brand is part of your cultural and social identity. It tells people a bit about who you are and what you like to do at weekends. Suddenly, you find out that it's done something terrible. It's associated with child labour, or damaging the environment, or collaborating with a dictatorship, or not paying workers a fair wage (all these are allegations that 'passion brands' have had to face). Your friends are talking about how they'll never use it again. They're deleting its app from their phones.

The brand has gone against your personal values, those 'core beliefs' that Gill Green talked to me about. And because you are so closely identified with that brand, you take it really personally. You remove the brand from your home; you cover up the tattoo. It's taken something away from you. You're in a relationship break up, and you're angry.

What triggers us to act when we're angry?

Behaviour essentially happens for two reasons. The first is positive reinforcement (behave in a certain way, get positively reinforced, keep doing it. The way a child learns, or a puppy). In a crisis or negative situation, that might mean you share a bad experience on social media, and people like or share your post. They positively reinforce what you've done. That makes you feel good, as though you belong, that others approve of what you're doing, or feel the same as you.

Green explains it like this: 'I was travelling on the train recently, and I was lucky enough to have a first class ticket. But the train company closed off the carriage, so I had to sit in the corridor next to the toilet. I posted a photo on Twitter. I got support from my friends, who liked my post. Each like reinforced what I'd done. Others had had similar experiences, which they shared. It felt like starting a movement.' Our bodies like it, too. We release endorphins (feel-good hormones) every time we see a like on a post. We get a kick from it, and a sense of taking control of a negative situation.

The second is negative reinforcement. Doing something bad takes away something bad. Attacking a brand might take away a sense of powerlessness, or a lack of control. If you attack the brand, that sense of powerless goes away.

That's a great motivator. We like to punish bad things, and kick back. If you treat me badly, I want to get back at you. It takes away my negative feeling of being out of control.

On this basis, shutting down negative conversations about your brand on social media, for example, will only make things worse. If you increase someone's sense of powerlessness by deleting their posts or shutting them down, you'll increase the motivation to keep attacking.

And then, of course, there's what OR Consulting calls the BMW club: the bitching, moaning and whining club. 'This is the most important club we can belong to,' says Green. 'Even if I've never bought anything from the brand, I want to join this club where people are moaning about a brand. It gives me a sense of purpose. I belong. And the people in that club might join me in complaining about another brand, too.'

What are the things a brand might do to trigger negative behaviour?

1 **It hits at its audiences' core beliefs and values.** Researchers Karlsson and Rodriguez at Umea University in Sweden examine brand hate in their research paper 'Why do we hate brands?'[11] In summary, if a brand creates a set of values that have deep appeal to you and your tribe, and then they do something that goes against those values, you will feel that as a personal affront. They have done that bad thing to you, not just to themselves. They've reduced your social currency, and damaged your very identity.

2 **It attacks our social norms.** We form tribes around ideas. If the tribe wants to disassociate with a brand, we will follow. We care about social norms, and don't want to be the one that's different. We want to be with people who share our echo chamber, even if we don't know them. We're attracted to belonging to the club.

3 **It goes against its own ethics and practices.** Amazon has been the subject of numerous boycotts, for issues from employee conditions to tax concerns. But Cale Guthrie Weissman, writing for Fast Company, says that Amazon has proven (so far) pretty much immune to boycotts.[12] Weissman says that if a company goes against its own set of stated values, it faces a reputational threat. But if it sticks to its stated values and is consistent in its delivery, then people probably won't change their buying habits, even if they disagree with what the company's doing. King says that the organizations most susceptible to boycotts are those who already have a reputation problem. But Amazon doesn't: it has a good reputation for delivery and service, and is consistent in how it behaves. So while it won't be completely immune to boycotts, it's likely to survive them. King says: 'If there was a boycott that was able to demonstrate that Amazon was acting in inconsistent ways, that may lead to internal strife.'

4 **It takes away our control.** If we trust in a company to protect our data, and it breaks that trust, we feel as though we've lost control of our own information. That's why data breaches – even those that don't result in the loss of financial information – attract such negative responses from people who feel they are not in control of their most personal information. And when our data is used for purposes that we don't believe we've consented to (even if, technically, we have), we feel manipulated.

   Ilka Gleibs, writing for the London School of Economics, talks about the importance of 'informed consent' in how data is collected and shared from social networks.[13] She gives this example: 'In a healthcare context, patients expect to share personal information on their health and they most likely accept that this information is shared with a specialist. Their expectations are violated, however, if they learn that the information is sold to a marketing company.' So we might understand from a company's terms that it will share our data, and be fine with that – but we'll infer that the company will only share our data in a way that we approve.

5 **It hurts something we relate to.** In 2018, commuters in the United Kingdom faced chaos as a number of rail companies changed their timetables, resulting in cancelled services and delays to thousands of people. You'd expect the commuters themselves to complain, of course. But pictures of overcrowded trains, people jostling for space at stations hit the national press day after day, accompanied by pictures taken by unhappy commuters with smartphones.

Why did this become such a big national story? It was something that everyone could relate to. People – even those not affected by the delays – identified with the commuters trying and failing to get to work. A story with a victim at the mercy of a huge corporate behemoth – in this case the rail company – is far more likely to attract attention.

And it's even more likely to attract attention when there's a clearly identified bad guy. In the case of Southern Rail, when commuters had been subjected to weeks of delays, the sight of a senior manager taking up two seats in a first class carriage on a packed and delayed train, while telling others that they couldn't sit in first class, was too much for many, who took to Twitter to vent their frustration.

Five things a brand does to trigger negative behaviour

1. Hits at core beliefs and values.
2. Attacks social norms.
3. Goes against its own ethics.
4. Takes away our control.
5. Hurts something we relate to.

Haters and trolls

Ed Latimore, the boxer and author, once said: 'Your failures make a hater happier than their own success. Haters need to see you go down to lift themselves up.'[14] There is one other reason that people love to hate people and brands, that has been facilitated by social media. Some people just love to be haters. Haters hate for a variety of reasons – social alienation, fear, a sense of injustice, powerlessness, a sense of having been wronged, a negative experience or inadequacy.

And then there are the trolls – the people who deliberately and maliciously act to bring people down, just for the fun of it. In my view, they're slightly different from the haters. Although they may exhibit some of the traits of haters, they may be less emotionally invested in their subject. They're troublemakers, lacking compassion, purely out to get a reaction.

Sometimes, it's not the brand we hate, it's the person behind it

In 2015, businessman Sir Philip Green sold his stake in UK retailer BHS for £1. According to Companies House, BHS had made a £70 million loss in 2013. It was considered to be out-dated and unfashionable. But there was a bigger problem. Its pension fund was running at a deficit. Ordinary, hard-working people were not going to get paid from a fund that they had contributed to. They would rely on a government bail out.

It was a story that gripped the UK public. BHS (originally known by its full name, British Home Stores) was part of the national identity. It represented the past in a way that people were nostalgic for, even though they hadn't shopped there for years. The story had victims: people who would lose their jobs. It broke trust: many of its employees had paid into a pension fund for years, and that money had gone. It had a villain: Sir Philip Green was portrayed as the greedy billionaire who had taken £400 million in dividends from a company that couldn't meet its pension requirements. It had a sense of unfairness, not just from broken pension promises, but also from reports that Green's dividends were paid to his wife in an offshore tax haven, so the United Kingdom – which would have to bail out the pension fund – had seen no tax benefit at all.[15]

There was a public outcry. In 2018, Green was the subject of a book, *Damaged Goods*,[16] which dragged his reputation through the mud. The High Court in the United Kingdom refused Green's request to take out an injunction to block a damning report by the Financial Reporting Council into financial misdoings at the firm ahead of its sale. Public opinion had turned firmly away from the failings of the company, and towards those they believed to be responsible.

David and Goliath: Social media is the new slingshot

In his brilliant book *David and Goliath*, Malcolm Gladwell says that we should rethink who was the likely victor and who the underdog in the legendary fight.[17] We all know the story, or at least we think we do. The Philistines and the Israelites faced each other to do battle in Judah. It was common in those days for two warring sides to fight and settle their differences by selecting two men, one from each side, to fight each other, and then letting that decide the outcome of the battle. It was efficient – risk two men, rather than waste the lives of many. Goliath was huge – the biggest warrior that the Philistines could produce to fight the Israelites, led by King Saul. His challenger was the young shepherd David, armed only with a sling and a handful of pebbles.

This is the classic story of the underdog, the improbable victor. Or is it? Gladwell says that David always had the upper hand. He was agile, and had a better weapon – a slingshot that could fire with the deadly accuracy of a modern-day handgun. Goliath, on the other hand, was laden with armour, his size making him slow and unwieldy. Gladwell also unearthed research that shows Goliath may have had a condition that led to overproduction of growth hormone, which would have explained his size. It could also have caused him to have limited vision. The comparison to brands is clear: Goliath's size hinders him, and means he can't see clearly.

The size of a brand being attacked by the little guy doesn't matter, if the little guy has the better weapon. Social media has empowered everyone with an internet connection to express their views to, and be heard by, brands that break their psychological contract. Where people were powerless before social media, they now have power to influence a brand's behaviour – or at least to make the brand sit up and take notice.

The lesson from David and Goliath is not that the underdog won, against probability. The lesson is that Goliath underestimated the power of David's weaponry. Social media is the new weaponry. And big, unwieldy brands would do well not to underestimate its power.

Summary of actions: Understand potential triggers for customers

1. Work out what is your psychological contract with your customers and with your employees. Make sure you're doing everything to uphold that contract.
2. Identify whether you have internal advocates of your brand. Are your people your brand's best promoters? List what you need to do to win them over.
3. Identify the areas of 'core belief' that matter to your audiences (and beyond). What in your business and its supply chain could impact those values, and how can you change it? Protect those core beliefs above everything.
4. Picture what your 'perfect storm' crisis might look like. What series of events could trigger negative behaviour?
5. Don't underestimate the 'new slingshot': the power of social media to start a movement. Listen carefully to what people are saying about you.

Notes

1. Preston, B (2015) Volkswagen scandal tarnishes hard-won US reputation as green company, *Guardian*, 25 September. https://theguardian.com/business/2015/sep/25/volkswagen-scandal-us-reputation-emissions.
2. Bryant, C (2017) Scandal, what scandal? *Bloomberg*, 2 November. https://bloomberg.com/gadfly/articles/2017-11-02/vw-s-40-billion-recovery-is-nothing-to-celebrate.
3. Robers, K (2005) *Lovemarks: The future beyond brands*, PowerHouse Books.
4. Hart, K and Fried, I (2018) Facebook favorability plunges, March, Axios/SurveyMonkey. https://axios.com/exclusive-poll-facebook-favorability-plunges-1522057235-b1fa31db-e646-4413-a273-95d3387da4f2.html.

5 Johnson, B (2010) Privacy no longer a social media norm, *Guardian*, 11 January. www.theguardian.com/technology/2010/jan/11/facebook-privacy.

6 Zuckerberg, M (2018) Facebook, 21 March. https://facebook.com/zuck/posts/10104712037900071.

7 Langton, K (2018) Retailers questioned by MPs over mislabelled fake fur, *Drapers Record*, 7 March. www.drapersonline.com/news/retailers-questioned-by-mps-over-mislabelled-fake-fur/7029424.article.

8 Thorpe, V, and Helmore, E (2015) Atticus Finch is a racist in *To Kill a Mockingbird*'s sequel, *Guardian*, 11 July. www.theguardian.com/books/2015/jul/11/atticus-finch-racist-go-set-watchman.

9 Barnhart, B (no date) The ultimate guide to social media for gamers, Sprout Social. https://sproutsocial.com/insights/social-media-for-gamers.

10 Zeki, S and Romaya, JP (2008) Neural correlates of hate. PLoS ONE 3(10): e3556. https://doi.org/10.1371/journal.pone.0003556.

11 Karlsson, D and Rodrigues, L (2015) *Why do we hate brands? A qualitative study of how the dark side of branding is influenced by group identification.* http://diva-portal.org/smash/get/diva2:868195/FULLTEXT01.pdf.

12 Weissman, CG (2018) Why Amazon is immune to almost any boycott, Fast Company, 2 March. www.fastcompany.com/40538592/how-amazon-is-immune-to-almost-any-boycott.

13 Gleibs, I (2018) The importance of informed consent in social media research, London School of Economics, 17 April. http://blogs.lse.ac.uk/psychologylse/2018/04/17/the-importance-of-informed-consent-in-social-media-research-2.

14 Latimore, E (2018) Why you have haters, 31 December. https://edlatimore.com/the-top-5-reasons-why-you-have-haters-if-you-arent-an-asshole.

15 Chu, B (2016) What's the real story, *Independent*, 25 April. www.independent.co.uk/news/business/news/bhs-whats-the-real-story-behind-the-collapse-a7000166.html.

16 Shah, O (2018) *Damaged Goods: The inside story of Sir Philip Green, the collapse of BHS and the death of the high street*, Portfolio Penguin.

17 Gladwell, G (2014) *David and Goliath: Underdogs, misfits and the art of battling giants*, Penguin.

The issue of declining trust in the spread of fake news

02

> The Investigatory Powers Act, 2016 (Commencement No 5 and Transitional and Saving Provisions) Regulations 2016: 'From tomorrow onwards there are new communications regulations. All calls are recorded. All phone call recordings saved. WhatsApp is monitored. Twitter is monitored. Facebook is monitored. All social media and forums are monitored. Your devices are connected to Ministry systems. Don't forward any posts or videos you receive regarding politics, government, PM etc. Writing or forwarding any message on any political and religious debate is an offence now, leading to arrest.' And then, my favourite bit: 'Take care not to send unnecessary messages.'

In 2017, variants of this message circulated on social networks and were shared on WhatsApp. I was forwarded it by a number of well-meaning friends who know I work in social media and communications. Of course it was entirely untrue, a hoax designed to worry and confuse people who are already suspicious of government policies on security and privacy. It plays on existing concerns and fears.

Some hoaxes, though, are unspeakably cruel. Following the devastating and tragic fire in the Grenfell tower block in London in which 79 people died, someone created a semi-official looking website with the story of a 'miracle' baby found alive after 12 days in the tower block.[1] Of course, the story was fake. Claims that the UK government was covering up the number of dead also circulated and were shared by people claiming that the media was being 'muzzled' (all media, presumably, apart from those sharing these stories).

The rise of fake news

The term 'fake news' went mainstream in 2016, when Craig Silverman, the media editor for online news site Buzzfeed, spotted a number of similar stories circulating on social media that were completely made up. Nothing new there, but these were interesting because they all originated from the same place – a small Macedonian town called Veles. Each story carried an outrageous claim about the hottest topic of the day: the election battle between Donald Trump and Hillary Clinton.

Headlines whipping round social media feeds included: 'Pope Francis forbids Catholics to vote for Hillary!', 'Breaking: Proof emerges that Obama was born in Kenya – Trump was right all along' and 'Robert de Niro switches to Trump!' They were almost all pro-Trump and they were designed to attract the social media attention of Trump supporters, and encourage them to share the claims on Facebook. It worked. The more outrageous the stories, the more they were shared. Buzzfeed's research shows that just one of these made-up stories generated 140,000 shares, likes and comments on Facebook. It was no accident that they were all pro-Trump; according to the report, pro-Trump stories performed better (ie were more shared) than pro-Clinton or Sanders stories. And, of course, the more they were shared, the higher their value. Algorithm-driven advertising revenue started to flow into Veles, and other people in the town rushed to capitalize on this new source of income.

Producing fake news can be a serious business. Buzzfeed found around 100 of these pro-Trump 'news' sites in Veles. They all had credible, vaguely familiar American-sounding names like WorldPoliticus.com, USConservativeToday.com and USADailypolitics.com, designed to dupe readers into believing that they were credible sources. This isn't the kind of fake news of satirical sites, designed to entertain and fool no one. This is seriously well thought through, manipulative news, designed to convince readers of its truth.

It works. Research from NewsWhip in April 2018 shows that one fake news site, Your Newswire, got more than 3.5 million Facebook 'engagements' (defined as shares, likes, reactions and comments) in February 2018 alone.[2]

Identifying and stamping out fake news is a constant battle for the likes of Facebook and Google. In 2016, both companies announced measures to restrict advertising on fake news sites.[3]

In Veles, the motivation for starting fake news sites was financial. But for others there is a darker motivation. Hackers and cybercriminals have long been the experts in social engineering – using psychology to persuade their targets to click on malicious links or download malware to their devices. Fake news is another weapon in their armoury. If it worked for Veles, it'll work for cybercriminals, too.

Why we share fake news

Why do we fall for this stuff? Mostly, because stories like these play to our fears, or to our hopes. We desperately want to believe that something good could have come from the tragedy of Grenfell Tower fire, so we'll accept a story that claims a baby has been found alive after an impossible number of days. They reinforce what we want to believe. It might suit some Trump supporters to believe the Pope had forbidden Catholics to vote for Clinton. UK citizens who don't trust their government could well believe there is a new law in place to monitor every message we send on social networks. Seemingly legitimate questions of Obama's birthplace appear to validate racist views. These are things that get straight to the core belief systems that Gill Green talked to me about in Chapter 1.

Filippo Menczer, Professor of Computer Science and Informatics at Indiana University, explains in an article for *The Conversation* in 2016 that human vulnerability to social engineering started with good reason: 'Trusting signals from our social circles and rejecting information that contradicts our experience served us well when our species adapted to evade predators. But in today's shrinking online networks, a social network connection with a conspiracy theorist on the other side of the planet does not help inform my opinions.'[4] That, he says, leads to the social media echo chambers that render us less likely to be able to distinguish real news from fake: 'Inside our bubble, we are selectively exposed to information aligned with our beliefs. That is an ideal scenario to maximize engagement, but a detrimental one for developing healthy skepticism. Confirmation bias leads us to share a headline without even reading the article.'

The three main types of fake news

According to research by Rubin et al at the University of Western Ontario,[5] there are three types of fake news:

1. Serious fabrications. These largely divide into two:
   a. Fraudulent reporting by journalists or other reporters, for example, a tabloid deliberately sensationalizing a crime story, or a celebrity scandal. This might generate headlines used as 'click bait', ie headlines that are written specifically to encourage people to click on them to read the full story
   b. Reporting where the facts are skewed or selected, because of the bias of the reporter
2. Large-scale hoaxes. Deliberate fabrication or falsification of news that may be shared by people who genuinely believe it to be true, either on social media or in some cases reported in mainstream media (for example, the fake news relating to the 2016 US election, coming out of Veles).
3. Humorous fakes, such as news satire or parody sites. These might include titles like *The Onion*, or *Private Eye*. They are not intended to deceive, but to satirise.

In July 2018, after a meeting between President Trump of the United States and President Putin of Russia, Trump faced accusations from his detractors, including Bernie Sanders, that he hadn't stood up to Putin.[6] To retaliate, Trump supporters posted on Twitter a photograph of a meeting between Barack Obama and Putin, where it appeared that Putin was pulling Obama's tie.

Of course, it was a doctored photo (what fact-checker website Snopes.com refers to as 'fauxography'). The original had been taken by White House photographer Peter Souza in 2014, at a service to commemorate 70 years since the D-Day landings. The tie-pulling had been added in later.[7]

If you stop for a minute to consider the story behind this and most other fake news headlines doing the rounds on social media, it seems pretty obvious that they are not true. Government agencies have enough to do to gather genuine intelligence, without worrying about monitoring all our cat photos on Instagram. It's unlikely that Putin would have grabbed Obama's tie in a public place with photographers watching. But we seek stories that feed our confirmation bias and reinforce our beliefs. We love a conspiracy theory.

The number of otherwise sane people who genuinely believe Princess Diana was murdered by the Royal Family never fails to astonish me.

But most people don't stop to think about whether a story is true. With a declining trust in media sources, people seek out news that they instinctively believe, and they share it. MIT research found that fake news is more likely to spread than real news.[8] It's not surprising. This isn't factual reporting. It's sensationalist story-telling, designed specifically to push all the right buttons to encourage people to share it far and wide. It's manipulative. And it's working.

Declining trust in media

Fake news itself isn't new. What's changed is the ability to share it at speed. A 2016 survey by the Pew Research Centre shows that 62 per cent of US adults get at least some of their news from social media. Fewer than 10 per cent of readers pay for their news, which means advertising models are realistically the only way forward.[9] So the drive for clicks, shares and likes isn't going to let up any time soon. If people read stories that either outrage them, or that confirm bias based on existing beliefs and experience, reporting will have to become more sensationalist in order to survive. It's not a happy picture.

No wonder, then, that according to the 2018 Edelman Trust Barometer, trust in media, governments and institutions are at an all time low.[10] That is in part a result of fake news. We know we're being served up information that isn't true. But how do we know what's true and what's a lie? Globally, nearly seven in ten respondents among the general population worry about fake news or false information being used as a weapon, and 59 per cent say that it is getting harder to tell if a piece of news was produced by a respected media organization. To add to the confusion, our definition of 'media' has changed. Increasingly, we see platforms (such as social media or search engines) as part of 'the media', together with publishers and news organizations. Once our trust has been broken – if we've been taken in by a deliberately deceptive news article, for example – we're less likely to trust a media source again. What we believe is based on our past experiences. So if we've been duped once, we're more likely to assume not just that the one article we read was bad, we'll assume everything we read is bad.

In the absence of authoritative media sources that we trust, where do we turn? The answer appears to be that we turn to individuals. The Trust Barometer shows something else that's interesting: although we don't trust institutions, we *do* trust individual experts. We may not trust the media but increasingly we trust journalists. We don't trust companies but we'll trust the CEO (at least, more than we did in 2017). The Trust Barometer finds that 'Technical experts, financial industry analysts, and successful entrepreneurs now register credibility levels of 50 per cent or higher.'

Fake news and brands in crisis

Brands are also falling victim to this fake news, and particularly brands in crisis. In almost every crisis we monitor and analyse, people will deliberately and maliciously spread false information and rumours to make the situation worse.

Starbucks faced this in 2018, after a real incident in one of its Philadelphia stores provoked outrage. Rashon Nelson and Donte Robinson, two young African-American men, arrived at Starbucks a few minutes early for a meeting. They asked to use the restroom but didn't buy anything, as they were waiting for a third man to join them. A Starbucks employee told the men the restrooms were for paying customers only, and asked them to buy something or leave. The two men brushed off the request, and the employee called the police. The two men were arrested.

The incident was filmed by customers (who confirmed that the men had done nothing wrong, other than possibly breaking the store's rule of not using the restroom without purchasing something) and the film went viral. People were outraged at their treatment, and accusations of racism were levelled at the company.[11]

Starbucks was quick to apologize. The firm took the unprecedented step of closing 8,000 of its US stores in order to deliver racial awareness training to all its employees. Starbucks' CEO, Kevin Johnson, met the two men, who both agreed to take part in the company's racial bias training. In May 2018 Nelson and Robinson agreed not to pursue a case against the city of Philadelphia, but settled for a symbolic payment of $1 each, asking instead that the city funded a $200,000 grant programme for young entrepreneurs.[12]

Shortly after the incident, rumours spread on social media that Starbucks was issuing free coffee vouchers to African-American customers by way of apology. A realistic-looking coupon spread on social media – Snopes.com believes that the coupon originated on internet forum 4chan, and was racially motivated.[13] Starbucks was forced to issue a statement to news website Business Insider confirming that the vouchers were fake. The news of the vouchers, of course, led to the story being repeated in media and social media.

Fake news is often politically motivated. A quick scroll through Snopes.com will show pages and pages of political stories that have been concocted to spread outrage to followers of one political party or another. That can also have a serious impact for brands, in the current climate of political passion.

In 2016, after the US election, PepsiCo's CEO Indra Nooyi was reported in right-wing blog Conservative Treehouse to have told Trump supporters in a *New York Times* interview to 'take their business elsewhere'. In fact, Nooyi had said in that interview that she was disappointed in the results of the election, and: 'I think we should mourn, for those of us who supported the other side. But we have to come together and life has to go on.'

Trump supporters called for a boycott on PepsiCo brands, and even on restaurants stocking PepsiCo brands. The furore led to a 5 per cent dip in PepsiCo stock through November 2016.

It seems that when we want to believe a story, we just don't stop to check the facts.

Summary of actions: Expect to tackle fake news in a crisis

1. Every time a false story is reported in the media (like the Starbucks voucher), it will resurface the original story that it's connected to. This prolongs reporting of the original crisis. Prepare your team.
2. Expect false information and rumours to spread after a crisis. Be prepared to deny it, quickly, publicly and repeatedly.
3. Inform all your staff of the truth in a crisis, regularly. If you hear something that isn't true, tell your team as well as correcting it with your public audience. They can help you spread the truth, and negate misinformation at the point of contact with customers.
4. If we don't trust institutions, but we do trust individuals, consider that when releasing a corporate statement. By using a named expert spokesperson, the statement could be more credible.
5. Be the source of truth. Always be open and honest, and release information quickly and often during a crisis. If you face fake news about your brand, you want to be the voice of authority that people turn to for the truth.

Notes

1 Farand, C (2017) Grenfell Tower fire: Fake story about miraculous baby found alive in flat sparks widespread anger, *Independent*, 26 June. https://independent.co.uk/news/uk/home-news/grenfell-tower-fire-baby-found-alive-flat-fake-news-miracle-london-north-kensington-a7809166.html.

2 Boland, G (2018) Who is still sharing fake news on social media? Newswhip, 24 April. www.newswhip.com/2018/04/still-sharing-junk-fake-news/#BsjBQSXh3CQmhbeD.99.

3 Love, J and Cooke, C (2016) Google, Facebook move to restrict ads on fake news sites, Reuters, 14 November. https://reuters.com/article/us-alphabet-advertising/google-facebook-move-to-restrict-ads-on-fake-news-sites-idUSKBN1392MM.

4 Menczer, F (2016) Misinformation on social media: Can technology save us? The Conversation, 28 November. https://theconversation.com/misinformation-on-social-media-can-technology-save-us-69264.

5 Rubin, VL, Chen, Y, and Conroy, NJ (2015) Deception detection for news: Three types of fakes, University of Western Ontario. https://onlinelibrary.wiley.com/doi/pdf/10.1002/pra2.2015.145052010083.

6 Bowden, J (2018) Bernie Sanders: Trump 'so tough' on child separations but not on Putin, The Hill, 20 July. http://thehill.com/homenews/campaign/398157-sanders-slams-trump-for-standing-up-to-migrant-children-but-not-putin.

7 Souza, P (2014) Obama White House. www.flickr.com/photos/obamawhitehouse/15518133424/in/photolist-cyUyNo-cNf8cb-dH3NUp-nsktbH-6E9GYB-cyUz67-jDLYto-oQQnv3-cNf87N-CVMsBX-7xfKHf-6E9GYr-nb8e7i-rgbJCn-cyUyZm-pDhn7W-kALgBR-pDhuqy-eahTRe-fc77U2-6Er5px-oQQtXF-bwcJ1C-nb8q8Y-6E9GYe.

8 Vosoughi, S, Roy, D, and Aral, S (2018) The spread of true and false news online, 9 March. http://science.sciencemag.org/content/359/6380/1146.

9 Matsa, KE, and Lu, K (2016) Ten facts about the changing news landscape, Pew Research Center, 14 September. www.pewresearch.org/fact-tank/2016/09/14/facts-about-the-changing-digital-news-landscape.

10 Edelman Trust Barometer (2018) www.edelman.com/trust-barometer.

11 Associated Press (2018) Black men arrested at Philadelphia Starbucks feared for their lives, *Guardian*, 19 April. https://theguardian.com/business/2018/apr/19/starbucks-black-men-feared-for-lives-philadelphia.

12 Siegel, R (2018) Two Black men arrested at Starbucks settle with Philadelphia for $1 each, Washington Post, 2 May. https://washingtonpost.com/news/business/wp/2018/05/02/african-american-men-arrested-at-starbucks-reach-1-settlement-with-the-city-secure-promise-for-200000-grant-program-for-young-entrepreneurs/?utm_term=.f047b3224090.

13 Evan, D (2018) Is Starbucks offering coupons for Black customers only? Snopes, 18 April. https://snopes.com/fact-check/starbucks-coupon-for-black-customers-only.

Who do I trust? 03

The rise of individual influencers versus declining traditional media

Influencers and trust issues

There's a strange thing happening in influencer marketing. A brand pays an 'influencer' to promote its product to the influencer's followers, because the followers trust the influencer's recommendations. But, in the case of many influencers, that recommendation isn't really theirs, because they've been paid by a brand to make it. In that scenario, what happens to trust (and, indeed, influence)? And what role do these influencers have in a crisis?

Let's start with what I mean by an 'influencer'. I think there's a problem with how we define influencers. Before the explosion in influencer marketing – a term coined by marketers to mean, broadly, paying a blogger or social media persona to promote a branded product or service to their followers – an influencer was just someone with... well, influence. Real influence. Not just lots of followers on social media. Someone who knew a subject inside out, and whose advice people listened to, valued and acted on. That advice was genuine, and could have been given in the office, in family circles or in the pub.

But social media has given everyone with an opinion a much wider reach, and influence has become a whole new industry. That's led, inevitably, to some exploitation, the creation of fake profiles and accounts that are available for hire in order to give credibility to messages, campaigns or even people, and skew that influence.

Influencer marketing, influencer advertising, influencer relations or brand advocacy?

Scott Guthrie is an influencer marketing consultant, writer and commentator. 'We need to agree the terminology,' he tells me. 'There's a difference between influencer advertising, influencer marketing, influencer relations and brand advocacy – but they're being used interchangeably. Take influencer advertising and influencer marketing. One is a one-hit wonder, and one is a longer burn, building a long-term relationship with someone who shares the same values and really understands your brand. It takes time. It might be about more than just selling products – it could be used to bring about change in opinion, or to promote a good cause, or healthy living.'

Influencer relations, he says, is commonly used by business-to-business (B2B) brands, and is more akin to media relations than to advertising. B2B influencers might be people who 'want their star to rise' as Guthrie says, but wouldn't consider being paid to promote a brand. Their income will come from something else, such as consultancy. (Guthrie himself is seen as an influencer on the influence industry, which takes me a moment to get my head around.)

Brand advocacy, on the other hand, is more akin to celebrity endorsement, says Guthrie. For example, a sports person might be an advocate for a sports clothing brand. They won't be an expert in the brand, but their celebrity is useful to the brand.

Influencer programmes: The terminology

1. **Influencer advertising:** Paying to advertise with an influencer (often a celebrity).
2. **Influencer marketing:** Creating a longer-term partnership with an influencer who shares your brand values. Co-creation of content and campaigns.
3. **Influencer relations:** Building a relationship with an influencer who does not make their money from influencer programmes, but as an expert in their field. No money changes hands.
4. **Brand advocacy:** More akin to celebrity endorsement. Long-term contract to leverage a person's celebrity to promote your brand (such as a sports personality promoting a brand of trainers).

The problem with influencers

In the same way that fake news is damaging our trust in traditional media, the issues of fake followers (self-proclaimed influencers buying likes and followers, and automating engagement in order to appear more popular) is damaging trust in influencer marketing. In 2018, Facebook launched an ad campaign that promoted its drive to eliminate abuse of the platform including deleting fake accounts. In May 2018, it revealed that it had disabled more than 1.3 billion fake accounts over six months. In August 2018, Facebook deleted 652 fake accounts and pages with links to Russia and Iran that it suspected of trying to exert political influence in the United States, United Kingdom, Middle East and Latin America.[1]

Paul Sutton is a digital marketing strategist and consultant, and runs training courses and conferences for brands and agencies, including on influencer marketing. 'The word influence and influencer marketing has been hijacked by marketers,' he tells me. 'Part of the problem we have now comes from marketers mistaking influence for popularity. If marketers will pay someone based on their follower numbers, it's not surprising that there's been a rise in people buying followers.' It's not a new issue, as Guthrie says: 'The issue of fake followers has been around forever. Some media fake their audience size to attract advertising.'

Why do people still obsess over the follower numbers, rather than looking at real influence? Sutton says it's to do with where we come from. 'Historically when we looked at media impact, we'd measure things like readership, reach and opportunities to see. So it figures that we'd do the same with influencers. It's based on eyeballs rather than behaviour.' Even the tools that emerged specifically to measure influence, he says, really only counted shares and followers. Klout, for example – which was merged into Lithium in 2018 and effectively shut down – looked at popularity and the propensity to influence, rather than measuring true influence. (It often got it wrong – I spent some time listed on the site as an 'influencer' in cooking. My friends and my partner thought that was hysterical. I'm a terrible cook.) 'Just because people are sharing, doesn't mean anyone's listening,' says Sutton. 'But at the time, Klout was all we had. Thank goodness there's a kickback now, but it's taken a long time to get there. We need to start looking at how influencers change behaviour, rather than counting followers.'

I ask him what we should count instead, to predict whether an influencer really has influence. 'There's no simple answer. But you can user trackers to see whether someone is having an impact, and how people are responding. Reach might be a small part of that. But brands want to know not just how many people a message reached, but how many people did what they wanted them to do. Did they buy something? If I reach fifty thousand people and not one of those people bought my product, what a waste of money! Track the things that matter.'

To predict that, of course, you need case study material from the influencers you work with. The good influencers, says Sutton, are already doing this. 'They treat it as a profession. They're not just taking the money and running. They'll ask a brand what they want from a campaign. They'll help you design something that hits proper objectives. They won't just sell you access to their fans. It's got to be authentic for them, too, and fit in with what they do. The better influencers, the ones who know what they're doing, are building up banks of case studies and testimonials to prove that what they does work, just like public relations agencies do, for example.'

Marketer Mark Ritson, in a brilliant column for Marketing Week (2018), quotes Facebook's head of agencies in Asia Pacific, Neil Stewart, who, when speaking at a conference in Singapore asked this question: 'Can I just ask that we don't keep using the word "influencer"? Because there's an assumption that they have influence. To be an influencer, you must have influenced something. I don't necessarily think that's true for a lot of influencers. There are plenty of influencers who have friends, followers; they have a blog and people who see their content. But until you can prove that they have influenced – so changed behaviour, an attitude or an action – I think we could almost sue them for using a false or misleading description.'[2]

Brands will soon get more savvy about which influencers to work with, avoiding those who are feigning influence where it doesn't exist. This is a relatively young industry, after all, and fraud is inevitable until the market grows up a bit. Until then, the onus lies with brands to do their research, and work with influencers who build loyalty and trust among their (real) followers. That trust could be critical if a brand needs to get a message out quickly through trusted intermediaries in a crisis situation.

But it's important to remember that trust doesn't necessarily equal influence. As Ritson says: 'Just because the person following you is human and trusts you does not mean they will be influenced by you.' And every parent will relate to his reasoning: 'My father, the inimitable Eric B Ritson, is certainly a real person (at least for the first two pints) and is a man I trust. But I would say that approximately 96 per cent of his attempts to influence my thinking during my adult life on topics as diverse as football, food, women, weather, Germans and pretty much every other topic known to humanity have ended in abject failure. Trust is not influence.'

What is real influence?

If trust isn't influence, what is? My definition, and for the purpose of this chapter, is this: a real influencer is someone who is trusted, *and* who actively changes behaviour – whether that's online or not, and whether that's the behaviour of one person or many people.

I went through the long and painful process of buying a house recently. When considering where to buy, my wife and I researched property articles, local forums, crime statistics and transport links. We went to local pubs and restaurants and talked to people about the area. When we wanted to know where to get the best deal on a mortgage, we went to an independent adviser whom we've known for years. We asked our friends to recommend a conveyancer that they knew and trusted. We turned to agents that we liked and who were respectful (we refused to buy through an agent that treated us badly in the past, even though we may have missed out on a great house). All those people and events had real influence on our decision. None of them had a huge social media following, but they had real experience that we valued and needed.

There's no doubt that some people have a serious influence over purchasing decisions and behaviour at scale. Whenever Meghan Markle (now the Duchess of Sussex) goes out in public, for example, the outfit she's wearing sells out, often in a matter of hours.[3] People want to style themselves like her, and so she has real influence over what they buy. Her influence doesn't stop at fashion. In 2018, she was named by *Vogue* magazine as one of the most influential women in the world. The magazine hailed her influence not just on fashion and style, but stated that as a 'bi-racial campaigning feminist from America, she is helping to forge a new 21st-century identity for the monarchy'.[4] A public figure in her own right, Markle's marriage to Britain's Prince Harry made her one of the most photographed and filmed women in the world. While influential in her own right before her engagement, the circumstances of her marriage propelled her influence to a whole new level. (It has nothing to do with social media: ahead of her wedding, she very sensibly deleted her social media channels and her online lifestyle site, The Tig.) What her lasting influence will be, only time will tell.

Public figures have always had the ability to change attitudes and behaviour. But they have to be genuinely passionate about the issue, or have a personal agenda, to make it real. Diana, Princess of Wales, is widely credited with changing attitudes to people with HIV when she shook the hand of an HIV positive patient in 1987, when many people didn't understand how the virus was transmitted and believed it could be caught through skin contact. After Angelina Jolie announced that she was having a double mastectomy, there was a significant increase in the number of people at risk of breast cancer going for screenings.[5] Neither issue would have had the same impact on behaviour if their proponents hadn't had a personal interest and connection with it. This is where influence is at its most powerful.

So the principle of real influence isn't waning. It's just that the term has been appropriated by marketers to mean something different.

And whether they're on social media influencers or not, we still turn to individuals – people we relate to, or aspire to be, or just believe – for advice on what to do, what to buy, how to behave. And how to respond in a crisis.

Working with influencers

In the modern definition of 'influencers', how they are categorized roughly depends on their follower and engagement numbers, and – to smart brands, at least – their potential impact on behaviour, measured by things like increased web traffic, sales and subscriptions. (I say smart brands, as research by influencer marketing platform, ZINE, shows that the majority of brands still don't ask their influencers for proof that their campaigns actually work.) ZINE's 2018 Influencer Marketing report divides influencers into four categories: 'micro influencers' (those with between two thousand and thirty thousand followers); mid-tier influencers (thirty thousand to 250 thousand followers); macro influencers (250 thousand to one million followers); and celebrity influencers (more than one million followers).[6]

And although, as Facebook's Neil Stewart said, trust isn't the be all and end all, it is, unsurprisingly, still important in influence. ZINE's research shows that people are more likely to buy from someone they feel they know and trust. And this is what will be the key to this new industry's success – people with genuine influence whose advice is trusted by those in their network, however big or small.

How to spot whether an influencer has fake followers or engagement

ZINE gives advice to brands that want to spot whether an influencer is the real deal or whether they have lots of fake accounts:

1 Check a random selection of profiles from the influencers' follower list. Check their follower to following ratio: fake accounts may look real, but they're likely to be following thousands of accounts, and only followed by a handful.

2 Check the engagement rates of the influencer. If they have thousands of followers but no engagement, they may have bought followers.

3 Check the types of engagement. It is possible to buy engagement, so if there is a similar pattern to the engagement, it could be a bot.

4 Look out for a sudden drop in follower numbers. If the social network has deleted lots of fake accounts, that could account for the drop in follower numbers.

5 Look at the location of your influencers' followers. If the influencer is writing about lifestyle in New York but all their followers are based in Iran, that should ring alarm bells.

Assuming you're working with influencers who have a real connection with their (real) followers, and are trusted by them, that could be a serious asset if you hit a crisis. Remember them in your crisis communications plans, if you need to get information out to their followers, quickly; this is something I'll explore more with Scott Guthrie again, in Chapter 19.

Don't let your influencers become the crisis

Whenever I work with a brand that uses influencer marketing, one of the scenarios they plan for is what to do if their influencers do something that reflects badly on the brand. If you're a fitness brand and you work with a sports personality, what happens if that person gets into a fight? Or an influencer for a health brand is caught doing drugs?

And sometimes the issue comes from someone else's actions entirely. YouTuber Logan Paul was dropped like a hot cake by sponsors and advertisers in early 2018 when he posted a video from Japan's Aokigahara forest (known as the 'suicide forest', because of the number of people who end their lives there). While filming, Paul came across the body of a person who had committed suicide by hanging from a tree. He carried on filming and uploaded the piece to YouTube. It went viral, and trended on YouTube, before a backlash forced Paul to take down the video.

A couple of apologies and a short stint off YouTube later, and the incident hasn't much damaged Paul. Fast forward eight months to August 2018, and a filmed fight between him and another YouTuber, KSI, generated an estimated $11 million, and drew more than 770,000 people to pay to watch it on YouTube (although The Verge reported that a million people watched it unofficially on Twitch). YouTube took the flack. Paul was part of its 'preferred programme' of YouTubers, and the platform was widely criticized for allowing the video to trend, and not paying due attention to its preferred programme members. It later severed ties with Paul, although in my view the very fact that we call Paul and others 'YouTubers' means there will always be a perceived association with the platform. Writing for The Verge in August 2018, Megan Farokhmanesh said: 'It's impossible to talk about YouTube in 2018 without examining the Aokigahara forest video. He wasn't just a disgraced YouTuber; he was a catalyst for changes to the platform.'[7] Few advertisers would want their brands associated with such controversy, and YouTube pledged to tighten up its rules on videos that were damaging to the community – including advertisers.

Media and trust

Media may be in decline, but it still has the power to effect change

Jonathan Bernstein, Head of Bernstein Crisis Management, Inc, said on his website in 2016: 'Social media's role should be to bring information to us quickly. Traditional media's role should be to bring information to us accurately.'[8]

My parents' generation would subscribe to a single newspaper, have it delivered every morning and read it over breakfast. Weekend papers were a real treat – long, lazy brunches flicking through glossy supplements and long features. My generation were more likely to buy a paper every day from a store than have one delivered, but I remember the pleasure of being led through a paper from front to back, getting my book recommendations from the review pages, and dreaming of holidays on the travel pages. Early on in my career I worked for travel firms, and I remember the phenomenal impact that being featured in a national newspaper, or on a TV travel programme, would have on sales – to the point where the companies would have to increase their call centre staff for a 24-hour period to deal with demand.

That world has largely changed – print circulation is dropping, which means 'directional' reading (being directed from one story to another by the paper's editor) has largely gone, replaced by headlines vying for attention on news sites that rely as much on social media to drive site traffic as they do loyalty from readers. As we saw in Chapter 2, fewer people than ever distinguish between news they get from newspapers and what they read on social media, and the issue of fake news means trust is at an all-time low. The truth isn't always as exciting – or as fast to uncover – as a story that's designed to elicit a response on social media.

But, despite this, traditional media still has the power to influence and effect change. The role of free media is, in part, to hold leaders, organizations and governments to account. That role has never been more important than in a 'post truth' world. While overall trust is decreasing, the Edelman Trust Barometer shows that individual journalists are seeing a resurgence in trust.[9] The biggest scandals of recent times have been uncovered by good investigative journalism. Canadian newspaper *The Globe and Mail* ran a project called 'Unfounded' in 2018 that investigated how Canadian police forces handle sexual assault charges. It won a series of awards, as did the journalist who spearheaded the project, Robyn Doolittle.[10] More importantly, it promoted law enforcement agencies to review more than 37,000 cases, and review their approach to how they deal with sexual violence. Carole Cadwalladr is the British journalist who spent two years researching and uncovering the story behind the Facebook and Cambridge Analytica scandal. Amelia Gentleman won the Paul Foot award for investigative and campaigning journalism for her research and reporting into the Windrush scandal in 2018, which resulted in the Home Secretary, Amber Rudd, resigning. Both Cadwalladr and Gentleman, together with the *Guardian*'s editor, Katharine Viner, were also listed by *Vogue* as among the most influential women in the world.

Perhaps traditional media are finding their voice. And there's hope for its future. In 2017, a Reuters report showed that, for the first time, Millennials were starting to pay for media in record numbers, at least in the United States.[11] The number of young Americans (aged between 18 and 24) who paid for online news rose from 4 per cent in 2016 to 18 per cent in 2017. Americans aged between 25 and 34 were also more likely to pay for news in 2017 than in 2016 (8 per cent in 2016 to 20 per cent in 2017).

Why is this happening in the United States? The report suggests two reasons: younger viewers are more comfortable with the idea of paying for quality content through streaming services like Netflix or music services like Spotify; and something that the report describes as the 'Trump bump' (an increase in young people seeking quality news that they can trust, since the US election). That's encouraging news for the media industry. The *New Yorker* is one of the publications that have seen a huge rise in subscriptions from younger readers. The US news site Politico reported in 2017 that this is in part to do with younger people identifying with the brand – and, importantly, its politics – much like those passion brands we saw in Chapter 1. It's a way of saying to the world: 'This is my political leaning. These are my values.'

Talking to Politico, Dwayne Sheppard, VP consumer marketing at Condé Nast, which owns the *New Yorker*, said that Millennials are opting for print versions of the publication at 10 per cent higher than older demographics. He is quoted as saying:

> Millennials are choosing print overwhelmingly, or digital and print. It's a physical manifestation of the relationship. You're on the subway or you're in the airport and you're carrying your *New Yorker*, that's another signal of what you care about and what you choose to read.[12]

Political movements, idealism and 'anti-intellectualism'

Just as an increase in print media subscriptions may be driven in part by left-leaning Millennials who take a stand against Trump, there are others who are moving away from seeking out expert opinion, driven by a different kind of idealist movement. Matt Motta of the University of Minnesota says that a move against intellectualism has led to a decline in trust in expert opinion. Writing for the London School of Economics blog, Motta says that, in the United States at least, intellectualism has long been associated with a so-called liberal elite at least since the days of McCarthyism, which associated intellectuals with Communism.[13] Anti-intellectualism is a reaction against that liberal elite. This is associated with the rise of populism in parties on both sides of the political divide.

Motta researched attitudes to experts over more than four decades. His findings show how divided the United States is along party lines. Take the scientific community as an example. In 1974, both conservatives and liberals had roughly the same trust for the scientific community (liberals 52 per cent and conservatives 50 per cent). But in 1994, this began to diverge. By 2014, some 53 per cent of liberals and 36 per cent of conservatives trusted scientific experts. So, while people are turning to individuals over organizations (as we've seen from the Edelman Trust Barometer in Chapter 2), it seems when it comes to passion subjects – politics, religion – people are seeking out the expert advice they want to hear. We put trust in people whom we perceive to be like us.

That has important implications for brands, organizations and legislators. If, in a populist world, the so-called liberal elite are those seen to be campaigning for environmental legislation to combat climate change, for example, anti-intellectual sentiment could scupper those plans. But the association of a person with influence that people relate to, trust or aspire to be, could be incredibly powerful in changing attitudes or behaviour.

Summary of actions: Understanding influence in a crisis

Who has real influence over your audiences? Judge this not by follower numbers, but by a change in behaviour over time.

Do your research into influencers. Make sure their followers and engagement are real. Background-check them for any potential crisis by association.

Include influencers in your crisis plans (more on this in Part Three).

Don't write off traditional media, particularly for their influence over younger audiences.

Who are your influencers talking to? Are they preaching to the converted, or genuinely changing attitudes and behaviour?

Notes

1 Solon, O (2018) Facebook removes 652 fake accounts and pages meant to influence world politics, *Guardian*, 22 August. www.theguardian.com/technology/2018/aug/21/facebook-pages-accounts-removed-russia-iran.

2 Ritson, M (2018) How 'influencers' made my arse a work of art, Marketing Week, 21 June. www.marketingweek.com/2018/06/21/mark-ritson-influencers/?nocache=true&adfesuccess=1.

3 Young, S (2018) Meghan Markle's entire outfit sells out just days after attending Audi Polo Challenge 2018, *Independent*, 3 July. www.independent.co.uk/life-style/fashion/meghan-markle-outfit-sold-out-audi-polo-challenge-2018-gingham-dress-panama-grear-sandals-a8428816.html.

4 *Vogue* (2018) The Vogue 25: Meet the women shaping 2018, *Vogue*, 31 May. www.vogue.co.uk/article/vogue-25-the-women-shaping-2018.

5 Hoffman, SJ, Mansoor, Y, Natt, N, Sritharan, L, Belluz, J, Caulfield, T, Freedhoff, Y, Lavis, JN, and Sharma, AM (2017) Celebrities' impact on health-related knowledge, attitudes, behaviors, and status outcomes: Protocol for a systematic review, meta-analysis, and meta-regression analysis, Systematic Reviews, 21 January. https://systematicreviewsjournal.biomedcentral.com/articles/10.1186/s13643-016-0395-1.

6 ZINE (2018) Influencer marketing science strategy and success. https://resources.zine.co/influencer-marketing-library.

7 Farokhmanesh, M (2018) Logan Paul's redemption is proceeding exactly as planned, The Verge, 29 August. www.theverge.com/2018/8/29/17785894/logan-paul-documentary-ksi-fight-redemption.

8 Bernstein, J (2013) Defining the roles of traditional vs social media, Bernstein Crisis Management. www.bernsteincrisismanagement.com/defining-roles-of-traditional-vs-social-media.

9 Edelman Trust Barometer (2018) Edelman, 2018. www.edelman.com/trust-barometer.

10 *Global and Mail* (2018) The *Globe and Mail*'s Unfounded investigation wins Canadian Journalism Foundation prize, 15 June. www.theglobeandmail.com/canada/article-the-globe-and-mails-unfounded-investigation-wins-canadian-journalism.

11 Schwartz, J (2017) Young subscribers flock to old media, Politico, 21 October. www.politico.com/story/2017/10/21/millennials-trump-paying-for-news-244001.

12 Schwartz, J (2017) Young subscribers flock to old media, Politico, 21 October. www.politico.com/story/2017/10/21/millennials-trump-paying-for-news-244001.

13 Motta, M (2017) Had enough of experts? Anti-intellectualism is linked to voters' support for movements that are skeptical of expertise, LSE US Centre Blog on American Politics and Policy, 30 August. https://blogs.lse.ac.uk/usappblog/2017/08/30/had-enough-of-experts-anti-intellectualism-is-linked-to-voters-support-for-movements-that-are-skeptical-of-expertise.

It's outrageous! 04

Understanding the new response to outrage and bad news, and the role of social media

'Is it ever OK to bully a bully?' I'm talking to Rohit Bhargava, an innovation and marketing expert, former Ogilvy strategist, and the founder of the Non-Obvious Trends Company. Each year, he writes his signature book *Non-Obvious Trends*, curating and predicting 15 trends that will impact brand marketing.[1] The thing I love about his book is that he reviews the previous year's trends – holding himself to account. These trends are real, and they're actionable. I first heard him speak in 2018, at SXSW, the huge interactive festival held annually in Austin, Texas, and was struck by how his trends analysis resonates with what I see happening on social media during a crisis.

One of the trends highlighted in his 2018 book is 'manipulated outrage'. This sees media, data analytics and advertising 'combining forces to create a perpetual stream of noise that is intended to incite rage and illicit angry reactions on social media and in real life'. Outrage in itself isn't new, of course. It's an ancient instinct that guards against one member of a group going rogue, providing an incentive for moral behaviour. If our ancestors went against the group, they would be ostracised, at a time when being part of the group was key to survival.[2]

We feel outrage when something hits at our core beliefs or values – religious, political, moral, ethical or nationalistic. And it's happening more and more. We're living in a world where outrage is political currency. Our political leaders use it to galvanize us into voting for them. Our world is becoming more polarized between left and right.

Social media has brought about a critical shift in how we express and share outrage. For a start, we don't have to face the person against whom our outrage is directed. It's far harder to be cruel to someone face-to-face than it is if you're protected by the relative anonymity of the online world. Online, it's easy to be unkind. There's no filter.

'There's this feeling – and it's something I've talked about with my kids – that it's OK to bully a bully. But is it?' asks Bhargava. 'Take Donald Trump. Is it OK to make fun of him just because he makes fun of other people? I think it just slides us deeper into a hole where we don't find any kindness.'

How do begin to talk to your children about navigating this world, I ask him. 'I had a funny conversation with my kids trying to talk about this idea of whether it's OK to tell Alexa to shut up, or whether it's rude,' he says. 'We have to rethink how we treat each other. We have to be kind. But we're constantly battling against what we all see every day from our leaders. There aren't many situations in the world where it's acceptable to act like a politician. The things they say! If I'm marketing tyres, I'm not allowed to say that your tyres are inferior. But in politics... it's all lies, attacking each other. It's a plague on the world. We have to teach our kids that's not OK, and that in the real world, if you treat people that way you'll fail. You won't create the relationships you need to survive.'

The trouble is, there's money in outrage, just as there is in fake news. In the mid 2000s, my company was approached by an agent for an online dating site that had been relatively successful in the United States. We discovered after agreeing to the meeting that its USP was encouraging extra-marital affairs. We turned down the opportunity to work with the business, but not before discovering that its PR objective was to upset so many moral crusaders that the *Daily Mail* (a mid-market tabloid with a quasi-moral agenda) would petition to have the site closed down. The agent knew, from his experience in the United States, that the side effect of inciting moral outrage would be increased awareness of the site – and increased signups.

Outrage and viral content

Social media's business model is, as Tim Wu, author of *The Attention Merchants*,[3] puts it, 'the attraction and resell of human attention.' The manipulation of what we see in our news feeds in order to influence behaviour (likes, comments, shares). Sound familiar? Manipulating news to influence behaviour is nothing new. During the First and Second World Wars, propaganda was a critical tool in influencing people to act – to join the forces, to do vital war work – and to keep up morale.

But what gets our attention is a story that outrages us. Research by Berger and Milkman shows that we're more like to share content that evokes 'high-arousal positive (awe) or negative (anger or anxiety) emotions'.[4] Conversely, content that evokes low-arousal, or deactivating, emotions (eg sadness) is less viral. Essentially, we're share things that make us feel so strongly we have a physiological response to them. We want to do something about it. That can be positive (we might go and help someone who's been unjustly treated, for example), or negative (we turn on someone who we perceive to be a threat).

This is relevant to brands. Berger and Milkman's research shows that we're more likely to share a customer service story that arouses anger than one that is good. As part of a study into what causes virality of content, Berger and Milkman set up an experiment to see how a customer service story with two different endings would be more shared. They took the (now infamous) story of a musician travelling on United Airlines, whose guitar was damaged by baggage handlers. Researchers presented two versions of the story to two randomly selected groups of people, to see which would be shared more. In the first version, entitled 'United smashes guitar', baggage handlers appeared not to care about the guitar, and United wouldn't pay for damages (what the researches termed the 'high anger condition' version). In the second version, entitled 'United dents guitar' (the 'low anger condition'), the baggage handlers dropped the guitar but United was willing to pay for the damage. Unsurprisingly, perhaps, those people exposed to the high anger version of the story were more likely to share it.

Social media means we see more of the stories that outrage us, posted by our networks whose outrage we share. In the normal course of our lives, we wouldn't come across a lot of them. But online we see them all the time. Maybe that's why – at least in Britain – we're getting angrier. Research from agency BMB in 2017 found that 21 per cent of adults said they were experiencing 'heightened rage' compared to the previous year.[5] Sharing these stories defines who we are. It's another stamp, a signal of how we identify ourselves. 'I abhor this; I am angry at that.' It's easy to share a story, sign a petition. Or to direct our rage at an individual.

I had a strange experience a few years ago, when I wrote a blog post for my company on a Christmas ad for John Lewis (a big UK retailer with a reputation for producing ads that capture the public imagination in the run-up to Christmas). Its ad had been about a young child who remembered a Christmas present for the family's dog, pictured in a kennel outside in the snow, lit by fairy lights. Animal rights campaigners protested, saying the dog shouldn't be shown in the snow, but in the family home. A small but vocal group started a campaign group on Facebook that got enough media attention to persuade John Lewis to reshoot the ending of the ad.

My blog post didn't judge whether or not the dog should have been outside. I was simply interested in John Lewis' response, and the power of a small group of campaigners on social media. But in the days after the blog was posted, I was the subject of real vitriol from the campaigners. My personal details were posted on the campaign group, and I was accused of being a stooge for John Lewis (I've never worked for the company). I was attacked on Twitter and in the comments of the blog, most of which I deleted. It died down within a few days, and there was never any threat to my safety, but it was enough to make me realize a little of what it's like to be on the receiving end of social media outrage.

The dangers of outrage and fringe groups

Bhargava says in his book: 'In this easily offended world, fuelling outrage can lead to credibility because it offers a fringe opinion the chance to reach the masses.' (How else would Nigel Farage, for example, hold any sort of media or political sway?)

Giving fringe groups credibility, fairly obviously, can be terrifying. I meet an old friend of mine for coffee to talk to her about a wave of outrage that's leading to beatings and murder in India, the country her family is from. Ana (not her real name) tells me of a rise in crime against those who eat, sell or transport beef in India, a predominantly Hindu country where cows are protected from slaughter in many states. Media reports document 'cow vigilantes' patrolling the streets, tracking, beating and even killing anyone suspected of smuggling beef.[6] Most of those attacked are Muslim. They are people like Allimuddin Ansari, a van driver, who was brutally beaten and murdered in June 2017. His lynching by vigilantes was recorded on a mobile phone and was played out almost live on WhatsApp, where his son and wife watched on a neighbour's phone, helpless. The police arrived, but it was too late for Ansari. He died shortly afterwards, on his way to hospital. His story, sadly, is not unique. Lynchings against (mostly Muslim) beef eaters or traders are increasing, and they're being filmed and viewed on social media, which is fuelling the violence.

I ask Ana, a food anthropologist and researcher, what motivates people to behave like this. She tells me the cow is more than a religious symbol; it's part of a national Hindu identity. It's also a symbol of independence. 'Eating beef was associated with the British Empire. It was done to show power. If beefeaters are associated with empire, then not eating beef is associated with asserting our rights and reclaiming traditions and beliefs after independence.' I'd never before considered eating beef to be a symbol of political power in the United Kingdom, but it's a light-bulb moment for me: one of Britain's biggest national icons is the 'Beefeater' – the Yeoman Warders who guard the Tower of London.

There has been a sharp rise in violent crime associated with eating beef since Narendra Modi's Hindu nationalist government, the Bharatiya Janata Party (or BJP), took power in 2014. The reason why is a complex topic for a whole different book, but Ana summarizes it for me: 'There's a new wave of nationalism in India (as we're seeing elsewhere in the world) that's rejecting secularism, and Nehruvian pluralism. That, combined with a fear of "westernizing" with liberalization in things like LGBTQ+ rights, women's rights and so on, creates a visceral response in some people. They want to reclaim Mother India, and the cow is a powerful symbol of that.'

Modi's government has been conspicuously slow to condemn the violence, and few crimes are punished. In 2018, eleven men were imprisoned for life for Ansari's murder; all eleven have since been released on appeal.

This has given rise to a new counter-protest – people raised as Hindu who reject the violence meted out in their names to those involved with the beef trade, and are making their voices heard, albeit with caution. Ana is one of a group who have decided to eat beef in protest at the treatment of Muslims. Until a few weeks ago, she had never eaten beef before. 'It's a small movement, but it's important,' she says. 'Not eating beef is part of my identity, but these lynchings are happening in my name, and I want to register that I'm not ok with that.' She says that people – including her – are nervous about talking about it. 'Putting that fork in your mouth is highly politicized. You could be lynched for it. It's highly charged both for Hindus in the diaspora and in India, but people are starting to think about the politics of the food on their plate. It makes a daily, personal decision political.' Social media plays a role here, too – it brings together people who feel the same, who can use their own Instagram or Twitter feeds to show pictures of themselves eating beef in protest. Food is, after all, one of the most photographed and shared things on social media.

Anger begets anger

Molly Crockett PhD is assistant professor of psychology at Yale University, and speaks of the 'moral norm violations' that cause moral outrage, and lead to shaming and punishment. She says that the heightened experience of moral outrage could lead to two things: outrage fatigue, or even more anger. If you vent about an issue, you get even more angry about it. Her research shows that people are more likely to learn about things that go against their moral norms (triggering outrage) online, than they are in person or via traditional forms of media (print, television and radio). Expressing our outrage brings us social benefits online. If we witness something in person, and we express outrage, only the people present will hear us. But to share something online shows our moral virtue to a much wider audience. In her 2017 paper 'Moral outrage in the digital age' Crockett notes that social media sites themselves encourage this behaviour, despite their arguments that they provide neutral platforms for social behaviours that already exist.[7] But if their algorithms increase the amount of content that outrages us, and encourage us to share that outrage by rewarding us with likes, comments and more shares, could that lead to greater polarization?

As Crocket says: 'Digital media may promote the expression of moral outrage by magnifying its triggers, reducing its personal costs and amplifying its personal benefits. At the same time, online social networks may diminish the social benefits of outrage by reducing the likelihood that norm-enforcing messages reach their targets, and could even impose new social costs by increasing polarization.' We express our feelings into the echo chambers of our own networks, where our beliefs are seldom challenged by networks of people who hold the same beliefs and outrage as we do. If we're not challenged, we have no opportunity to widen our views. We become more polarized. I know that I've seen this in my own networks in the lead-up to Brexit – there was no room for discourse or debate, or to see the other side's point of view online. Even being seen to be open to another point of view could be enough to see you blocked or trolled by someone with an opposing view.

Bhargava told me he hopes the platforms will take more responsibility for their content, but we also have to show individual responsibility to get out of our own echo chambers: 'Individually and as a culture we have to make teaching media literacy more of a priority. We must get out of this habit of believing something's true, just because we see lots of people seeing, sharing and believing it.' In this world we have all the information we could possibly want at our fingertips, but, says Bhargava, 'It's possible to be both more informed and more narrow-minded. You can find anything to reinforce what you already think. Check out stories that aren't all connected. Get beyond the algorithm. Choose to read and consume things that don't fit your world view.' That includes reading foreign media sources. 'Get beyond the bias of media in a particular country,' he says. 'When I go outside of the United States, I might read *Al Jazeera* or the *Guardian*. It gives you a different perspective.' We should challenge everything: 'If we read three reviews on Amazon that say a product sucks, we'll think it must be true. But we don't know those people, and there's nothing to say they're trustworthy. That mentality of numbers becomes more of a problem when they're presented based not on merit, but on someone cheating the algorithm.'

Molly Crockett asks whether we are getting into a habit of outrage, encouraged by the algorithms of online media and social media sites. She says that we receive positive feedback for our outraged responses (likes, shares, comments) at unpredictable times, which is a pattern of reinforcement 'well-known to promote habit formation. And just as a habitual snacker eats without feeling hungry, a habitual online shamer might express outrage without actually feeling outraged.' Could we be going through the motions of outrage without really feeling it, just to be part of a group? Or, as the other theory Crockett espouses, could we be so over-exposed on social media to stories that offend us that we're experiencing more outrage? It's a frightening live experiment.

Outrage for good

Of course, there's a positive side to outrage, too. Movements like #blacklivesmatter or the #MeToo movement show the power of the crowd when views extend beyond our own echo chambers. Being part of a movement can be immensely healing for people who are survivors of crimes like rape or abuse, which – particularly in sexual abuse cases – often carry with them a residual feeling of shame or powerlessness for those affected. Knowing that you're not alone, that you have a voice, and you can bring about real change, is powerful. And, as we'll see in Chapter 7, brands can be part of that movement to great effect.

The outrage cycle

Research from Stanford psychology Professor Benoit Monin and graduate student Takuya Sawaoka in 2018 shows that when outrage goes viral, it triggers another backlash, from those who see it as bullying.[8] There's outrage

Figure 4.1 The outrage cycle

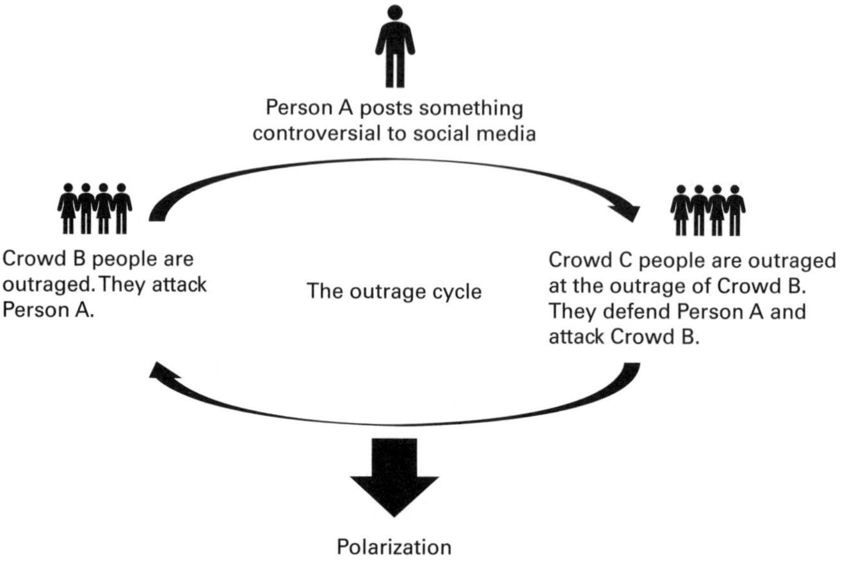

against the initial outrage. Monin and Sawaoka's research tested how people respond to public outcry at an offensive or controversial post on social media. When one person commented on the offending post, taking the originator to task, that was seen as a good thing. But when a lot of people started wading into the comments, the research participants were more likely to feel sympathy for the poster, even feeling more negative to the original person who spoke out against it.

How do we begin to counter this? I'll let Bhargava have the final say: 'We're individuals to come together for different reasons. We can disagree about politics, but we still have other things in common – sports, music, travel – our common passions. They give us moments that can bring us together. We just have to find more of them.'

Summary of actions: Dealing with the new challenges

1. Taking a stand on an issue can make good business sense – but consider carefully what the consequences might be.
2. Track the real emotions and feelings of people on social media, not those of fringe groups, or habitual outrage.

3 If you do something that causes outrage, pause before you act. Let the outrage cycle play itself out so you see a true picture of consumer feeling.

4 Create moments for people to share that bring them together, not drive them apart.

Notes

1 Bhargava, R (2019) *Non-Obvious 2019: How to predict trends and win the future*, Ideapress.

2 Crockett, MJ (2018) Modern outrage is making it harder to better society, *The Globe and Mail*, 2 March. www.theglobeandmail.com/opinion/modern-outrage-is-making-it-harder-to-bettersociety/article38179877.

3 Wu, T (2017) *The Attention Merchants*, Atlantic Books.

4 Berger, J and Milkman, K (2012) What makes online content viral? American Marketing Association, *Journal of Marketing Research*, 1 April. https://journals.sagepub.com/doi/10.1509/jmr.10.0353.

5 McLaren, H (2017) British Consumers much 'angrier' than they were in 2016, BMB, The Drum, 1 December. www.thedrum.com/news/2017/12/01/british-consumers-much-angrier-they-were-2016-finds-bmb-study.

6 Gowen, A, Sharma, M (2018) Rising hate in India, *Washington Post,* 31 October. www.washingtonpost.com/graphics/2018/world/reports-of-hate-crime-cases-have-spiked-in-india.

7 Crockett, MJ (2017) Moral outrage in the digital age, *Nature*, 18 September. www.nature.com/articles/s41562-017-0213-3#auth-1.

8 Sawaoka, T and Monin, B (2018) The paradox of viral outrage, *Psychological Science*, 9 August. https://journals.sagepub.com/doi/10.1177/0956797618780658.

I want it now 05

Managing consumer expectation for instant information

The human instinct for instant gratification

We're hardwired to want things now, and not to wait for them. In prehistoric times, we didn't know where the next meal would come from. Life depended on making quick decisions, and taking quick action. It didn't come from delaying gratification. If you're hungry, and you're offered food, you'll take it. You don't wait to see if there will be better food round the corner. We seek pleasure over pain, and delaying gratification leads to anxiety. It is only as we get older that we learn that, in some situations, delayed gratification might be better.

Shahram Heshmat, an associate professor emeritus at the University of Illinois, says in an article for *Psychology Today* (2016):

> Generally speaking, we want things now rather than later. There is psychological discomfort associated with self-denial. From an evolutionary perspective, our instinct is to seize the reward at hand, and resisting this instinct is hard. Evolution has given people and other animals a strong desire for immediate rewards... Like other animals, humans would survive and reproduce if they had a strong tendency to grab the smaller, immediate reward and skip the larger but delayed reward.[1]

This desire for immediate gratification is known in psychology as the pleasure principle. The phrase was first coined by Sigmund Freud, and although many of Freud's other theories have fallen out of favour, this one has stuck around. Broadly, the pleasure principle is the theory that our driving force is to seek immediate gratification for the most basic human needs and urges: air, food, water, shelter, sex. It responds to the need to breathe, to eat, to drink, to reproduce. If we can't satisfy those urges, we feel anxiety and tension.

But those urges and needs have evolved, too. Now, we might 'need' a new phone, or a bigger house, or a glass of wine, or a new suit. And as we're in the information age, we need information.

The importance of trust in delaying gratification

In the famous Stanford marshmallow experiments of the 1960s and 1970s, a psychologist called Walter Mischel conducted a series of tests to see how well children could delay gratification. He put marshmallows in front of children, and gave them each a choice: they could eat the marshmallow now, or they could wait 15 minutes and they'd be rewarded with a second marshmallow. The children came up with ingenious ways of trying to wait – hiding the marshmallow, covering their eyes, playing with their hair to distract themselves from temptation. For most, the urge was too strong. Only one-third of the children waited for the second marshmallow.

In 2012, Celeste Kidd, a doctoral candidate in brain and cognitive sciences at the University of Rochester, replayed the experiment, with a few important changes.[2] She wanted to see whether creating an environment of trust or mistrust would have an impact on the children's decision to eat the marshmallow straight away (giving into the pleasure principle) or delaying gratification in order to reap the bigger reward: a second marshmallow.

The children were split into two groups. Both were given a container of used crayons, and told that if they waited for a few minutes without using the crayons, the researcher would bring them a bigger and better set of art supplies that they could use. One group was brought the better supplies. The other was told by the researcher that she was sorry, but there weren't any other supplies. They could still use the crayons that were there, and the researcher helped the children open the box. Kidd repeated this experiment, but with stickers – both groups were given a sticker, and the researcher said she'd get more stickers from the room next door. One group was given more stickers, and the other was told there were no stickers after all.

Then she reran the marshmallow experiment. The children who had been denied the better crayons and stickers immediately ate the marshmallow. They didn't trust the researcher to bring them a second one.

The lesson here is that if we don't trust someone, we won't wait for them to do what they say they'll do. Apply that principle to a brand managing a crisis. Joe Smith contacts a retailer that has had its customer database hacked. He's concerned that his financial information has been stolen and compromised. Joe has been a loyal customer of the store for many years, and has a good relationship with it. He trusts it. Jane Brown also contacts the retailer. She too is worried that her data has been compromised. But she's had a different experience from Joe. She shops in another branch from Joe, and there have been a few times that the store has let her down. She doesn't trust it.

The retailer's social media team contacts both Joe and Jane with a holding statement, something along the lines of: 'We're aware there has been a breach, and we're looking into it. We take customer security extremely seriously and we'll let you know as soon as we have more information.' (We see a lot of these kind of statements: this is a variation of a typical holding statement from a brand at the beginning of a crisis.)

Joe and Jane respond very differently to this statement. Joe believes that the retailer is looking into it, and will let him know as soon as it knows more. Jane, however, thinks the retailer is incompetent at best, and covering up a lie at worst. They're basing their responses on their previous experiences with their local store.

The only way for the retailer to get both Jane and Joe to trust them isn't in the wording of a holding statement. It's in everything that retailer has done in the years leading up to the crisis, to build up trust. Trust is the single most important factor in determining whether your customers will wait for you to give them the information they want. It determines whether they'll ride it out, and stay with you through the bad times, or leave you, dragging your name through the social media mud on their way.

Social media is driving our expectation of instant information

In the age of Amazon and Netflix, we don't have to wait for anything, anymore. If we want something delivered, we can get it from Amazon in an hour. If we want to watch the next episode of a TV series, we don't have to wait a week, we can binge watch the whole series on Netflix. We record live TV so we can fast forward through the ads. Even our TV shows are all about instant gratification: talent shows that rocket someone from obscurity to stardom overnight; makeover shows that transform a life in a few days. Technology has changed our expectations, and allows us to indulge our instinct for instant gratification. When we post to social media, we get instant feedback from our friends as they like, share and comment. Constant feedback is addictive: that little dopamine hit as we refresh the page to see more likes, shares, comments.

Social media has had a massive impact on the amount of information we get from brands, and the speed at which we get it. Before social media, if we wanted to challenge a brand, we had to make a phone call, or write a letter, or later, send an email. Mostly, we wouldn't bother – it would take too long to get a response. But now, it's easy to fire off a tweet or a Facebook post. Email changed our expectation of a response to within 24 hours. Facebook and Twitter have changed that expectation to 15 minutes.

If we don't get the immediate response that our pleasure principle wiring wants, we'll feel anxious (or worse, in a crisis situation, angry). We don't want delay. We want certainty in a world where we've learned to become uncertain of others' reliability.

Speed is a measure of responsiveness in Facebook's own recommended standards for brands. In 2018, to be accredited by Facebook as 'very responsive to messages' (and to be able to show the official 'very responsive' badge on your company page), you must have responded to 90 per cent of messages, and responded within 15 minutes, over the last seven days. Fifteen minutes! Imagine having to keep that up in a crisis.

Sadly for brands, that's setting the expectations of consumers. If you've worked hard to get Facebook's badge, and put all that effort into being responsive to your customers, they'll come to expect it. If you usually respond in 15 minutes, that's what they'll look out for. If you don't respond to them in that timeframe during a crisis, they'll think you're either out of control, or hiding something.

Honestly, it's unlikely that you'll be able to keep the responsive badge during a crisis. Sheer volume will mean that you probably can't respond to everyone; and you almost certainly won't be able to respond with 15 minutes of a crisis breaking – you simply won't have the facts in time unless the crisis was predicted. Responding initially within an hour is a good guide at the start of the crisis – the 'Golden Hour' that crisis communicators often talk about.

But speed is important. During a crisis, you want to establish your brand as the voice of authority – the place people will come to get information. If they don't see it from you, they'll turn to others, who will certainly be posting, but may not be posting the right information.

Dealing with volume, at speed

'How do we deal quickly with the number of queries we get on social media in a crisis? And should we respond to all of them?' These are two of the most common questions I get asked by brands' crisis teams when we're running crisis simulations. It's a difficult thing to address for most brands. During a crisis, you should expect the volume of all contacts – calls, emails, live chat conversations and posts – to increase significantly. But nowhere will you see that more than on social media; one of the signals that alerts brands to an impending crisis is an increase in posts to social media.

Let's assume that during a crisis you'll receive so many posts and comments on social media that you can't respond to all of them. A good strategy would be to do everything you can to reduce the number of posts on Facebook about the crisis. That means a proactive information strategy: posting regular updates so people don't have to come to you to ask for information.

Group responses by the type of query you're getting, and let that inform your response. If you have hundreds of people asking when your business will reopen, for example, post the answer to the top of your social media pages, as well as on your website. Prepare variations on template responses to different groups of queries, to make posting quicker (but personalize them where possible).

Join up your responses. Make sure that information that is available on your website is also available on social media, to the press, and also to you call centre and customer-facing employees.

Manage people's expectations. If you really can't provide information when your customers and audiences want it, tell them so, and explain why. Give them clarity on when they can expect information – this will reduce the anxiety of waiting.

Do what you say you'll do. Don't fall into the trap that I see so many companies caught by when they're rehearsing their crisis response: saying they'll update people and then getting distracted with managing the crisis, and not delivering on the promise.

If you can, bring in additional team members. That could be through a specialist agency, or people you know and trust in-house.

Don't sacrifice truth for speed

The most important thing is to make sure you don't lose the truth in the rush to communicate quickly. In May 2017, BA's computer system crashed, just as thousands of families were travelling on holiday during the half-term break. It affected more than 1,000 flights, and 75,000 people whose holidays, and in some cases weddings, had been ruined. Others couldn't access medication that was in their hold luggage, while BA struggled to match bags to passengers. BA's statement read:

> There was a loss of power to the UK data centre which was compounded by the uncontrolled return of power which caused a power surge taking out our IT systems. So we know what happened, we just need to find out why. It was not an IT failure and had nothing to do with outsourcing of IT, it was an electrical power supply which was interrupted. We are undertaking an exhaustive investigation to find out the exact circumstances and most importantly ensure that this can never happen again.

However, Scottish and Southern Electricity, which is responsible for the local power grid, said publicly that there had been no issues with the power supply and no power surges. In the absence of detailed information from BA, media turned to other experts to explain what had happened. Data centre experts interviewed by journalists criticized BA for not having surge protection built into the data centre. A report from *The Times* on 2 June confused the issue even more by reporting that the system failure had been caused by an IT worker accidentally switching off the power supply. A blistering report in *The Economist* said that BA's CEO, Alex Cruz, was 'Better known as a cost cutter than a communicator, and it shows.'[3]

Summary of actions: Think customers first during a crisis

1. Think customers first, not media first, during a crisis. How do your customers feel? Can you make them feel less anxious by communicating with them regularly?
2. Are you responding within your usual timeframe (more or less)? If you've set expectations of speed ahead of the crisis, your customers will expect a fast response during it, too. Try to respond within the hour of the crisis breaking.
3. Triage which queries you respond to first, by the immediacy and importance of their need. Deal with the most important ones first – the ones that, if left unanswered, would cause the most anxiety to the

person asking. In the most serious crisis, that means ensuring that everyone directly affected by the crisis has the information they need to be safe. Then widen that net out to those indirectly affected: families, friends, customers.

4 Group queries, and respond to multiple questions in one response. Let your customers' queries inform your response.

5 Try to answer as many genuine queries and posts as you can. That might mean you have to scale up your social media team during a crisis so you can manage the volume.

6 Make sure you get your facts right. Don't post something that's inaccurate, for the sake of posting quickly.

Notes

1 Heshmat, S (2016) 10 reasons we rush for immediate gratification, *Psychology Today*, 6 June. https://journals.sagepub.com/doi/10.1177/0956797618780658.

2 Kidd, C (2013) Rational snacking: Young children's decision-making on the marshmallow task is moderated by beliefs about environmental reliability, Science Direct, January. www.sciencedirect.com/science/article/pii/S0010027712001849.

3 *Economist* (2017) British Airways botches its response to its latest technical woes, 3 June. www.economist.com/business/2017/06/03/british-airways-botches-its-response-to-its-latest-technical-woes.

Profile of a troll 06

Understanding and dealing with trolling behaviour

What trolling is, what motivates trolling behaviour and how to deal with it

In 2013, Caroline Criado-Perez, a journalist and feminist activist, successfully campaigned for Jane Austen's face to be printed on the United Kingdom's new £10 notes. Her campaign followed a decision to replace the face of Elizabeth Fry on £5 notes with that of Winston Churchill, which would mean there were no women other than the Queen featured on British banknotes.

The reaction was extraordinary. Criado-Perez became the target of a vicious campaign on social media (particularly Twitter), facing a torrent of abusive tweets, including threats of rape and murder. Soon, other women who had supported the campaign for the new £5 note also found themselves subjected to abuse on social media. One was Labour Member of Parliament Stella Creasy, who, like Criado-Perez, received rape and death threats.

In January 2014, two people – a 25-year-old man and a 23-year-old woman – were found guilty of sending menacing tweets to Criado-Perez. A BBC report in January 2014 suggested that the woman, Isabelle Sorley, had told police she was 'off my face on drink' when she sent the tweets. The man, John Nimmo, was, according to his defence, a social recluse, who had been bullied at school, and had learning difficulties. Both were sent to prison.[1]

In September 2014, a 33-year-old man, Peter Nunn, was prosecuted and found guilty of sending rape threats to Creasy. According to the BBC, when Nunn was asked why he'd done it, he said: 'It is just a joke. It came into my mind at the time and I thought it was really, really funny.' Nunn was jailed for 18 weeks.[2]

What motivates a troll?

The dictionary definition of trolling is 'someone who posts unkind or offensive messages on social media sites, and often tries to start arguments with other users'. What kind of person behaves like this online, and why? After Isabelle Sorley had served her time in prison, the BBC brought her face to face with a young woman, Natalie, who had been the victim of trolling for years. The interview was fascinating. Natalie asked Sorley whether she had 'felt powerful' sending the messages. Sorley's response was 'I'd be lying if I said you didn't kind of have the upper hand against the victim.' She says she didn't do it for the reaction, but it was a '10-minute Twitter splurge' while she was drunk after a night out. She didn't completely blame the drink, she said, but she 'stupidly followed the crowd'. It has made her question her mental health, and how, even when under the influence of alcohol, she could have written such explicit threats.[3]

I asked clinical psychologist Gill Green why someone might behave like this. She told me: 'Most people looking at that behaviour find it unimaginable. We can't make any sense of it. And it's done in an environment we're all familiar with.' But social media gives a public voice to people who perhaps wouldn't otherwise have one. 'Social media has mobilised and given people with mental health disorders a vehicle, a way to act on their behaviours. It opens up avenues for people to act upon impulses and express themselves in a way they couldn't have done before,' says Green.

In part, this is about attention. 'We all love attention,' Green says. 'Think about how you respond to a toddler – one of the worst things you can do is ignore them. And in the absence of positive attention, negative attention will do.' So if you can't be heard by being good, be bad. It commands attention, gives you the 'upper hand' that Sorley talked about in her interview.

For some, even the threat of punishment may not be a deterrent. 'Even if they're punished, they were nobody, and now they're somebody,' says Green. 'Potentially the perpetrator could be under huge amounts of distress. It could be a sign of a serious underlying mental health issue.'

Research in 2017 by psychologists at the School of Health Science and Psychology at Federation University in Mount Helen, Australia, suggests that 'trolls' may have high levels of cognitive empathy (the ability to understand someone's emotions) but lack affective empathy (the ability to experience and respond to those emotions).[4] They also exhibited higher than average levels of psychopathy (a lack of care about other people's feelings) and sadism (the desire to hurt someone). Combining cognitive empathy with psychopathy and sadism gives you a toxic mixture of being able to understand what will upset someone, while not caring that they're upset, or even actively trying to hurt them.

Federation University's research also said that, as psychopathy can be associated with thrill-seeking, a possible motivation for trolling is simply to create mayhem online. This is borne out by research in 2014 by Erin Buckels at the University of British Columbia.[5] According to Buckels, one of the characteristics that discriminates trolling from other forms of antisocial online behaviour (cyberbullying, for example) is its 'deceptive and 'pointless' disruptive nature. Trolls' identities and intentions are typically less clear than the average hostile internet user.

In his research into what motivates behaviour, psychologist Richard Ryan states that there are essentially two types of motivation: intrinsic (finding something 'inherently interesting or enjoyable') and extrinsic ('doing something because it leads to a separable outcome').[6] Ryan talks about 'introjected regulation' as an extrinsic motivation: being motivated to perform an action by a feeling of pressure to avoid anxiety, or to enhance their ego. In other words, trolls might be motivated by trying to improve their feeling of self-worth, or taking control, or seeking approval from others in their community.

Taking away that feeling of self-worth by ignoring them could make the problem worse. Working in communications and social media, I often hear people say 'don't feed the trolls' – in other words, don't respond, you'll only encourage them. (I have a problem with this approach in that it lays the blame at the target's door, rather than the troll's.) But if a lack of self-worth is a motivator for trolling, ignoring them isn't going to make them go away. Perhaps the aim of the troll is not to elicit a response, but simply to be heard.

Trolling as sport

Tamara Littleton is the CEO of social media agency, The Social Element, and my business partner and co-founder of crisis training company, Polpeo. She defines trolls as people who deliberately make mischief to be disruptive and annoying. 'Their end purpose is trying to disrupt others,' she told me. 'They're trying to get an emotional reaction.'

Littleton has worked in the world of digital and social media since 1995, when she was involved in managing the early chat rooms and forums that preceded social media. She remembers getting involved with Microsoft cartoon chat rooms, where you'd adopt a cartoon character as your persona, and 'speak' as that character in the chat room. It became a competition of wit.

'It could be hilariously funny, but if you didn't know what you were doing, you'd get decimated,' she says. 'People were trying to prove how quickly they could outsmart each other. If you weren't clever enough, you'd get knocked down. You had to be funny. It was a kind of sport.' But it soon turned into what Littleton describes as an early form of online bullying. 'Because everyone was hiding behind a character, no one knew who they were. In the real world, this person might be the kind of person you'd have a drink with in the pub. But online they had another persona.' Eventually, in the quest to outsmart each other, the jibes turned vicious. 'It ended up with bullying, threatening behaviour, and even encouraging suicide,' says Littleton.

The essence of trolling, she says, is 'A group of very smart people who are sarcastic and biting, but who end up going to a place that you wouldn't, just to get the last word, or to win the competition for who's the most quick-witted. That competitive streak can mean things turn nasty.'

Littleton told me about Godwin's Law – a theory from the 1990s that at some point online, someone will end up calling someone else a Nazi, or comparing them to Hitler. It can be used as a check among community managers for how healthy the community is. The longer it takes for someone to resort to calling someone else a Nazi during a heated debate, the better the health of the community. There's also an unwritten rule that once you call someone a Nazi, you've lost the argument. 'There's a sublevel of trolling, where people try to goad others into calling them Hitler,' says Littleton. 'This is trolling as an intellectual sport.'

It gets darker. If trolling is a sport, you have to have a 'winner'. That leads to trolls competing with each other for who can go the furthest. 'There's always someone who goes too far,' says Littleton. 'There was always that one kid in school who'd throw something at the teacher rather than just badmouth them. Someone who wanted that bit more attention, and who'd go the extra step to get it.'

Those extra steps are terrifying. The kinds of behaviours that Littleton and her team see online include rape threats, death threats and people encouraging behaviours like self-harm or suicide. Group behaviours even have their own words in this new world. Doxxing is where trolls deliberately share other people's personal details online, so that they'll be besieged by phone calls or even people turning up at their door. 'This is about releasing people who are worse than you,' says Littleton. 'A doxxer might not want to phone someone and threaten them themselves, but they can give out their phone number so someone else does it.'

Swatting is another relatively new phenomenon that's well known in the gaming industry. Many online games now are played with groups of friends who can hear and see each other live, even if they're not in the same room. They're connected online, and chat via headsets or video. If a player wants to prank another player, they call the police and tell them there's a hostage situation. Armed police (the SWAT team) turn up at the house, terrifying the target, and the rest of the gamers can see or hear what's going on, live. At best this is an appalling waste of police time and resource. At its most extreme, it has tragic consequences. In December 2017, Tyler Barriss, a 25-year-old man from California, made a hoax call to the police after an argument between two people playing Call of Duty escalated. At the request of one of the players, Barriss called the police and claimed there was a gunman and hostage situation at the other player's house. Armed police turned up at the address Barriss gave them. A young man called Andrew Finch opened the door. Police shot him dead when he reached for his waistband (he later turned out to be unarmed, and unconnected to either of the players – Barriss had given police the wrong address). Barriss and the two players were all charged by police.[7]

How do you determine what's a joke and what's a serious threat? If someone tweets they're going to blow up an airport, presumably you always have to take it seriously. It's a common occurrence. Littleton's agency manages the social media feeds for some of the biggest public events. During a high profile event in 2011, someone left a public comment on a social media channel saying they'd left a bomb under a seat at the venue. Littleton phoned the Metropolitan police personally, and fortunately it turned out to be a fake. But this kind of behaviour is becoming normal: threats, abuse, bullying. Managing it has become part of a social media manager's job.

Littleton says that polarizing issues such as Brexit or the US elections have made it almost acceptable to attack people. 'We form tribes online. That's great when you're in a community of people who are supporting each other. But it's terrible when there are families who can't speak to each other because of their political differences, for example. Social media allows us to have conversations that we'd avoid offline.' Littleton has her own experience of trolling, too. She and her team were brought in to manage a branded online forum for IT professionals. It had never been properly managed, and had descended into a place where anything was tolerated. 'It was full of people sharing racist and misogynistic jokes, and sexual content, and the brand had lost control,' she told me. 'The female members of the forum had all left because they couldn't take the abuse. It was a terrible place.' It didn't take long for forum members to work out that moderators had been brought in to clean up, and they didn't like it. 'They started out just pushing our boundaries, but then they got abusive. No one wanted us there spoiling their fun.' Finally, it got personal. They turned on Littleton. 'They posted pictures of me and made comments on my physical appearance. They found and published my home address. I felt unsafe then.' She called time on the project, and finally the forum was closed down.

Trolling as a group activity

'Deindividuation' – the shedding of individual identity, when we're anonymous, or part of a group – may play a role in the hostile behaviour of some users online. In the 1970s, a psychologist called Edward Diener conducted a field experiment to see whether children were more likely to break rules if they took on a different identity.[8] He studied the behaviour of 1,000 children going 'trick or treating' in costumes at Halloween, tempting them to more candy from homeowners than they'd been told they were allowed. In summary, the study found that children who were in a group were more likely to take the candy. If a child was addressed by name by the homeowner, they were less likely to take the candy. So if we're being spurred on by a group, or we're anonymous, we're more likely to break rules.

As early as 2004 – before the widespread use of social media – psychologist John Suler recognized that people are more likely to exhibit intense, expressive behaviours online as a result of what he refers to as the 'online disinhibition effect'.[9] Some of this manifests itself as what Suler calls 'benign disinhibition', where users 'show unusual acts of kindness and generosity, sometimes going out of their way to help others'. But at other times, it leads to 'toxic disinhibition', often resulting in 'rude language, harsh criticisms, anger, hatred, even threats'. This is the world of the troll.

Suler outlines six significant factors in online disinhibition:

1 'Dissociative anonymity', the disconnection between a user's online doings and their real-life identity. The user doesn't feel responsible for their actions.

2 'Invisibility', where the lack of a physical presence online provides the individual with a false sense of anonymity on the internet. In person, disapproving body language from another person might stop you saying or doing something. Without it, people are given the confidence to act

out. As Suler puts it, 'Text communication offers a built-in opportunity to keep one's eyes averted.'

3 The 'asynchronicity' of online communication. This allows people to step away from their comments. Unlike a normal conversation, you don't need to deal with someone's immediate response.
4 'Solipsistic introjection'. This is where a user unconsciously creates a character of the person they are interacting with. This persona is defined in part by the way they present themselves through messages, and in part by the subjective representation of the user. What remains is a caricature that exists almost as a fantasy – which makes it much easier for the user to aggravate them.
5 'Dissociative imagination', which allows the user to look at online interaction as more of an imaginary game than a true interaction with another human.
6 A lack of clear authority figures. The internet makes it easier for people to ignore authority. Without anyone moderating or guiding conversation online, a community is likely to have more toxicity.

I think Buckels et al (2014) have the best definition of trolling: 'cyber-trolling appears to be an internet manifestation of everyday sadism.'[10] Whatever a troll's reason for attacking another person, the internet and social media gives them the chance to behave in a more extreme way than they ever would in person. When I was researching this chapter, I had the help of a brilliant young natural sciences student, Stan Campbell. I asked him whether he thought society could solve the trolling problem, and, if so, how should we approach it. He said: 'If we are truly looking to solve the problem of trolling, we should undo this online disinhibition effect. What appears to connect most of its contributing factors is the ability of the troll to dissociate from their actions. If you bridge the gap between two real human beings, the troll and the victim, it dissolves the protective glass barrier that stands between the two. It makes it much harder for the troll to continue.'

So, if we keep communities human, a troll is more likely to realize the tangible emotional impact of their actions. Isabella Sorley's remorse was evident when she came face-to-face with a victim of trolling. She was no longer invisible, nor, as Campbell puts it: 'a caricatured figment of their psyche'. The person behind the façade is the root of the problem. Trolling, at its worst, is more than a social media issue. It's a society issue.

Summary of actions: Tips on deterring trolls and fostering healthy communities

1. Create an online community where there are clear authority figures, to show trolls they are not welcome. Have really good, strong and visible community management,
2. Set out your community rules early on. Reward and encourage good behaviour.
3. Blocking people may not prevent them coming back. It's common for people to create another account if they've been blocked from a site. Technology means you can do things like IP blocking, but it becomes a game of whackamole. If someone really wants to say their piece, they'll find a way to be heard. One option is to set the troll's posts so that no one else can see them but the originator (who is unaware). That way, they won't feel they're being silenced, but they have no negative impact on the community.
4. Take control of your own page. You can delete abusive posts. Don't confuse free speech with abusive speech. Agree what you're prepared to tolerate, and stick to it.
5. Have clear and visible community management by real people to set the standards. As Littleton says: 'You can automate the doors of a nightclub, but if you have a real person on the door, they create a first impression and a welcome.'
6. Distinguish someone with a genuine problem from a troll. Sort out any underlying problem that might be triggering bad behaviour. Differentiate between someone who's trolling and someone who's frustrated after a bad experience of the brand.
7. Confront someone who's behaving badly and tell them that if they continue, they can't be part of the community. They may moderate their behaviour.
8. Create a clear purpose. Communities can be a self-fulfilling prophecy. If everyone says it's a great community, it attracts people who want to be part of a great community.

Notes

1 BBC (2014) Two guilty over abusive tweets to Caroline Criado-Perez, BBC News Online, 7 January. www.bbc.co.uk/news/uk-25641941.

2 BBC (2014) Troll Peter Nunn guilty Of MP Stella Creasy rape tweets, BBC News Online, 2 September. www.bbc.co.uk/news/uk-england-london-29034943.

3 Thomas, E (2014) Twitter troll: What I said was utterly appalling and disgusting, BBC Newsbeat, 16 November. www.bbc.co.uk/newsbeat/article/30075370/twitter-troll-what-i-said-was-utterly-appalling-and-disgusting.

4 Sesta, N and March, E (2017) Constructing the cyber-troll: Psychopathy, sadism, and empathy, Science Direct, 1 December. www.sciencedirect.com/science/article/pii/S0191886917304270.

5 Buckels, EE et al (2014) Trolls just want to have fun, *Personality and Individual Differences*, 67, September, pp 97–102.

6 Ryan, RM (2000) Intrinsic and extrinsic motivations: Classic definitions and new directions, *Contemporary Educational Psychology*, 25, pp 54–67.

7 Johnson, A (2018) Three – including the intended victim – charged in Kansas 'swatting' death, NBC News, 24 May. www.nbcnews.com/news/crime-courts/three-including-intended-victim-charged-kansas-swatting-death-n876946.

8 Diener, E, Fraser, SC, Beaman, AL, and Kelem, RT (1976) Effects of deindividuation variables on stealing among Halloween trick-or-treaters, *Journal of Personality and Social Psychology*, 33(2), pp 178–83.

9 Suler, J (2004) The online disinhibition effect, *Cyberpsychology and Behavior*, 7(3), pp 321–26.

10 Buckels, EE et al (2014) Trolls just want to have fun, *Personality and Individual Differences*, 67, September, pp 97–102.

The conscious consumer 07

The question complex and pressures of brand transparency

In the Center for Civil and Human Rights in Atlanta, Georgia, you can read the story of how, in 1964, the Coca-Cola Company put pressure on Atlanta's society to honour its resident and civil rights leader, Martin Luther King.

King had won the Nobel Peace Prize that year, and the City of Atlanta threw a gala dinner to mark the occasion, inviting the city's society and business figures to buy tickets. But King was still a controversial figure in the city, and racism was rife. None of the city's elite would attend.

The organizing committee contacted Coca-Cola, which had (and still has) its headquarters in the city. Coke's then president was J Paul Austin, originally from Georgia, who had spent time in South Africa where he had seen first-hand the negative effects of apartheid on the economy. He agreed to intervene. A letter in the Center records his response: 'It is embarrassing for Coca-Cola to be located in a city that refuses to honor its Nobel Prize winner... We are an international business. The Coca-Cola Company does not need Atlanta. You all need to decide whether Atlanta needs the Coca-Cola Company.'

The dinner sold out.

It was a significant moment. Coca-Cola wasn't just a big employer in Atlanta, but part of a soft drinks industry that was politically charged. Soda fountains were segregated, and King himself had taken part in a famous sit-in protest with students at the Magnolia Tea Room at Rich's Department Store in 1960 – a protest that saw him arrested and jailed. (King later called for a boycott on the company for racial inequality in its employment practices; the company changed its policies, and the boycott was lifted.) The brand's intervention meant the seeds of connection between the company and its city's battle for civil rights were sown for good; the Civil Rights Museum is now located on land donated by the company.

Was this stand a moral imperative for Coca-Cola, or was it motivated by future profit, seeing the way the world was changing, and getting on the right side of history? Who knows. Whatever the motivation, the action was, of course, the right thing to do. It shows that getting involved in politics is nothing new for brands, and is a great example of how they can make significant and positive contributions to society. That can make good business sense. And, like Coke, it can mean landing up on the right side of history.

Fast-forward to 2018, when Nike ran an ad campaign featuring Colin Kaepernick, the American football player who had caused controversy by kneeling during the national anthem played before games started, in protest at a number of police shootings of unarmed African-Americans. The #takeaknee campaign gained traction, support and opposition (most notably from President Trump) and when Kaepernick ended his contract with the San Francisco 49-ers in the spring of 2017 he wasn't taken up by any other NLF team. After a reportedly heated debate internally, Nike decided to keep him under its sponsorship contract, even though he had no team. In 2018, he featured in an ad campaign with the strapline 'Believe in something, even if it means sacrificing everything.' It was a brave decision. Nike faced a serious backlash from some quarters. Nike trainers were burned in the street across the US, it faced protests and boycotts, and its stock price took a hit, initially. But within weeks a counter-protest emerged. Nike's share price reached an all-time high and digital sales were up by 36 per cent. It seems Nike's customers responded positively to it taking a stand.

'This was perfectly on brand for Nike,' says trends predictor and author, Rohit Bhargava, whose 2018 edition of his book *Non-Obvious Trends* identified a key trend as 'brand stand' – brands taking a stand on issues that their consumers care about.[1] 'There was nothing accidental about the Kaepernick campaign. This is a master marketer brand we're talking about. Nike knew what was going to happen. One of the things a brand will do if it's smart is to do an exercise ahead of a campaign to see what's the worst thing that could happen. You get five smart people in a room talking about this one, and they'd come up with people burning trainers.'

He's right. This isn't the first time that trainers have been burned to make a political point. A few weeks after the US elections in 2016, Matthew LeBretton, Vice President of Public Affairs for shoe company New Balance found himself in hot water after he told a journalist from the *Wall Street Journal* that he supported President Trump's opposition to the Trans-Pacific Partnership trade deal. The *Wall Street Journal* tweeted his view: 'The Obama admin turned a deaf ear to us & frankly w/ Pres-Elect Trump we feel things are going to move in the right direction.' Trump's opponents boycotted New Balance, and some posted videos of themselves burning or trashing their New Balance trainers on social media.

According to the *New York Times*, New Balance clarified its position in a statement that said it 'publicly supported the trade positions of Hillary Clinton, Bernie Sanders and Donald Trump prior to Election Day that focused on American manufacturing job creation'.[2] It soon faced another issue. A website known for its racist, anti-Semitic and homophobic views publicly supported New Balance's political stance, but went a step further, claiming New Balance shoes were 'the official shoes of white people'. This prompted the company to release a statement saying: 'New Balance does not tolerate bigotry or hate in any form. One of our officials was recently asked to comment on a trade policy that was taken out of context. As a 110-year-old company with five factories in the US and thousands of employees worldwide from all races, genders, cultures and sexual orientations, New Balance is a values-driven organization and culture that believes in humanity, integrity, community and mutual respect for people around the world. We have been and always will be committed to manufacturing in the United States'. I can't imagine New Balance predicted this outcome, no matter how many smart people were in the room: how many brands expect to have to rebut claims of supporting white supremacy?

The key to getting this right is understanding your audience. The message has to connect with brand values. That is what made the Kaepernick campaign work for Nike, despite the bumpy road. The message was on brand. Nike knows what its audience wants from it. And – and here if the difference between Nike and New Balance – it knew that in this case, its detractors wouldn't hurt the brand value. 'If you took Kaepernick out of the ad, there's nothing controversial in it,' Bhargava says. 'It's exactly what you expect Nike to say. So for them, it's another way to remind people who they are.'

Marketing genius, or moral imperative? As with Coca-Cola, who knows? But it sent an important message to people who wanted to hear it – and who bought Nike trainers as a result.

The age of the conscious consumer

On 20 January 2017, the day Donald Trump was inaugurated as President of the United States, Expedia released an ad called 'The Train', which shows a woman travelling the world, at first having fun, seeing new and beautiful places, but then encountering barriers, fear and hostility. She is seen joining a protest and helping refugees landing on a beach, and experiencing different cultures. The message is clear: open your heart to different cultures, broaden your view and your mindset, and welcome your neighbours without prejudice. The timing can't be a coincidence.

In November 2018 British food retailer, Iceland, released an ad that was billed as being 'banned' from being shown on television for breaking political advertising codes in the United Kingdom. (In fact, the ad was not banned, as such – it simply wasn't cleared for broadcast by Clearcast, the body responsible for assessing ads against the UK code. But 'banned', of course, is a much stronger message.) The ad was a cartoon-style film made by Greenpeace, featuring a character called Rang Tan, a tiny orang-utan who's taken up residence in a young girl's bedroom, and causing havoc. The girl is upset at the mess Rang Tan has left, and asks her why she's there. The girl listens, wide-eyed, as Rang Tan tells her that she doesn't have a home, that humans have destroyed her habitat. Narrated by Emma Thompson, Rang Tan says: 'There are humans in my forest, and I don't know what to do. They're burning it for palm oil, so I thought I'd stay with you.' The video ends with the girl promising to fight for Rang Tan's home and her future.

The message isn't party-political, and it doesn't call for specific action, other than to save the little orang-utan, who lost her mother to the destruction. It carries the retailer's pledge to ban palm oil from all its own-brand products, so there's a clear brand message there. The issue, according to Clearcast, is that the ad was made by Greenpeace, which is a political lobbying organization. The video had been running on its website for months.

While Iceland claims it genuinely wanted to get the ad on TV (pointing to a £500,000 TV spend as evidence), it seems unlikely to me that it didn't at least suspect that the ad would be blocked. Greenpeace had made the film as part of a wider campaign against the use of palm oil, and it had been blocked then – so, in my view, there would have been no reason to believe it would pass under Iceland's brand name.

Whether Iceland knew or not, it was great PR. The ad's so-called banning led to far more publicity than it would have generated had it been aired on TV. Within a couple of weeks of the ad going viral on social media, every major news outlet in the United Kingdom had covered the ad; according to The Drum (2018) it had more than 30 million shares on social media; a petition calling for the ad to be aired on national television gained three-quarters of a million signatures; and celebrities were calling for the ad to be approved for broadcast.[3] It put the supermarket ahead of a Greenpeace campaign against companies who use palm oil, positioning them with, rather than in conflict with, Greenpeace.

Getting it wrong

Edelman's 2017 'earned brand' survey shows that 57 per cent of consumers around the world buy or boycott products because of a brand's stance on political or social issues, according to the *Financial Times* (2017).[4] There have always been a few brands who've spoken out on issues that matter to them – ice cream company, Ben & Jerry's, which has long carried political messages supporting environmental and societal causes, is one good example – but, on the whole, the idea of a brand expressing a political opinion is relatively new. And it's picking up traction.

I ask Rohit Bhargava whether brands should take a stand on issues. His response is: 'It's like asking, should people have a point of view? Everyone does.' The point, he says, is whether that view is relevant to the brand. 'You can have a view, but if it doesn't relate to anything you're doing, it creates cognitive dissonance.'

As Bhargava says, nothing in Nike's campaign was unexpected or off brand. And although of course everything it does is, presumably, designed to sell more sports gear, its message was relevant and authentic to the brand. It connected with its consumers.

Not all brands get it right. Pepsi had a very different public reaction when it ran an ad that showed Kendall Jenner leaving a photoshoot on a whim, to join civil rights protesters. She walks up to a police officer and hands him a can of Pepsi, diffusing any tension in the crowd. The officer smiles with the whole crowd (who are all rather beautiful and, it would seem, very easily appeased). Against a backdrop of #blacklivesmatter and accusations of police brutality, the ad was widely condemned as being 'tone deaf', and trivializing an important issue. Perhaps most painful of all, Bernice King, the daughter of Martin Luther King Jr, tweeted a photo of her father being confronted by a police officer at a civil rights march. 'If only Daddy would have known about the power of Pepsi,' her tweet said.[5]

The issue of funding hate

Jake Dubbins is the CEO of social media agency Media Bounty, and the co-founder of the Conscious Advertising Network (CAN). Brands are concerned, he says, that by using programmatic advertising with the big networks

(Google, Facebook, YouTube) they risk their ads appearing on (and funding) sites that include hate speech, prejudice or abuse. The networks need to take more responsibility for the sites that benefit from their advertising technology, and come up with a way to block such content. He created CAN in 2018 with communications strategist Harriet Kingaby to put pressure on them to do just this.

The issue of not funding hate is clearly important to brands; CAN has some big global companies supporting it. I ask Jake what made him start this campaign alongside his regular job of running an agency. 'My kids are six and three,' he says. 'The IPPC report on climate change says we've got till 2030 to drastically change how we view climate change if we're to restrict global warming to 1.5 degrees. My kids will be eighteen and fifteen by then. I need to be able to answer them when they ask me, "Dad what did you do?"'

It's a powerful motivation. Dubbins believes that hate speech is fundamentally linked to climate change. 'There's been a huge effort by some groups to discredit climate change,' he says. 'It's all linked to division and hate. Migration is the most divisive issue, and migration is fundamentally linked to climate change. It will significantly increase if we don't sort out global warming, which will lead to more division and hatred. We live in a world where some of the mainstream media spread division and hatred of migrants, and tell us we should fear them. The longer we spend on outrage and division, the more we retreat into tribes and nationalism. And then we start denying the real problems.'

As we saw in Chapter 4, the media operates on a business model where outrage sells. This is what CAN is set up to address, says Dubbins: 'If you de-fund the model of click bait and outrage, then you make the internet a kinder place. We need a kinder media, and kinder social media discourse – right across the political spectrum.'

Dubbins calls himself a 'relentless optimist,' determined that humans will face up to the challenge ahead. 'Our collective consciousness is waking up,' he tells me. 'I'm hopeful that we'll look back and say, "We faced this significant challenge."' His optimism wavers momentarily: 'We have to,' he says, simply. 'We can't keep batting it away.'

What's stopping us from taking action? 'Everyone has their own, smaller, more immediate battles. Are my children happy at school? Can I get through what I have to do today? Until an issue hits you directly, you tend not to act. But more and more, it does hit us directly.' He points to the increasing number of huge weather events, public awareness of the impact of plastics in our oceans, the devastating wildfires that destroy homes and livelihoods. At some point, we'll all be touched directly.

The underlying principle of CAN is that brands have a role to play in this waking of public consciousness. 'Brands don't live in a vacuum,' says Dubbins. 'They're not devoid of human influence. The have an impact on people, the planet and society. They can't abdicate responsibility.' I ask him about the rise of the conscious consumer, and brands' response to it. 'Conscious brands will be the only game in town,' he tells me. 'The brands that will flourish are those where purpose is fundamental to how they behave.'

He talks, too, about the rise of 'ultra-transparency'. 'Brands can't get away with a purpose wash or green wash. They'll get found out. These days, people find out very quickly if you're saying one thing and doing another.' Not everyone can get it right all the time, but that's fine, he says. 'The important thing is communicating where you are on a journey. Don't set yourself up to be a paragon of virtue, but be clear about where you want to get to. Be honest about your ambition.'

Is there really a role for brand activism, I ask him. 'Why not? I worked with The Body Shop for years. Anita Roddick [the Body Shop's founder] was an activist, who ran a very successful business. Even when she sold it to L'Oréal, the spirit of what she did went through the acquiring brand. L'Oréal changed how it sourced many of its products.' The Body Shop has now been sold by L'Oréal to Natura, which was the first publicly listed company to achieve B Corp status (accreditation that requires businesses to 'consider the impact of their decisions on their workers, customers, suppliers, community and the environment'), according to Ethical Corporation magazine.[6]

Dubbins started CAN after one of his neighbours was beaten up in a local pub, simply for being Turkish. He was compelled to act, to do something to address a rising tide of hatred and nationalism. He got involved with Stop Funding Hate, a campaign group that puts pressure on brands not to advertise with media titles that promote division and fear (the UK's *Daily Mail* is one of the campaign's biggest targets). He met Kingaby, and the two set up CAN. It focuses on six areas: hate speech; fake news; advertising fraud; consent; diversity; and children's well-being. Advertisers sign up to the CAN manifesto and report back on how they've implemented the principles through their brands, including their advertising briefs.

'Industry ethics need to catch up with the technology of modern advertising,' says Dubbins. 'Advertising funds the internet. If we want to address the big problems of the internet – fake news, hate sites and so on – we need to address advertising. And the platforms will only take responsibility if advertisers put pressure on them.'

Do advertisers want to do this? Dubbins says they do: 'When you ask someone the simple question, whether they want the money they spend on advertising to fund hate speech, people say no, of course not. It's not just an ethical choice; it's a brand reputation issue. If your brand appears next to a message that incites racism and violence, you're associated with that message. So we're giving brands a way to put collective pressure on the platforms and media titles to sort this problem out.' I ask him how realistic is it that they'll succeed. His response is unequivocal: 'Imagine if advertisers pulled out of Twitter for a week. How long do you think it would take to find a technical solution?'

It makes sense to me. After all, brands want what their consumers want. And if consumers are becoming more conscious about how they spend their money, this isn't just an ethical issue for brands. It's a financial one.

Summary of actions: Taking a stand

1. If you're going to take a stand, do so on something that makes sense for your brand and its values. Make sure it's something that your customers genuinely care about. To do this, of course, you have to know what they care about.
2. Avoid the 'brand dissonance' that Rohit Bhargava talks about. Does your stand jar with how you behave every day? Are you trivializing an important issue?
3. Advertise with a conscience. Know where your ads are appearing, and make sure those sites reflect your brand values.
4. Bring your team on board with you, if you're taking a stand, particularly if it's something potentially divisive. If it makes sense for the brand (rather than the political view of a leader), they'll probably get behind it. Don't blindside them with it.
5. Never, ever use 'purpose wash'. If you say you stand for something, you have to mean it. If you don't, you'll get found out. Remember Gill Green (in Chapter 1) who said that the people who care about these issues will be into the detail. They'll find out if you're not genuine.

Notes

1 Bhargava, R (2018) *Non-Obvious 2018: How to predict trends and win the future*, Ideapress.

2 Maheshwari, S (2016) Statement on Trump puts New Balance shoe company in cross hairs, *New York Times*, 15 November. www.nytimes.com/2016/11/16/business/statement-on-trump-puts-new-balance-shoe-company-in-cross-hairs.html.

3 Tompkins, G (2018) Iceland's ad was never banned – but the publicity is no bad thing, The Drum, 13 November. www.thedrum.com opinion/2018/11/13/iceland-s-ad-was-never-banned-the-publicity-no-bad-thing.

4 Bond, S (2017) Consumers turn shopping into a political statement, *Financial Times*, 19 June. www.ft.com/content/7aef7e9a-52af-11e7-bfb8-997009366969.

5 King, B (2017) If only Daddy would have known about the power of Pepsi, Twitter, 5 April. https://twitter.com/berniceking/status/849656699464056832?lang=en.

6 Slavin, T (2017) Under Natura The Body Shop will return to its activist roots, Ethical Corporation, 13 September. www.ethicalcorp.com/exclusive-under-natura-body-shop-will-return-its-activist-roots.

PART TWO
The role of changing consumer behaviour in crisis management and response

The new challenges 08

Understanding the impact of changing consumer behaviour on crisis management strategies

The fundamental principles of good crisis communications and crisis management haven't changed in twenty-five years. However, the context and the environment in which those principles have to be applied has dramatically changed.

(JONATHAN HEMUS, MANAGING DIRECTOR OF SPECIALIST CRISIS MANAGEMENT CONSULTANCY INSIGNIA)

Social media has fundamentally changed how companies and consumers communicate. As we've seen, it has had a significant impact on how consumers behave in a crisis: people are more expressive of outrage, trust is at an all-time low, expectations of transparency are high, consumers are able to put unprecedented pressure on companies to raise their ethical standards, people want information immediately and fake news is spread more widely than the truth. And, against this backdrop, companies have to deal with more information than ever before.

As Jonathan Hemus, Managing Director of Insignia Communications, a specialist crisis management consultancy, says to me: 'This is a more transparent world than we've ever known. A world in which bad news knows no geographic boundaries, stakeholders are less deferential and trust is at a premium (and more easily and quickly lost than ever before). Social media has imposed additional pressures on crisis teams to deploy the same skills and principles as they've always done, but with less time, and with greater risk.'

Let's look at the impact those challenges have had.

Impact one: Information overload

'All businesses are struggling with the ways in which customers are communicating with them... they're struggling to keep up with what customers are saying. Customers aren't feeling that they're heard, at all.' I'm speaking to Dale Roberts, a customer experience expert and author, formerly Head of Customer Experience at Clarabridge. In 2017, a survey of airline passengers by Clarabridge found that 73 per cent of UK consumers and 69 per cent of US consumers have never complained to their airline. Why? Because they didn't think there was any point. In both countries, two-thirds of people reported that even when they did complain, they didn't get any response.[1]

I ask Roberts why so many people don't bother to complain any more, in a world where we have more channels than ever over which to do so.

That, says Roberts, is precisely the problem.

'The sheer volume of information we all get now means we're half listening to everyone,' he says. 'And the rawest filter of data is to ignore it completely.' As my own inbox reaches 1,500 unread emails on a fairly regular basis, I can relate to this. Ignoring it feels like a valid choice. Roberts tells me I'm in good company, which makes me feel marginally better. 'We're all overwhelmed. All the barriers have been taken away. In the past, if my flight were delayed, I'd call and get through to a real person. Now, I know I'll be directed to a contact centre. I'm one of millions, my call probably won't be answered immediately – and when it is it won't be by someone with authority to do anything for me – and I'll be put into a holding pattern. So what's the point?' Isn't that what Twitter's for, to get your complaint heard? I ask. 'It was,' Roberts says. 'But even that's overwhelming now. Just because it's on Twitter and it's public, doesn't mean it's important to an organization. There's just too much to be able to care about everything. So companies triage posts and queries to deal with what they believe to be the most important ones. Inevitably, that means missing or ignoring a lot of genuine issues.'

I feel vaguely guilty. This is exactly what I advise companies to do in crisis situations: prioritize those people who are most in need first, and then those who are likely to have the biggest influence. (Although I never advise ignoring genuine posts, of course.) In the early days of social media, I would regularly speak to brand managers in a panic because the CEO's child had seen a solitary critical post on Twitter, and the whole business had gone into crisis overdrive. Now brands are dealing with such high volumes of posts, Roberts tells me, that they probably only see the extremes – the very positive or very negative reviews and messages; those from people who are really angry and vocal; or those that a machine judges to be critically important (early rumblings of an issue that affects public health, for example).

The idea that you're more likely to be heard if you're really angry interests me. It explains why people are so vocal, so furious – to get past the filters. It's changing the way we complain. Being politely cross doesn't get you anywhere. But if you don't have the appetite for that level of anger, you probably just give up. We've all experienced the heart-sinking feeling when you know you have to speak to your local water board, or your phone provider (why is it so hard to speak to telephone companies by telephone?). If you know you're going to struggle to speak to a real person, and if the issue is marginal, why bother? We only have a finite amount of time.

Being overwhelmed by information has a negative impact on our mental health, too. Roberts tells me: 'One day recently, I had nine or ten meetings. Some of them with customers, some internal. My job is to make decisions, mostly. But by the end of the day, I couldn't function, let alone make a decision. There was too much information.' We talk about how, in the past, you might have travelled to a meeting and had a break when you could digest information. We'd never have reached what Roberts calls our cognitive limit. But in these days of video calls and remote working, we do, regularly. The same principle applies to dealing with constant information, particularly in a crisis situation, where facts change rapidly and each decision is critical. 'We don't know what the long-term effect is of dealing with information overload,' says Roberts. 'We don't take breaks any more. We're taking mental health more seriously, but we're contributing to its damage by giving ourselves too much information to take in. We're experiencing more anxiety.'

It's true that we don't have the constraints we used to have. We're always on, always accessible, with no clear boundaries. We used to talk about 'work–life balance': now the phrase is 'work–life merge'. We check work emails regularly from home, and never really switch off. We have flexibility at work, but at what cost?

'We don't have the emotional tools to deal with this constant flow of information,' says Roberts. 'Working at the weekend used to mean going into the office, taking a break for lunch, and stopping at a set time. Once you left the office, you switched off from work. But now we never really leave the office. We check your email, pick up a complaint from an unhappy customer, and we can't unsee it. Technology changes our behaviour, and our behaviour changes because of technology. We haven't developed the tools to deal with it yet.'

Impact two: Changing values

Jonathan Hemus talks to me about the change in values that has eroded trust in recent years. 'Fifty years ago, people were brought up to respect and defer to authority figures – royalty, the church, politicians, journalists, business leaders. You bestowed your trust in them, and didn't question whether they deserved your respect.' That, he says, has changed – in part because of social media: 'Media has become more probing and challenging, and social media has opened the curtains on people, organizations, institutions. Over time, we've seen that not everyone in authority is worthy of our trust and respect. So it's eroded. We've heard stories of corrupt politicians, media hacking the phones of children, celebrities who are sexual abusers, businesses avoiding tax. We don't take anything at face value any more.'

While our trust has decreased, our power (or our perception of power) has increased. 'People feel empowered to criticize and challenge authority. They have the tools to express how they feel. They have a voice that they didn't have before. In theory, they can put pressure on organizations using social media.' He agrees, though, with Roberts' view that the sheer volume of posts on social media means that the pressure takes longer to be felt: 'So many people are saying so many negative things that the threshold for something to become a genuine issue for an organization is much higher than it used to be.'

But when that volume does reach a higher threshold, it can be incredibly powerful. 'The #metoo movement couldn't have happened without social media,' says Roberts. 'Our values around gender and power have changed incredibly quickly, because we understand the scale of issues like #metoo. We learn and adapt very quickly, and this was an intergenerational value shift.'

Impact three: Doing the right thing (and being seen to be doing it)

If social media has exposed the flaws of the institutions we used to trust, and changed our values at a more rapid pace than ever before, then the impact on brands is that they must be transparent about how they operate, particularly in crisis situations. They must keep pace with these changing values.

Dale Roberts says that organizations must do right by their customers, not necessarily by their stakeholders. 'There's nothing to be lost by doing the right thing,' he ways. 'Social media and the transparency that it brings could force really positive change. Companies have to be more open when they get it wrong.' He talks about how Dido Harding, formerly CEO of TalkTalk, dealt with customers in the wake of security breaches at the firm that resulted in two record-breaking fines from the UK's data privacy watchdog, the Information Commissioner's Office. TalkTalk told customers they could only get out of their contracts if they could prove they'd had money stolen as a result of the data breach. Customers who were concerned at TalkTalk's lack of security couldn't break their contracts without facing a penalty. 'That put the burden of proof onto the customer,' says Roberts. 'It shows no desire to put things right.'

Part of the issue, he says, is that companies are set up in such a way that their responsibility is primarily to themselves. A company has to act in the best interest of itself and its shareholders, not to its customers. This is, to me, a fundamental issue in good crisis management and communications. If a company will act to protect itself and its shareholders above its customers, it has a conflict of interest. Transparency may not appear to be in the best interest of the company, or to deliver shareholder value in the short-term. A company's initial instinct might be to cover up a misdemeanour. But a combination of a media that is far more focused on investigation than breaking news, and a sceptical public disinclined to trust big corporations and ready to share bad news on social media, means that cover-ups get found out. That leads to the kind of betrayal and outrage that I examined in earlier chapters.

Roberts says consumers want companies to be more human. 'Say "I'm sorry we screwed up, and we'll find a way to put it right," rather than behaving only in the short-term interests of shareholders or the company,' he says. 'That used to work – it got companies this far after all – but social media is exposing this kind of behaviour. And it has to change.'

Impact four: The speed at which brands have to work in a crisis has changed

In Chapter 5 I looked at how consumers are not prepared to wait for information; in fact, it can cause anxiety to do so. That puts enormous pressure on brands to act fast in a crisis. We know that Facebook expects brands to respond to queries within 15 minutes to be a fast responder.

But unless you are fully prepared for the crisis, 15 minutes is unlikely to be enough time to gather all the facts. It's plenty of time, however, for consumers to bombard you with queries, criticism, rumours and even abusive posts from trolls.

Resisting the urge to respond too quickly can be difficult. When we run crisis simulations, we often throw in a scenario where some of the facts can't be verified immediately, to see how communications teams respond. The more pressure our role-players put on the crisis teams, the more likely they are to make assumptions that may turn out to be wrong. We run one scenario, for example, where a senior manager is accused publicly of unethical or even criminal behaviour by a former employee. Often, the crisis teams will respond to the pressure of public outrage by reiterating that it doesn't tolerate such behaviour, apologizing publicly, launching an investigation or even suspending the manager. They act fast to get ahead of the story. Later, the company's head of human relations confirms that the former employee had a history of making such accusations. An investigation finds no evidence of unethical behaviour. The crisis team has to backtrack, fast – and deal with the fallout from current employees who are unhappy that it was prepared to throw one of its managers under the bus so readily.

Speed may be of the essence in a crisis. But not at the cost of truth.

Impact five: The critical need for clarification and verified facts

At a conference for communications directors in late 2018, I heard the journalist and author Kate Adie OBE speak. Adie has reported on most of the big news events in my lifetime, breaking barriers for women reporting from war zones. She has been a hero of mine since I watched her report from Beijing's Tiananmen Square in 1989, as Chinese troops fired on protesters. She has reported from the ground in the war zones of Iraq, Bosnia, Northern Ireland, Rwanda and Sierra Leone; and brought to our TV screens some of the defining news events of the second half of the 20th century, such as the Iranian Embassy siege in London in 1980, the Dunblane massacre, the US bombing of Tripoli, and the *Herald of Free Enterprise* disaster at Zeebrugge. Now in her seventies, she is still reporting for the BBC, and is as full of energy and passion for her craft as ever.

She spoke of the changing environment in which news breaks, and the dangers of relying on third parties for information, particularly in a world of social media and 'fake news'. It is even more important now, she said, for communicators (she included herself in that bracket) to focus on facts, plainly told, to build trust. 'Clear, factual and trusted information, is the bedrock of democracy,' she said.

What does that mean for corporate communicators? Adie issued a plea: 'Do not use emollient words... audiences appreciate candour.' If journalists are to trust their sources of information, those sources must speak plainly and honestly. No wonder, she said, the journalists of some hard-hitting news programmes (she mentioned BBC Radio 4's flagship news programme, *Today*, in particular) are so 'gruff' (Adie's word) with their interviewees.

Adie says that she abides by four principles of journalism: get to the story, find the facts, verify the facts and report the facts. They struck me as being as critical for crisis management as for journalism, and are a good structure to use in approaching a crisis.

- **Principle one: Get to the story.**
  In a crisis, don't rely on third parties, or hearsay – find the story yourself. Go to the source of the issue, and talk to the people affected. Experience first-hand what's happening.
- **Principle two: Find the facts.**
  There will be a lot of hyperbole, emotion and rumour in a crisis. Strip all that away and get to the facts of what's happened.
- **Principle three: Verify the facts.**
  In a crisis, what appears to be fact often turns out to be wrong. If you've gone public with what you believe to be true, but it turns out later to be wrong, you will lose the confidence and trust of your audience. In her talk, Adie said that the first fact is what people remember. You have to get it right first time.
- **Principle four: Report the facts.**
  This holds as true for communicators in a crisis as it does in journalism. Nobody trusts someone who obfuscates the facts (more on the importance of truth-telling in Chapter 12). There is nothing more important that factual communication in a crisis to build trust.

Summary of actions

1. Deal with information overload. It may seem impossible to deal with the volume of data a brand is faced with, but not dealing with customers will lead to behaviour becoming more extreme in order to cut through the

noise. Invest in good social listening tools, triage who you need to respond to, and ultimately ensure everyone who needs to, feels heard.

2 Be aware of changing values. Listen to the values your customers hold close, and review them regularly. In these days of consumer movements enabled by social media, values change quickly. Brands need to keep up.

3 Do the right thing, and be seen to be doing the right thing. Know what the right thing is. Never cover up a transgression – it will be found out, and lead to brand betrayal.

4 Work at speed. Be prepared to move quickly in a crisis – but never so quickly that you can't get to the truth of the issue.

5 Clarify and verify the facts of the crisis. Adie's four principles (above) are a good guide to communicating in a crisis. Get to the story. Find the facts. Verify the facts. Report the facts.

Note

1 Clarabridge (2017) Clarabridge's unique study shines a light on customer attitudes to airlines, 25 September. Available from www.clarabridge.com/press/clarabridges-unique-study-shines-light-customer-attitudes-airlines.

What is acceptable in a crisis?

09

How to differentiate business as usual versus crisis management

In January 2015, New York City was facing what many described as a 'historic' blizzard that was scheduled to hit the city. Expecting 26 inches of snow, Mayor Bill de Blasio and Governor Andrew Cuomo made the unusual decision to shut the subway and impose a travel ban after 11pm. 'This could be a storm the likes of which we have never seen before,' de Blasio told a news conference. 'Don't underestimate this storm. Prepare for the worst'.[1]

The city was spared the full impact of the blizzard. Many accused Cuomo and de Blasio of overreacting, but not to prepare would have been far worse. In 2013, Toronto was hit by an ice storm. Thirty millimetres of freezing rain fell on the city, taking down trees, and with them telephone and power cables. Swathes of the city were left without power – and in freezing conditions that can be life-threatening. Toronto was widely criticized for not calling an emergency quickly enough, and for not preparing its citizens.[2]

Deciding when to activate a crisis plan can be tricky. Without the benefit of hindsight, you have to make a call on the facts as you know them at the time – and it's always better to be safe than sorry.

What is a crisis?

Let's go back a bit. Before you put your crisis plan into place, you need to know you're in a state of crisis. And for that to happen, you need to know what a crisis looks like for your organization. The Institute for Public Relations defines it as:

> a significant threat to operations that can have negative consequences if not handled properly. In crisis management, the threat is the potential damage a crisis can inflict on an organization, its stakeholders, and an industry. A crisis can create three related threats: (1) public safety, (2) financial loss, and (3) reputation loss.[3]

So when I talk about a crisis, I mean something that has the potential to have a serious negative impact on your brand. To damage sales, company valuation or share price, or even threaten the company's ability to operate. At its most serious, it could cause (or threaten to cause) loss of life, or pose a threat to health. It certainly has the potential to damage your reputation, if it's poorly handled.

What I don't mean is an issue that's become routine for the business, even if it's serious. (More on that later.) And I certainly don't mean what people often refer to as a 'social media crisis' – like a rogue tweet, or a few negative comments on Facebook – that might be difficult to manage for a short time, but that ultimately doesn't pose a real threat to the business. How you define a crisis will mean different things for different organizations, and that's a good place to start in your crisis communications planning: what does a crisis mean to you?

Crisis management specialist Jonathan Hemus says that one definition (although not the only one) of a crisis for a company is if an event renders you unable to conduct your core business. This came up in a discussion we had about whether a fast food restaurant running out of chicken (as happened to KFC in the United Kingdom in 2018) was really a crisis – a few people might have had to go to a different restaurant, but no one got hurt. But, as Hemus says, 'If your core business is based on selling chicken, and you are unable to source it for an extended period of time, that certainly constitutes a crisis for your business.' Fortunately for KFC, the issue was resolved quickly – and after the appropriate apologies, it was able to get back to business as usual.

The important thing is to know what a crisis might look like for your business, and define that as part of your crisis preparation.

What is an issue, rather than a crisis?

Not everything that's difficult to manage is a crisis. By reversing Hemus' definition, we can assume that an organization is not in crisis if its core business – or the reputation that effectively gives the business permission to function – is not affected. That means that anything you have to manage as part of your day-to-day business constitutes an issue, rather than a full crisis. That might seem like semantics – but if you're about to push the button on a full crisis plan, it's useful to understand the difference.

I often hear companies say they are in a permanent state of crisis, constantly putting out fires of one sort or another. But usually what they mean is they're managing issues that are so common, they've become routine. They may be serious, but they don't stop the business functioning.

Nestlé is a great example of a company that routinely has to manage some extremely serious issues. It is under constant fire from campaigners for how it is perceived to market baby milk products, and faces regular boycotts by consumers. The baby milk boycott has been going on for so long (it first started in 1974) that it has become ordinary for the company. It might flare up, and it needs close management, but it (mostly) doesn't materially affect day-to-day operations. Many of those who boycott Nestlé will be too young to remember the original issue, and will never have bought from the brand in the first place – so although the boycott might limit its audience, it doesn't necessarily affect sales. It still needs managing, of course; left alone, it could have a negative impact on reputation.

And then there are less serious issues that all companies now have to deal with – issues that bubble up on social media, and die away just as quickly. Random tweets, groundless rumours, sudden outrage. The 'social media crisis' that I hear so many companies talking about.

Lisa Barnett is Head of Crisis Services for social media agency The Social Element. She says to me: 'There's really no such thing as a pure social media crisis – a crisis might break and spread over social media, but it's rarely confined to it.' Social media can have a devastating impact on the spread of information during a crisis. And it can be used to great effect by campaigners against a brand. But, as Barnett says, 'Someone posting something from the wrong account is unlikely to herald the fall of the company.'

How do you know if you are in crisis?

Some crises are obvious (an accident, a death, a fire, a scandal, an outage). Others creep up on you. Barnett advises companies to think of a crisis as 'something out of the ordinary.' So you have to know what ordinary looks like. Social media is a great way to gauge that. What is the usual level of activity for your brand, what is the usual tone, who are the usual people that talk about you? It will be different for every company. 'If you're a utility company, for example, ordinary can mean a few hundred or even a few thousand complaints and negative posts on social media per day,' Barnett says. 'But if you're a manufacturer, tens of negative posts could indicate a serious problem with a product that you need to investigate.'

Barnett advises companies to pause before they activate their full crisis plan, if they see an issue on social media. 'Take a breath,' she says. 'Ask yourself: does this go against the core values of the company? Could it cause reputational or financial damage? If the answer is no, your crisis plan can stay put, for now.'

If your crisis planning has been effective, you'll have set criteria that define when you're in crisis, and when to activate your crisis plan. These criteria might include:

- Someone has been seriously injured.
- The incident is not localized, or it has the potential to spread.
- There is a threat to public health.
- It goes against people's core values (as Gill Green talks about in Chapter 1).
- It involves emotionally charged subjects such as animal welfare or children's welfare.
- It affects or has the potential to affect the company's ability to function, either in part or entirely.
- It will cause financial damage.
- It affects or has the potential to affect the company's reputation.
- It goes against core company values (such as animal products being found in a vegan brand).
- It could happen again.
- It connects or has the potential to connect with an issue that is high in the public consciousness (such as the #metoo campaign).

What is the right balance between business as usual and the focus on the crisis?

One of the most common questions I'm asked when running crisis training is how to get the balance right between concentrating on the crisis, and business as usual. Unless the entire business grinds to a halt during the crisis, it will still need to provide customer service and sell products.

Getting the balance right really means being led by what your customers want from you (listen to them, to find out). If people are still trying to buy your products, then you have a duty to ensure they can do that in the usual way, and with the usual level of customer care. But you must also make sure those people affected by the crisis have all the information they need, too.

It might be appropriate, though, to adapt your tone to fit the crisis, across all your communications. Assume that everything is public. Even your private messages can be made public – leaks are common in a crisis. Make sure you're consistent across all channels, even internal emails. If your usual tone is jokey and informal, it might jar during a crisis. Change it so it reflects the seriousness of what's happened. Stop any scheduled ads and social media posts; delay that product launch; postpone the Christmas party; cancel the sales team's bonding activity. Assess everything that's planned across the business, and view it with a critical eye, in the context of the crisis – how will it look to an outsider?

What does success look like in a crisis?

Barnett says that when she advises companies on communicating through a crisis on social media, there are a number of ways to measure whether the crisis communication has been successful.[4] She outlines three key metrics for before, during and after the crisis:

1. **Before the crisis**
   Can you avoid the crisis altogether? In an ideal world, success is avoiding the crisis in the first place – spotting an issue early on and managing it so effectively that it never escalates into a crisis. That's not always possible, but in some cases (for example, a customer service issue), managing it well averts something more serious. As Barnett says: 'Many issues can be spotted early, with the right tools and the right people. Social listening technology will help you scan the conversations people are having on social channels, and gather the data to find any deviance from the norm.'

2 During the crisis

Do you have the right information to hand in order to communicate clearly and consistently? Barnett says: 'During the crisis, you should look at whether you have the information to hand that you need in order to be able to communicate clearly and consistently, both to your external audiences and internally.' She gives examples of indicators of success:

- *Success indicator 1:* The ability to operate as a single team, rather than in silos, so you can collect the information you need from across departments, quickly – and know with absolute certainty that it's the right information.
- *Success indicator 2:* Having clear lines of communication internally, a clear and consistent tone of voice and a clear and rapid escalation process.
- *Success indicator 3:* Having not just the data, but insight from that data to enable you to act quickly.
- *Success indicator 4:* Being clear about roles and responsibilities, so everyone plays their part in the crisis. Barnett says: 'No company should be scrambling to assign roles and responsibilities when a crisis breaks. When we run training sessions on crisis preparation, it is the teams who really understand their roles in a crisis – and what the company expects from them – that fare better in a crisis situation. Everyone should be rehearsed well enough that they know exactly what to do as soon as the crisis hits.'

3 After the crisis

You must know how to get back to normal quickly from a state of crisis. In, a crisis, you might lose customers temporarily. One measure of success might be how quickly they come back to you. Barnett says: 'Again, you need to know what normal looks like, and assign a clear timeframe to when normality should be resumed. Social media can be a useful indicator of customer intent.' She advises brands to track intent-based metrics such as: the number of complaints (compared to pre-crisis); customer intent (are your customers looking at your competitors, or are they considering moving?); and conversations around 'trigger' topics – things that could show an underlying discontent, despite apparently normal activity.

When can you resume business as usual?

The crisis might be over, but it's now that the hard work begins. For many businesses, there will be no such thing as going back to business as usual.

Don't assume that what applied before the crisis will apply afterwards. You may have lost the trust of employees, customers, stakeholders and observers. Your audiences certainly won't be as receptive to your positive marketing and PR messages as they were before the crisis. You should expect to feel the fallout on all your social media channels (even on marketing posts that have nothing to do with the issue). Your customers may be more hostile than they were before.

Your crisis communications plan should include a recovery plan. Start by telling people that your service is back up and running, your stores have reopened, your fast food shop is once more stocked with chicken. Acknowledge the impact the crisis has had on people, in its aftermath. Apologize (more on this, later). And then communicate action – what have you done to put it right, and what will you do to ensure it doesn't happen again?

Focus on initiatives that start to rebuild trust, rather than behaving as if the crisis never happened, and revisit planned PR, marketing and advertising programmes to make sure they're still appropriate in light of the crisis. Expect to deal with queries about the crisis for a long time afterwards – this is completely normal.

Associate Professor Nicole Gillespie is an expert in organizational trust at University of Queensland Business School. Her research shows that there are six approaches that work for organizations to rebuild trust after a crisis:[5]

1. Make sense of what's happened, in order to restore trust. Gillespie recommends a process of 'sense-making' to establish what went wrong, and how to stop it happening again. That means publicly facing up to the issue, explaining what happened (without 'scapegoating') and tackling the root cause of the problem.
2. Make amends. This might include a public apology (that is genuine and heartfelt); accepting punishment (such as fines); and offering compensation. Outrage will only subside if the company is seen to face up to its mistakes, and to do the right thing.
3. Be seen to be adopting high standards and acting in accordance with rules and regulation; particularly by signing up to voluntary standards.
4. Build an ethical culture, where misdemeanours by employees are less likely (and if they do happen, they'll be nipped in the bud). Remind people of the company values, and what is and isn't accepted. Lead by example.

5 Be transparent and accountable. If you want to show you have nothing to hide, you have to open the doors. If you say you will make a change within a year, report back regularly on what you're doing to effect that change, and confirm when the change has been completed.

6 Consider what Gillespie calls 'transferring trust' – associating with a respected trusted figure or institution to help restore credibility.

Summary of actions: Getting back to business as normal

1. Agree what a crisis looks like for your business. What is normal, and what is deviation from normal?
2. Determine, in advance, at what point you activate your crisis plan.
3. Include a recovery process in your crisis communications plan. Don't assume you can simply get back to business as usual once the crisis has ended.
4. Listen to your customers through the crisis, to ascertain what they need from you. You can do this with customer service software and social listening tools.
5. Review all current and planned activity to ensure it doesn't jar with the crisis. This includes scheduled events, advertising and PR activities.
6. Assess your crisis actions against success metrics that have been agreed in advance.
7. Consider how you will rebuild trust in the aftermath of a crisis and include that in your recovery plan.
8. Acknowledge, apologize, act.

Notes

1 Woolf, N (2015) Overreaction or justified caution? New Yorkers question city's storm response, *Guardian*, 27 January. www.theguardian.com/us-news/2015/jan/27/overreaction-prudence-winter-storm-juno-response-new-york.

2 Crowe, C, and Kemper, A (2013) Toronto should call the ice storm what it is: An emergency, *The Star*, 27 December. www.thestar.com/opinion/commentary/2013/12/27/toronto_should_call_the_ice_storm_what_it_is_an_emergency.html.
3 Institute for Public Relations (2007) Crisis management and communications, 30 October. https://instituteforpr.org/crisis-management-and-communications.
4 Barnett, L (2018) What does success look like in a crisis? The Social Element Blog, 4 December. https://thesocialelement.agency/what-does-success-look-like-in-a-crisis.
5 Dietz, G, and Gillespie, N (2011) Building and restoring organisational trust, Institute of Business Ethics, January. www.researchgate.net/publication/265623168_Building_and_Restoring_Organisational_Trust.

The social media Hydra

10

Principles of transparency versus suppression of information in crisis mitigation

Free reporting, privacy and superinjunctions

In 2011, Ryan Giggs was outed as the subject of a so-called superinjunction, taken out to prevent him being named in UK media as the UK Premier League footballer who was having an affair with a reality TV personality and former model, Imogen Thomas. The injunction initially prevented newspapers from naming Giggs, but didn't work for social media; around 75,000 people on Twitter reportedly broke the injunction. A British MP, John Hemming, used parliamentary privilege (which protects MPs and peers from prosecution for statements made in Parliament) to name Giggs during a discussion on privacy orders, saying, 'With about 75,000 people having named Ryan Giggs it is obviously impracticable to imprison them all.'[1]

The injunction itself – and its failure to be applied to social media – became the story. Privacy law had a long way to go to catch up with the way people spread information online. Giggs' name was plastered over international media. People who had no interest in football knew about Giggs' affair. He effectively became the test case for how ineffective injunctions could be. It can hardly have been the outcome he wanted.

Fast-forward to 2018, and parliamentary privilege was once again invoked in the United Kingdom to name an individual at the centre of a scandal. Peter Hain, a peer and former cabinet minister, named Sir Philip Green as the businessman at the centre of sexual harassment and bullying allegations (allegations that Green denied). The UK courts had granted an injunction stopping the *Daily Telegraph* from naming Green after it published allegations from a number of his employees who had signed non-disclosure agreements. As in the Giggs case seven years earlier, social media was awash with speculation and rumour that couldn't be stopped by an injunction. A number of newspapers, unable to name Green under the terms of the injunction, again made the injunction the focus of the story. And again, Ryan Giggs found himself front-page news (as a friend of mine said to me, 'You think superinjunction, you think Ryan Giggs' affair'). Eventually, Green was named.

There are instances where an injunction has held up. In a well-documented case in 2016, a married celebrity couple with young children successfully prevented media from publishing the details of extra-marital affairs. The names – and details of the affairs – were widely available on social media, but the courts agreed that the story was not in the public interest. The media attention from disclosing their names would be an unnecessary further invasion of the couple's – and their children's – privacy.

I must stress here that I am not a lawyer, and am not commenting on legalities of an injunction. But in each of these cases it was easy to search social media and find the identities of those involved. No matter what the law says, you can't stop people from sharing gossip. It's impossible to say definitively whether the injunctions increased the public's interest in each story. But in the case of Giggs, it certainly prolonged it.

This is the principle of the social media Hydra: that for every story you delete, another two will replace it. In Greek mythology, the Hydra was a water monster with many heads; for every head chopped off, it would regrow two more.

The thorny issue of deleting content

Managing a crisis can be stressful. If you've been dealing with an angry mob for days, and you're tired, it's really easy to drop your guard and hit back. You post something in anger, and it makes the situation worse. When you calm down, you quietly delete it. But it doesn't go away – people have taken screenshots. Posts appear with the caption 'This is the post that [company/celebrity/politician] doesn't want you to see!'

Nothing is ever really deleted online. Someone, somewhere, will have a stored copy of it. Sometimes the only thing to do is to fess up, say sorry and explain why you deleted the post.

In June 2018, Buffalo Wild Wings had its Twitter account hacked, and crude, racist tweets sent out in its name. Journalists and others took screenshots of the posts, which appeared in news articles.[2] In 2017, McDonald's Twitter account was hacked, and a tweet posted that read:

'@realDonaldTrump You are actually a disgusting excuse of a President and we would love to have @BarackObama back, also you have tiny hands.' Many threatened to boycott McDonald's, but the brand responded quickly, saying in a statement sent to *Fortune* magazine: 'Twitter notified us that our account was compromised. We deleted the tweet, secured our account and are now investigating this.'

Be careful who you take on

Uniontown, Alabama, is one of the poorest communities in the United States, with half of its residents living below the poverty line. In 2016, those residents faced a $30m lawsuit for defamation from a Georgia-based company, Green Group Holdings, which dumped four million tons of coal ash into a 1200-acre landfill site, Arrowhead landfill, on the edge of the small town. The coal ash had been moved from Kingston, Tennessee, after its previous site collapsed, contaminated nearby rivers and land, in what the Environmental Protection Agency said posed 'imminent and substantial endangerment to the public health'.

Residents protested, and formed a group called the Black Belt Citizens Fighting for Health and Justice, saying that the coal ash caused health problems, citing increased issues such as asthma, rashes and headaches.

Green Group Holdings objected to how the Black Belt Citizens used a website and social media accounts to describe what it was like to live so close to the landfill site. It got heavy-handed, threatening four of Uniontown residents with a defamation lawsuit. It offered a deal, according to the *Guardian*: it would drop the lawsuit in exchange for 'access to their electronic devices, access to the group's future social media postings, and extensive details about Black Belt Citizens' membership, advocacy and communications with other environmental groups'. The paper goes on to report that the company asked for apologies from each of the four, and for them to withdraw from the complaint to the Environmental Protection Agency.

Fortunately for Uniontown, the co-founder of the American Civil Liberties Union (ACLU) was native to the town. The ACLU intervened, saying the lawsuit was designed to suppress free speech, and the lawsuit was dismissed.[3]

This heavy-handed approach can make the problem worse. Not only does it make the company look like a bully (and we know from Chapter 1 how people love a David and Goliath story), but long legal battles can create their own backlash. Nestlé learned this the hard way in 2010 when it asked YouTube to remove an emotive video by Greenpeace as part of a campaign

against unsustainable palm oil production (the video showed an office worker biting into what he thought was a KitKat chocolate bar; it was the bloody fingers of an orang-utan, displaced by deforestation). Greenpeace removed the video, but published it on other sites, and on social media pages, encouraging people to view and share it. Arguably, the action led to more views of the video, not fewer. Nestlé ended up changing its palm oil sourcing policies.[4]

Even asking nicely for content to be removed on your behalf doesn't go down well unless there's a really good reason for it. According to a report on Buzzfeed in 2013, a representative of Beyoncé emailed the publication to request the removal of 'unflattering' photos of the star performing at that year's Superbowl. The publication responded by reposting the photos and asking readers whether they agreed they were unflattering.[5] Donald Trump did something similar in 2016, according to website Politico, when he complained to NBC that the network wouldn't use a 'nice' picture of him. The internet responded in true style, finding the most unflattering photos and reposting them with captions like this one: 'I hear Donald Trump really hates this photo. So make sure not to retweet it. Ever.'

Intent is key

Your intent should be your guide in deciding whether to remove or censor content. Why do you want it gone? Is it because it's inaccurate, untrue, abusive or a genuine error (all good reasons)? Or is it just inconvenient? And are you being honest in your request? Invoking copyright law to remove content that criticizes your company's human rights record, for example, might be a legal solution, but it could damage your reputation further by making you look like a corporate bully, and as if you're trying to cover up an unpleasant truth.

When to delete content from your own feed:

- Because it's untrue. State why it's untrue, explain why you've deleted it, and go on record with the facts.
- Because it's (genuinely) the result of a hack. Explain that you were hacked, and why the content went against your values.
- Because it's abusive, and goes against the rules of your page (see below).

- Because it was a mistake and you don't want your brand associated with it. Apologize, explain you're deleting the post, but accept that it will be shown by others on their feeds. The best you can hope for is that your apology will appear alongside the original post.

When to request content is deleted from another's feed:

- When it misrepresents the facts. State why you want the content removed, and state the facts.
- Do not ask for content to be removed if it is true, or just because you don't like it. It could inflame the situation.

When not to delete (or request deletion):

- When the facts are correct, but you don't want them being made public.
- When you don't like the way you are being portrayed.

Dealing with fake content

In December 2018, videos circulated on social media that appeared to show the liquid from a can of Bang energy drink bursting into flames. The brand told fact-checking site, Snopes: 'It was a hoax. The user who made the video poured lighter fluid in the can. There are multiple videos online debunking that one video.'

Fans of the drink created their own videos trying – and failing – to set light to the drink. That was a far more effective way of dealing with the issue than an official statement from the company alone.

But, as we'll hear in Chapter 11, it is critical to correct misinformation whenever you encounter it, even if it appears to be harmless, or so obviously fake that you don't think you need to do anything. If you leave it alone, it will hang around in search engines, and could come back to haunt you in the future. You might need a correction to be on record.

Dealing with abusive content on your communities and social media pages

Your page, your rules, at least in the case of abusive content. I never advocate deleting critical posts, but if someone is using hate speech, or showing

abusive or bullying behaviour, you are perfectly within your rights to delete that content if you feel you can't respond to it. Best practice is to have clear guidelines and terms on your pages that state you will not tolerate abuse, with detailed information about the process you will go through to delete posts. Enforce those terms – but do so even-handedly. If you only delete posts using swear words that are critical of your brand, but not those that praise it, your motives will quite rightly be called into question. If you're seen to be transparent, and you have a good track record of responding positively to criticism – by answering questions politely and openly, and putting right any underlying problem where you can – the community will benefit from your actions.

Tell the culprit why you have deleted their post, before they ask. We know from Gill Green in Chapter 1 that simply silencing someone may not be as helpful as it seems. If you explain what it was about their post that went against your terms, it gives them the chance to post again, but without the abusive language.

But sometimes there is an opportunity to reinforce your values by responding to, rather than deleting, hateful posts. In 2018, Nationwide (a UK building society) ran a campaign called 'Voices', which featured socially and ethnically diverse spoken word poets. It performed well, and underlined the value that Nationwide places on diversity. But, predictably, it attracted haters, too – racist, homophobic and misogynistic comments appeared under the campaign posts.

Instead of deleting those comments, Nationwide responded to them. It not only reinforced its own values of inclusion, but publicly showed that it was supporting those who appeared in the campaign. Along with two other brands, Maltesers and McCain, who had both had similar experiences, Nationwide took some of the abusive social media posts they'd received in response to the campaign, and overlaid them on an ad that aired on Channel 4, to raise awareness of online abuse. Instead of sweeping the comments under the carpet, the ad conveyed a powerful message about the importance of standing up to hate.

Dealing with abusive content on other people's communities and social media pages

You don't have the same privileges on others' pages, however. Again, intent is key. If you ask for a post to be removed because you just don't like what

it says, forget it. But if it is genuinely abusive, potentially dangerous or a downright lie then you can ask for it to be removed or report it to the relevant site owner (or authorities).

Transparency is your end goal

On the whole, deleting posts is best avoided where you can. In a crisis you need to earn trust. You have to be open and honest – and be seen to be both those things. For everyone who posts, there will be another who is a silent observer. Your responses to criticism aren't just intended for the critic, but for everyone who may think the same thing, but not post it.

Summary of actions: Being transparent in communications

1. Getting content removed from a site, or imposing a gagging order, is unlikely to stop people talking about the issue. Don't just think about what's possible legally; think about the longer-term reputational impact of your actions.
2. If you're thinking about deleting content, consider why you want it gone. Is it genuinely untrue, or just inconvenient? How will it make you appear?
3. Always correct lies and misinformation. You may need a statement on record if the content resurfaces in the future.
4. Avoid deleting posts unless they are abusive, threatening or hateful (even then, you might be able to reinforce your values by calling out hate speech and taking a stand). Never delete a post simply for criticizing you.
5. Remember, transparency will help you build trust in a crisis. And trust is what you'll need to rebuild your brand once the crisis is over.

Notes

1 BBC (2011) Ryan Giggs named by MP as injunction footballer, BBC News Online, 23 May. www.bbc.co.uk/news/uk-13503847.
2 Pullen, JP (2018) Buffalo Wild Wings' Twitter was hacked and its tweets were wilder than anything on its menu, Fortune, 1 June. http://fortune.com/2018/06/01/buffalo-wild-wings-twitter-hacked-racist-tweets.

3 Shankman, S (2017) Alabama town that fought coal ash landfill wins settlement, Inside Climate News, 8 February. https://insideclimatenews.org/news/07022017/coal-ash-environmental-justice-uniontown-alabama-green-group-holdings-aclu.
4 Hickman, M (2010) Online protest drives Nestlé to environmentally friendly palm oil, *Independent*, 19 May. www.independent.co.uk/environment/green-living/online-protest-drives-nestl-to-environmentally-friendly-palm-oil-1976443.html.
5 Buzzfeed contributor (2013) The 'unflattering' photos Beyoncé's publicist doesn't want you to see, Buzzfeed, 5 February. www.buzzfeed.com/buzzfeedceleb/the-unflattering-photos-beyonces-publicist-doesnt-want-you-t.

Crises in action 11

Lessons learned from crisis responses from five major brands

United Airlines Flight 3411

On 10 April 2017, David Dao, a 69-year-old physician from Kentucky, was on his way home from Chicago. He boarded United Airlines flight 3411 to Louisville and settled into his seat. A few minutes later, at around 5pm local time, airline representatives boarded the plane to ask passengers for four volunteers to give up their seats to airline staff. In return, the airline said, they would receive $400 travel vouchers, a hotel stay and a rebooked flight. When no one volunteered, the offer was increased to $800. The airline still didn't get the volunteers it needed, and so passengers were chosen by a computer system to be removed from the flight.

Dr Dao was one of those chosen. He refused to leave, saying he had to get home: he was seeing patients the following day. Security officers (employed by the City of Chicago, rather than United) forcibly removed him from the aircraft, dragging him along the floor of the aisle. His face hit an armrest, he was left with two broken teeth, a bloody face, a broken nose and concussion. He was taken to a nearby hospital to recover.

The incident was filmed by a passenger on the flight, Jayse D Anspach, and posted to Twitter. The video was shared 154,000 times from Anspach's account alone (Anspach has around 1,500 followers on Twitter). The issue spread internationally. One of the passengers on the flight said they thought Dao might have been removed because he appeared to be of Chinese origin (he is actually Vietnamese American). Within 48 hours, 'United forcibly removes passenger from plane' was the most popular topic on Weibo (China's microblogging platform), with more than 550 million views and 240,000 comments, according to the *New York Times*.[1]

The issue soon hit mainstream media. Within hours of the incident, journalists were contacting Anspach on Twitter to ask for the rights to use the film.

At around 4pm, United's CEO, Oscar Munoz, issued a formal response on Twitter. He apologized, but the apology was seriously undermined by the rest of the statement, which read in full:

> This is an upsetting event to all of us here at United. I apologize for having to reaccommodate these customers. Our team is moving with a sense of urgency to work with the authorities and conduct our own detailed review of what happened. We are also reaching out to this passenger to talk directly to him and further address and resolve this situation.

Let's take a look at that statement in more detail, for a moment. First, 'This is an upsetting event to all of us here at United.' I imagine it was more upsetting for Dr Dao and his family, and even for the other passengers on the aircraft. No one had sympathy with United here, and certainly no one cared if United was 'upset'.

Next: 'I apologize for having to reaccommodate these customers.' Reaccomodate? Really? Munez was called out relentlessly on social media for his choice of words. Dao wasn't reaccommodated, he was dragged off the aircraft, and injured in the process.

Then: 'Our team is moving with a sense of urgency.' What does that mean? Moving where? What is a sense of urgency? And finally 'We are reaching out to this passenger to talk directly to him and further address and resolve this situation.' The word 'further' here implies that the situation has, to some extent, been addressed and resolved already. This was obviously not the case.

Plain, clear language is so important in a crisis. Who trusts someone who uses 'reaccommodate' to mean forcibly removing someone from an aircraft? I'm sure that statement was the result of many drafts and rounds of approval. The result comes across as a deliberate attempt to sanitize a deeply unpleasant situation.

Munoz listened to opinion. Compare his first 'apology' to the one that followed 24 hours later:

> *Statement from United Airlines CEO Oscar Munoz on United Express Flight 3411*
>
> The truly horrific event that occurred on this flight has elicited many responses from all of us: outrage, anger, disappointment. I share all of those sentiments, and one above all: my deepest apologies for what happened. Like you, I continue to be disturbed by what happened on this flight and I deeply apologize to the customer forcibly removed and to all the customers aboard. No one should ever be mistreated this way.

I want you to know that we take full responsibility and we will work to make it right.

It's never too late to do the right thing. I have committed to our customers and our employees that we are going to fix what's broken so this never happens again. This will include a thorough review of crew movement, our policies for incentivizing volunteers in these situations, how we handle oversold situations and an examination of how we partner with airport authorities and local law enforcement. We'll communicate the results of our review by April 30th.

I promise you we will do better.

Sincerely,

Oscar[2]

It was a bad week for United. Its stock price dropped, reducing its market cap by $770 million.[3] Consumers called for a boycott, and even President Trump said treatment of Dao was 'horrible', in an interview with the *Wall Street Journal.*

Unsurprisingly, public sympathy was with Dao initially. He had fled Vietnam in 1975; he was a doctor trying to get back to his patients. He later reached a confidential settlement with United to compensate him for his ordeal.[4] But what happened next was interesting – and typical of what we see in a crisis situation (remember the 'cycle of outrage' I mentioned in Chapter 4?).

Within 24 hours, journalists were digging up everything they could on the man behind the story. Reports spread like wildfire: Dao had faced criminal charges for unauthorized drug prescriptions to a former patient with whom he had a sexual relationship and his patient contact had been limited as a result. The tabloid media and social media went into meltdown.

Whatever the truth of Dao's past, it is quite clear that it had absolutely nothing to do with his removal from the aircraft. But it's an interesting pattern, again: an initially sympathetic mob quickly gets its pitchforks out. The victim becomes the villain.

One year on, what did this incident change? A few things for the airline industry, not much for United, everything for Dao. United has ended its policy of involuntary removal of passengers, except when necessary for safety reasons. It has increased the payment cap it will offer passengers to volunteer for re-booking, and across the airline industry 'bumping' passengers off a flight is down. Media sites were still referring to the incident a year later,[5] and it comes up every time United comes under fire for another incident (such as the time later in 2017 when airline staff insisted on a passenger's puppy being put an overhead bin – the animal suffocated). But, despite all this, there has been no real long-term damage to United. Within a month of the incident, its share price had not only recovered, but reached a record high; and passenger numbers were up on the previous year. We don't know how much the settlement with Dao cost the airline, or whether it was a life-changing amount of money for him. Whether it was or not, he was hospitalized, became infamous overnight, had his past dragged through the international media, and his (bruised and bloodied) face plastered all over the internet.

Did this have a long-term impact on United? Was it, technically, a crisis for the airline, or a short-term issue? I'm sure it felt like a crisis for those managing it. It hit the company's share price and had the potential to hit sales. It cost the company in terms of reputation damage, settlement, and time and effort in handling it. Ultimately, the share price bounced back. Importantly, Munoz wants the airline to remember it – and that says a lot about his leadership. Addressing a conference in Chicago in 2018, Munoz said: 'We had a truly horrific event last year that everyone in the world frankly heard about. It was flight 3411, with the doctor that was dragged off the plane. And people say, "Aren't you glad that's over? Can't you wait for that thing to go away?" That is the furthest thing from my mind and our mind. We want it front and center. We constantly want to be reminded of how things can go wrong so quickly.'[6]

What a contrast from the statement at the beginning of the crisis. This is the kind of leadership that will pull a company back from crisis.

Lessons from United Airlines Flight 3411

1. Even if you're not technically responsible for an incident, if you're the brand delivering the product or experience to the consumer, you're the one that has to deal with the crisis. Review every process and procedure around your brand, not just those delivered by the brand. Where are the potential issues lurking?
2. Everything that your customers experience has the potential to be filmed and go public. Assume everything is public. It doesn't take an influencer to break a story.
3. Take action, even after a one-off event, to avoid anything similar happening again. You might survive one incident, but a second will be more damaging and gives media an excuse to rake over the past.

4 Remember who is the victim of the incident. It's probably not the brand. Make sure your statement reflects that. Use plain language and don't obfuscate the facts. Think carefully about your statement. Endless rounds of edits and approvals can turn it into something more damaging than helpful.
5 Learn from the crisis. Keep it 'front and centre' as Munez says, so it doesn't happen again.
6 Could this crisis have been avoided? Probably, with better processes and dialogue between the airline and its partners on the ground (who ultimately represent the airline to customers). But in an organization of United's size, there will always be incidents you can't foresee. What matters is your response.

Uber and #DeleteUber

In January 2017, Uber stood accused of profiting from a protest against Donald Trump's executive order banning refugees and immigrants from certain (mostly Muslim) countries from entering the United States. In protest at the executive order, New York City taxi cab drivers went on strike at JFK airport. Uber continued to pick up passengers from JFK, and even turned off its usual surge pricing. In contrast, rival firm Lyft released a statement against the ban and in support of its 'community members, their families and friends' who were directly impacted by the executive order, and announcing that it would donate $1million to the American Civil Liberties Union.[7]

Journalist and writer Dan O'Sullivan, was the first person to post the hashtag #DeleteUber, in a tweet encouraging people to use their local taxi service. In an interview with The Daily Beast in January 2017, he said: 'Let this be a warning: if you are a corporation who thinks you will ride out Trump, and quietly make money at his side, you will be made to pay a price.'[8]

Uber's then CEO, Travis Kalanick, was widely criticized for supporting Trump (he was then part of Trump's Strategy and Policy Forum). Overnight, the hashtag caught hold, and celebrities (including actress Susan Sarandon, Perez Hilton and George Takei) shared the hashtag or screenshots of themselves deleting the app to millions of followers, comparing Uber's response to that of Lyft. In total, according to the *New York Times*, around 200,000 people deleted the app. More worrying, perhaps, was the impact on Uber employees and drivers. Kalanick had his work cut out to persuade them that the company was not 'anti immigrant'.

Uber was caught unprepared. It couldn't handle the volume of deletions. Until this point, the company had deleted users manually; It had never had to cope with more than a handful of people wanted to wipe their accounts. It had to create an automated process to cope.

The next day, in an announcement on his Facebook page, Kalanick pledged $3 million to assist drivers affected by the ban, calling it 'unjust'.[9] A week later he resigned from the Strategy and Policy Forum, something his own employees had been asking him to do.[10] It was too late to undo all the damage, perhaps unfairly (the *New York Times* in 2017 points out that two of Trump's major supporters and advisers, Peter Thiel and Carl Icahn, own a significant number of shares in Lyft).[11] Uber's real mistake was in not understanding the strength of feeling among its customers and drivers.

Uber recovered. As Gill Green said in Chapter 1, you can disagree with a company at a corporate level, but still support it on the ground. But the #DeleteUber hashtag won't go away easily. It emerged again in February 2017 after Susan Fowler, a former Uber employee, wrote a 3,000-word essay on her experience of sexual harassment at the firm; and it resurfaces every time the company faces another issue.

Lessons from #DeleteUber

1. Listen to what your customers, employees and partners really care about, and act on it, fast. Uber came out in support of its drivers, but too late to stop the perception that it supported the immigration ban.
2. The truth doesn't necessarily mean anything in a crisis – it is how you are perceived publicly that matters. Kalanick knew that the executive order would harm his drivers, but he wasn't seen to support them quickly enough.
3. It is not possible to separate the personal, the political, the business. The actions of a CEO will be picked apart and attributed to the company.
4. Could this crisis have been avoided? Yes, if Uber had listened more closely to its customers.

TalkTalk's cyber attack

On 21 October 2015, UK media began to report an outage at UK-based internet company TalkTalk. By the following day, it became clear that the company had suffered a 'significant and sustained cyber attack'. Initial reports over the next 24 hours said that the personal data of up to four million customers had been accessed. Public reaction to the story was immediate and negative (according to research from The Social Element for this book, social media mentions averaged 2,000 per hour, overwhelmingly negative).

TalkTalk released a number of statements over the coming days, which did little to clarify the situation. First, it said its website had been taken down because of an attack, to protect customer data. Next, a statement said that law enforcement was investigating the cyber attack, and there was 'a chance that some of the following data has been compromised: names, addresses, date of birth, phone numbers, email addresses, TalkTalk account information, credit card details and/or bank details'. It attributed this loss of data to a distributed denial of service (DDoS) attack. This did nothing to reassure people that the company knew what it was doing. As The Register pointed out: 'A DDoS is only capable of increasing the load on a network resource – and thus taking a website offline – and not capable of retrieving information from that resource.'[12] On 23 October, TalkTalk said it had received a request for money from the attacker, but it was still not clear on the details of the attack – how many customers were affected, or what customer data was encrypted on its systems.

TalkTalk's CEO at the time, Dido Harding, gave a number of media interviews and posted videos online addressing the attack, but did not offer any specific details. She couldn't answer basic security questions; she didn't know how many people were affected, but potentially every single TalkTalk customer was. With no hard information available, rumours were rife that the cyber attack was carried out by, variously, the Mafia, ISIS, or the Russian secret services. TalkTalk had completely lost control of the story. BBC Radio 4's *The Money Programme* told stories of customers contacted by scammers pretending to be from TalkTalk, asking them to hand over payment details in connection with the breach.

Figure 11.1 TalkTalk's stock price had been in steady decline since slightly prior to the data breach. There have been several sharp dips over the course of the last three years, most of which can be tied back in some part to the data breach

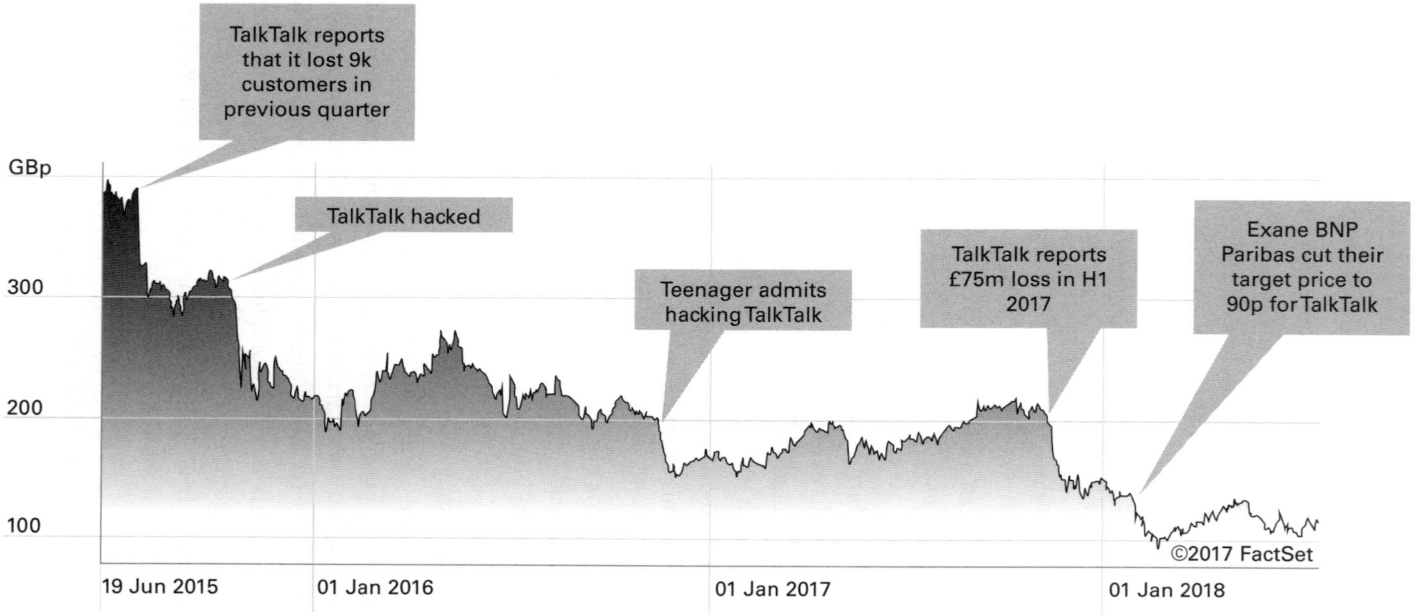

SOURCE Reproduced with permission of The Social Element

By November, it transpired that the details of 157,000 customers (not the four million originally thought) had been compromised. In around 15,500 cases, the hackers had access to bank details. In January 2016, a teenager from Antrim, in Northern Ireland, admitted responsibility for the hack. In November 2018, two men in their 20s were also sentenced for their role in the attack.[13]

The impact of a crisis so badly handled was felt not just over the period of the hack, but for years later. TalkTalk's stock price took a number of hits, starting with the breach, and then suffering pronounced drops at key points of the crisis, the most notable being when the teenager admitted responsibility, and when the company announced its half-year losses.

The hack is estimated to have cost TalkTalk £77 million, halved its profit and lost it 10,000 customers. In 2017, the UK's Information Commissioner's Office (ICO) fined TalkTalk a record £400,000 for the breach. Its report was damning. Information Commissioner Elizabeth Denham said: 'TalkTalk's failure to implement the most basic cybersecurity measures allowed hackers to penetrate TalkTalk's systems with ease.'

Lessons from TalkTalk

1. It's good to put your CEO up to address issues in a crisis – but make sure they have the facts they need to hand. If you're hit by a cyber attack, the CEO needs to understand what security you had in place. That means getting the right people in the room, quickly.
2. Every board member should understand the basics of security, and the potential risks associated with them.
3. If you get some of the major facts wrong at the beginning, you lose all credibility. Harding bravely fronted all the media interviews – but she had lost the trust of the public, security commentators and customers.
4. Deal only in facts, not in rumour.
5. Could the crisis have been avoided? We can't know for sure. But certainly TalkTalk's security was not fit for purpose, so the scale of the crisis could have been averted.

Wells Fargo, fraud and the whistleblowers

Jessie Guitron started working for Wells Fargo in 2008. Soon after she joined the bank, she noticed that colleagues, keen to meet their new business quotas, were opening premium accounts for customers without their permission. 'It's fraud,' Guitron told CBS. 'I kept complaining and complaining.' She was fired in 2010. A two-year lawsuit against the bank was dismissed, and she gave up fighting.

Guitron was not the only person to notice the fraud, nor was she the only one to be fired for complaining. In August 2016, Wells Fargo was ordered to pay $5.4 million to a bank manager who was fired after he reported what he suspected was fraud being committed by two people in his team. By September 2016, Wells Fargo was engulfed in scandal, facing allegations of systemic fraud. It emerged that as many as 700 whistleblowers had told their stories, going back to 2010.[14] The bank reached a $190 million settlement with regulators, and reports said that 2.1 million unauthorized accounts had been opened on behalf of customers. Politicians and influencers took to social media to express their outrage. US presidential candidate Bernie Sanders tweeted to his 7.8 million follows: 'It's a disgrace that while Americans were defrauded by Wells Fargo, the executive in charge received $124 million.'

The bank's culture was called into question. Aggressive sales targets were blamed for creating an environment where fraud was routinely committed and ignored. The US federal bank regulator, the Office of the Comptroller of the Currency, held an internal review to find out why it missed the warning signs (it had been made aware of complaints as far back as 2010), and removed the individual responsible for overseeing the bank.

John Stumpf, Wells Fargo's CEO, felt the brunt of the outrage. In 2015, he had told *Fortune* magazine that he was proud of the company's work ethic, and was the 'keeper of our company's culture'.[15] At a Senate hearing in September, Senator Elizabeth Warren publicly called for his resignation. Afterwards, Jeffrey Sonnelfeld, an authority on corporate governance at Yale University, told CNN that Stumpf seemed to be a 'deer caught in the headlights with a tin ear in understanding, addressing, and communicating the problem.' In 2016, he agreed to give up much of his salary, his bonus and dividends in 2016 in the wake of the scandal (he earned $19.3 million in 2015). But, in October 2016, he bowed to the pressure and stepped down, saying it was it in the interests of the company to do so. CNN reported that 'The hearing, and another similarly blistering dressing down of Stumpf before House lawmakers a week later, may have helped speed up Stumpf's demise.'[16]

> **Lessons from Wells Fargo**
>
> 1 Wells Fargo's overly aggressive sales culture and willingness to turn a blind eye to fraud created the perfect environment for the scandal.
>
> 2 If the CEO is the keeper of company culture, then the CEO will be in the firing line when that culture is exposed.
>
> 3 A poor performance at a Select Committee or Senate Hearing will, ultimately, lead to the demise of the CEO.
>
> 4 Could this crisis have been averted? Yes, if the bank had listened sooner to its employees, spotted early patterns of behaviour, paid more attention to culture and acted to stamp out fraud.

TSB and IT chaos

In April 2018, TSB began a planned upgrade to its information technology (IT) systems. Customers had been informed that some banking services would be shut down as data was migrated from the old system to the new one. The switchover was done at the weekend, and by Sunday evening the new system was ready to be used.

But there was a problem. When some customers logged on to their accounts, they could see not only their own accounts, but other people's, too. The bank quickly fixed that issue, but there were more problems to come. Social media was flooded with complaints from people who couldn't access their bank accounts, or transfer money between accounts. The bank was overwhelmed, and customers complained of long delays reaching customer service. The ICO launched an investigation into the data breach, and consumer watchdog Which? Money posted advice to social media for customers to claim compensation from the bank. The UK regulatory body, the Financial Conduct Authority, said that the IT failure led to 10,600 fraud cases. Media reports told stories, taken from social media accounts, of people unable to pay their mortgages, going into debt, and unable to run their businesses.

Soon, customers were reporting that they had been contacted by scammers purporting to be from TSB, asking them for their account details and PINs. The FCA announced that TSB's IT failure led to 10,600 fraud cases.[17]

Andrew Bailey, the FCA's CEO, told Parliament's Treasury Committee that he was 'dissatisfied with TSB's communications with its customers' and 'had concerns that TSB was not being open and transparent about the issues experienced'.[18] The bank should, said Bailey, have shown greater caution, and avoided an overly optimistic view of the breach.

In June 2018, letters from TSB to customers (many of whom had been affected by the breach) were sent out with the wrong customer details on them. Then, in September 2018, TSB suffered a second outage, with thousands of people unable to access their online or mobile accounts. These gained disproportionate attention from media and social media users on the back of the earlier crisis.

The issues in 2018 cost TSB a reported £175 million (wiping out its profit), and the CEO his job. Paul Pester stood down in September 2018 – with a £1.2 million severance package, and a £500,000 bonus, much to the outrage of customers. He had forfeited a £2 million bonus shortly after the incident.[19]

Lessons from the TSB crisis

1. Stick to the facts. Avoid trying to make the situation sound better than it is.
2. Expect to have to deal with scammers exploiting the situation.
3. A second issue, even if it's seemingly minor, will inflict disproportionate damage on an already weakened organization. Be prepared.
4. Ultimately, the CEO is held personally accountable for a crisis. And his or her pay will be called into question in the wake of a crisis.
5. Could this crisis have been averted? We can't know. A data breach is likely to hit all organizations at some point, but TSB could have done more to contain and shorten the crisis by being more open with consumers.

Patterns in behaviour during a crisis

In the summer of 2018, I asked social media agency, The Social Element, if it would conduct research for this book into these five brands to see if there were patterns in behaviour by consumers in response to each crisis. The purpose of doing this was to ascertain if a brand could understand – and plan for – the peaks and troughs of a crisis. The Social Element's insights team looked at patterns in social media volumes, influencer involvement, how a crisis breaks and the cost of a crisis.

How a crisis breaks

All these crises broke on Twitter first, followed by mainstream media, with the exception of TalkTalk, which broke in mainstream media at the same time as on social media.

The cost of a crisis

United:

- Damage to share price: $770 million (share price recovered quickly).
- Business cost: None in sales; fines and compensation undisclosed.

TalkTalk:

- Damage to share price: 10 per cent drop.
- Business cost: £77 million plus £400,000 fine.

TSB:

- Damage to share price: unknown (TSB owned by Sabadell).
- Business cost: £175 million.

Wells Fargo:

- Damage to share price: minimal.
- Business cost: around $200 million.

DeleteUber:

- Business cost unknown; but a reported 200,000 people deleted the app.

Impact of a crisis on the CEO

The impact of a crisis is felt not just by the business, but also by the CEO. Of the five crises we examined, only one CEO was still in place six months after the crisis ended.

The personal cost of a crisis on the CEO

- United: CEO Oscar Munoz was initially criticized for poor handling of the crisis. He showed strong leadership after the crisis, and reportedly has the support of his employees.[20] He kept his job, but volunteered to halve his pay in 2017 (compared to 2016).
- TalkTalk: CEO Dido Harding lost credibility by appearing not to understand the scale of the crisis, or the basics of security. She resigned four months after TalkTalk was fined by the ICO.
- Wells Fargo: CEO John Stumpf resigned in 2016, less than one month after appearing in front of the Senate. He had been widely criticized for his handling of the crisis, and – more importantly – the culture of the business that allowed the crisis to happen.
- TSB: CEO Paul Pester stood down in 2018 in the wake of the crisis. He had forfeited a £2 million bonus (but left with a large and equivalent severance package).
- Uber: Founder and CEO Travis Kalernick stepped down from Donald Trump's Advisory Board in the wake of #DeleteUber; he resigned in June 2017 following a raft of scandals that started with the #DeleteUber campaign.

Other notable patterns

1. Influencers. The single most influential group of people in spreading the crisis on social media was, in all cases, media. In the case of Wells Fargo, a significant number of politicians posted about the crisis; and during #DeleteUber, celebrities escalated the conversation.
2. Memes and humour. Unless your crisis involves loss of life, expect people to laugh at you. Spoof tweets mocking the brand appeared in every one of these examples.
3. Your crisis will peak again on social media whenever significant news emerges. United saw a peak in the number of conversations on social media when it came to a settlement with Dr Dao (volume decreased after Munez' second apology). TalkTalk's peaks came when it announced it had had a ransom demand, and when a teenager was arrested. Wells

Figure 11.2 Social media patterns from five crises

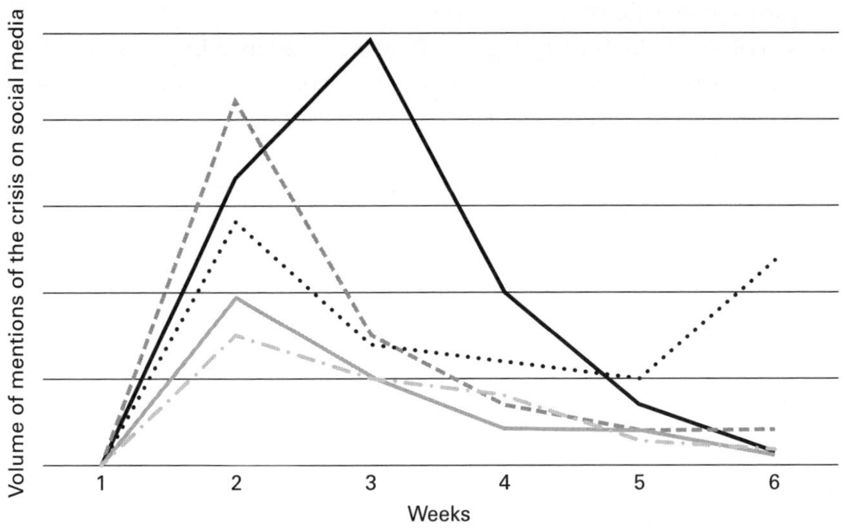

Fargo saw a peak when it was fined. Uber sees the re-emergence of #DeleteUber after Susan Fowler's revelations (and every subsequent discussion of drivers' rights). TSB peaked when Visa had similar IT problems – and people made the comparison to TSB; and when the FCA announced that the TSB failure had led to 10,600 fraud cases.

Overall, each crisis has a similar pattern – a high volume of activity in the first two weeks, dropping away significantly and then only peaking again when there was a significant development in the crisis (Figure 11.2).

It is worth noting, though, that the long-tails of these crises are significant. If a crisis is perceived to be unresolved, it will crop up again and again.

Notes

1. Hernandes, JC and, Li, C (2017) Video of United Airlines passenger creates furor in China, too, *New York Times*, 11 April. www.nytimes.com/2017/04/11/world/asia/united-airlines-passenger-dragged-china.html.
2. Mutzabaugh, B (2017) United Airlines CEO issues second apology, 'I promise you we will do better', *USA Today*, 11 April. https://eu.usatoday.com/story/travel/flights/todayinthesky/2017/04/11/full-text-united-ceo-munoz-apologizes-flight-3411-pledges-review/100336992.

3 Wile, R (2017) Here's how much United Airlines stock tanked this week, *Time*, 14 April. http://time.com/money/4739880/united-airlines-fiasco-overbooked-passenger-dragged-stock-price-value.

4 Tangel, A, and McGroarty, P (2017) Doctor dragged from United Airlines flight prepares lawsuit, *Wall Street Journal,* 13 April. www.wsj.com/articles/doctor-dragged-from-united-flight-suffered-concussion-will-probably-sue-1492097423.

5 Gulliver (2018) A year after United's public-relations disaster, *The Economist*, 12 April. www.economist.com/gulliver/2018/04/12/a-year-after-uniteds-public-relations-disaster.

6 Murphy, B (2018) With 6 short words, the CEO of United Airlines just taught a major lesson in successful leadership, Inc. www.inc.com/bill-murphy-jr/united-airlines-ceo-we-constantly-want-to-be-reminded-that-a-passenger-was-dragged-off-our-plane.html.

7 Lyft (2017) Defending our values, Lyft blog, 29 January. https://blog.lyft.com/posts/defending-our-values.

8 Collins, B (2017) #DeleteUber's creator: Resist Trump or 'pay a price', The Daily Beast, 29 January. www.thedailybeast.com/deleteubers-creator-resist-trump-or-pay-a-price.

9 Kalanick, T (2017) Standing up for the driver community, Travis Kalanick Facebook post, 29 January. www.facebook.com/traviskal/posts/1332784556742710.

10 Isaac, M (2017) Uber CEO to leave Trump advisory council after criticism, *New York Times*, 2 February. www.nytimes.com/2017/02/02/technology/uber-ceo-travis-kalanick-trump-advisory-council.html.

11 Isaac, M (2017) What you need to know about Delete Uber, *New York Times*, 31 January. www.nytimes.com/2017/01/31/business/delete-uber.html.

12 Martin, AJ (2015) TalkTalk incident management: A timeline, The Register, 27 October. www.theregister.co.uk/2015/10/27/talktalk_incident_management_review.

13 Abel, R (2018) Pair of friends sentenced for 2015 TalkTalk Hack, SC Magazine, 20 November. www.scmagazine.com/home/security-news/a-pair-of-friends-who-were-responsible-for-the-2015-talk-talk-data-breach-were-sentenced-monday.

14 Egan, M (2017) Feds knew of 700 Wells Fargo whistleblower cases in 2010, CNN, 19 April. https://money.cnn.com/2017/04/19/investing/wells-fargo-regulator-whistleblower-2010-occ/index.html.

15 Stumpf, JG (2015) How Wells Fargo's CEO built the team at the world's most valuable bank, Fortune, 23 July. http://fortune.com/2015/07/23/john-stumpf-culture.

16 Egan, M, Wattles, J, and Alexci, C (2016) Wells Fargo CEO John Stumpf is out, CNN, 12 October. https://money.cnn.com/2016/10/12/investing/wells-fargo-ceo-john-stumpf-retires/index.html?iid=EL.

17 Azeez, W (2018) 12,500 TSB customers leave after IT Meltdown, Sky News, 6 June. https://news.sky.com/story/tsb-it-failure-led-to-10-600-fraud-cases-fca-says-11396580.

18 Bailey, A, (2018). Letter to Parliament's Treasury Committee, 30 May. www.parliament.uk/business/committees/committees-a-z/commons-select/treasury-committee/news-parliament-2017/tsb-sabadell-fca-letters-17-19.

19 The Week (2018) TSB IT crisis: Bank chief Paul Pester steps down with £1.7m payout, *The Week*, 4 September. www.theweek.co.uk/93365/tsb-it-crisis-news.

20 Murphy, B (2018) With 6 short words, the CEO of United Airlines just taught a major lesson in successful leadership, Inc. www.inc.com/bill-murphy-jr/united-airlines-ceo-we-constantly-want-to-be-reminded-that-a-passenger-was-dragged-off-our-plane.html.

The importance of telling the truth and its role in crisis and reputation management 12

The only way to get consumer trust is to open all the doors.

JOHN BROWN, FOUNDER, DON'T CRY WOLF

Lies and deception: Good and bad

When I was a child, I met a man in his seventies who had been a highly decorated wartime bomber pilot. A crash after the war left him without sight in one eye. 'How did you carry on flying, if you couldn't see with both eyes?' I asked him. He grinned. He told me that he simply never declared it in his medicals. Testing his right eye was no problem. He'd cover his left eye with his left hand as instructed, and read from the sight test. Testing his left eye took a bit more skill. 'Cover your right eye with your right hand,' came the instruction. Instead, he covered his left eye with his right hand. He got away with it. Of course, everyone he flew with knew he had limited sight. But he was a great pilot. Everyone wanted him to pass his medical. The deception was allowed to stand.

I loved that story as a child. I still do. It's David and Goliath again. The story of one man who outsmarted a bigger, unwieldy system.

An older colleague of my father's, a soldier, famously feigned deafness when he was captured by German troops during the Second World War. If he were war-wounded, and useless to his captors (if he couldn't hear questions during interrogation, he couldn't give answers), he would eventually be let go. His captors used to shoot a pistol behind him to test his reactions, and he never flinched. After a year, he was released. (The story goes that the only time he nearly gave himself away was when he was given his release papers. He had to stop himself from saying 'Thank you.')

These stories of deception are brave and extraordinary. They're the stuff of spy novels and films. We grow up on them, fascinated by heroic tales of escaping capture, spying on the enemy, deceit and intrigue, where the deceiver sits firmly on the side of good.

Why do we lie?

We learn to lie from about three years old. These lies are mostly selfish, to get us out of trouble, or to avoid the consequences of our actions. 'It wasn't me. She broke it.' It's a positive sign of our brains developing what psychologists call 'theory of mind' – the ability to distinguish our own thoughts from other people's. According to research by Kang Lee (2013), a psychologist at the University of Toronto, it is at about that age that we know we should tell the truth, but we also realize we don't have to.[1] Later (around seven years old), we start to tell 'prosocial' lies, or 'white lies'. This is another sign of brain development. Prosocial lies are those we tell to make someone else feel better. 'That's delicious', 'That's a great picture', 'I love my birthday present.' They require compassion – we don't want to hurt someone else's feelings. From this age, in a struggle between honesty and compassion, compassion wins.

So, lying is part of our development, and can indicate our ability to empathise. But as we get older, it gets more complicated. Kang Lee talks about 'blue lies' – lies that are both selfish and selfless. These are lies that protect people in your group at the expense of outsiders. For example, you might lie to cover up a crime committed by a family member to protect the family unit, or to protect a member of your football team who cheated, but whose exposure would damage the whole team. Interestingly, Lee's research shows that there may be cultural differences at play here. He cites a study in China where children between seven and eleven years old were told that their class had broken the rules of a chess competition that would put their school at a competitive advantage.[2] When each child was interviewed individually, they were more likely to lie in order to protect their school's interest. Lee says that in China there is a strong culture of the importance of group harmony and collective interests. Lee suggests that 'socialization to the rules of one's culture influences children's willingness to lie accordingly.'

We've all deliberately deceived someone during our lives. When is telling the truth essential, and when is it OK to deceive? When do we love a deception, and when does it damage us?

Sisella Bok is a philosopher and the author of a book called *Lying: Moral choice in public and private life*.[3] She defines a lie as 'any intentionally deceptive message which is stated.' But deceit can be a virtue in some situations, for example during times of war. Here, the 'blue lie' theory comes into play. Writing for the *Scientific American* in 2017, JA Smith asks why lies told by leaders are accepted by their followers, using Donald Trump as his example.[4] He quotes George Edwards, a political scientist at Texas A&M University: 'People condone lying against enemy nations, and since many people now see those on the other side of American politics as enemies, they may feel that lies, when they recognize them, are appropriate means of warfare.'

Could this theory explain why so many companies deliberately deceive their audiences in a crisis situation, perceiving the crisis almost as a state of war? To protect the company, you feel you have to tell a blue lie. You believe that such a lie could be the difference between your company surviving the crisis, or going under. Do you choose the truth, or the lie? In lying, you protect the people you care about, and the organization that gives both them and you a livelihood. But you also deliberately deceive people outside that organization who could suffer as a result.

Whistleblowing

Telling blue lies is always murky ethically, and particularly so in the context of whistleblowing, which can be critical for companies to identify and stop unethical or even illegal practice within the business. If an employee sees fraud happening within their team, do they instinctively lie to protect their close colleagues, or do they blow the whistle in order to protect the wider business?

I spend a lot of time examining major corporate scandals, in order to train organizations on what they should expect in a crisis, and how to respond. Most involve a whistleblower of some kind. It could be a disgruntled employee (or a 'source close to the company') speaking anonymously to the media, a former employee or contractor going on the record about their time at the company, or a full-blown Wikileaks-style exposé.

The only way for organizations to deal with this is to encourage whistleblowing in a controlled way. And yet, culturally, many oppose it. In 2017, Wells Fargo faced allegations that it had opened two million accounts on behalf of customers, without their permission. In September 2017, the bank agreed to pay a $185 million fine and give back $5 million in fees to customers. CEO John Stumpf, faced a Senate Banking Committee where he took full responsibility for 'all unethical sales practices'. (He retired shortly afterwards, in October the same year.)

In October 2016, the *New York Times* reported that a number of Wells Fargo employees had raised concerns about unethical sales practices, some as far back as 2005.[5] According to the paper, one employee, Julie Tishkoff, then an administrative assistant at the bank, kept complaining for four years until she was fired in 2009. Many of her colleagues did the same. Some called the bank's ethics hotline (one employee claims he was fired after doing so); some even wrote directly to Stumpf. The bank didn't act, although it did update its manual in 2007 to remind employees that they had to have a customer's consent before opening a bank account on their behalf. After it accepted responsibility in 2017, the *New York Times* reports, 'dozens' of former employees came forward to tell their stories. Wells Fargo blamed its lack of action on the fact that each complaint was dealt with individually, but it didn't join the dots between each. It was unaware that there was a bigger problem until 2013, when it set up an internal investigation.

The term 'whistleblower' still has a whiff of disloyalty about it for many organizations. When we run crisis simulations that include a whistleblower scenario, often the first thing a brand team will do is to find ways to discredit the whistleblower, rather than seek to fix the underlying problem. It can be hard to hear criticism, much harder to act on it. But imagine if Wells Fargo had listened to the complaints in 2004, and acted then to stamp out any wrongdoing. The cost of not doing so was high: not just millions in fines and returned fees, but the associated reputation damage of the bank and of its former CEO.

The UK Government's Department for Business, Innovation and Skills lists the following in its 'whistleblowing code of practice':[6]

1 Have a whistleblowing policy or appropriate written procedures in place.
2 Ensure the whistleblowing policy or procedures are easily accessible to all workers.
3 Raise awareness of the policy or procedures through all available means, such as staff engagement, intranet sites and other marketing communications.

4 Provide training to all workers on how disclosures should be raised and how they will be acted upon.

5 Provide training to managers on how to deal with disclosures.

6 Create an understanding that all staff at all levels of the organization should demonstrate that they support and encourage whistleblowing.

7 Confirm that any clauses in settlement agreements do not prevent workers from making disclosures in the public interest.

8 Ensure the organization's whistleblowing policy or procedures clearly identify who can be approached by workers that want to raise a disclosure. Organizations should ensure a range of alternative persons who a whistleblower can approach in the event a worker feels unable to approach their manager. If your organization works with a recognized union, a representative from that union could be an appropriate contact for a worker to approach.

9 Create an organizational culture where workers feel safe to raise a disclosure in the knowledge that they will not face any detriment from the organization as a result of speaking up.

10 Undertake that any detriment towards an individual who raises a disclosure is not acceptable.

11 Make a commitment that all disclosures raised will be dealt with appropriately, consistently, fairly and professionally.

12 Undertake to protect the identity of the worker raising a disclosure, unless required by law to reveal it and to offer support throughout with access to mentoring, advice and counselling.

13 Provide feedback to the worker who raised the disclosure where possible and appropriate subject to other legal requirements. Feedback should include an indication of timings for any actions or next steps.

Telling the truth

What does it take to be honest in business?

John Brown is the founder of Don't Cry Wolf, a consultancy that works with brands to put honesty at the heart of their communications. He is passionate about why brands should be honest, and clear about why most aren't. In a world of social media, he says, it is fear that stops brands being open and honest. It takes courage to be open. Over lunch, I ask him why it is so important for brands to be honest. As I say it, it seems a strange question. Surely it's obvious that companies should tell the truth? But we live in a 'post-truth' world, now, and research from the University of Essex (2011) indicates we may be becoming more tolerant of a certain level of deceit, so nothing is taken as given.[7]

'It's a market share issue,' Brown says. 'It's a competitive issue. You couldn't slide a credit card between one brand's product and another in most cases. So competitive distinction comes from the way the brand behaves, and how it communicates.' Companies know they need to change when they see their audiences going off to a competitor. 'This is about trust. Audiences who have trust in a brand are loyal.' He cites a TKMaxx advert from 2018 as an example of a brand that is brutally honest about what it offers – and what it doesn't. Narrated by Bill Nighy, the ad starts with the line: 'I know what you're thinking. Why would anyone shop at TKMaxx?' It answers the question immediately. 'It might feel a little haphazard in there, but where else do you stumble on a designer dress while looking for a frying pan?' It's honest, it's refreshing. 'It's not like one of those swanky shops with complimentary lattes,' Nighy says in the ad. 'But who cares? Look at these shoes.' This, says Brown, is bravery. 'It shows brutal awareness of what they're actually offering and who they're talking to. People believe it.'

Brown works as much on changing the culture of brands as he does on their communications. It's tough for a brand to be honest. It takes a complete change in culture. 'The only way to get consumer trust is to open all the doors,' he says. 'That means showing everything, warts and all. You show your vulnerability in order to be honest, and that's incredibly brave.'

Why is it brave? Why are brands so fearful? Brown believes that brands have retreated back into themselves with the rise in social media. 'The amount of vitriol spewed at brands when they do something wrong is astonishing,' he says. 'So brands withdraw from the public if they've messed up. We're in this situation where the public demands honesty, but they won't accept mistakes made by humans. And before anything else, a brand is a collection of humans.'

Brown believes that with the decline in the major tribe – religion – we're finding micro-tribes around beliefs, things we care passionately about. 'We're outraged about everything,' he says. 'The opportunity for rational debate has gone, in favour of tribal politics.'

And so, often, brands respond by putting up barriers. But, says Brown, they'd be better off showing their human side: 'The one thing that counteracts this vitriol is human nature.'

It's far harder, in most cases, to attack an individual who's trying to help you, than a brand that's trying to hide or obfuscate. That means being held accountable. If there's fraud within an organization, someone must take responsibility for it. If a business dodges its responsibilities, it will lead to a lack of trust.

> The three main stages to changing the culture of a brand to be more open, according to Brown, are:
>
> 1. Show vulnerability.
> 2. Be honest.
> 3. Be accountable.

Tell the truth during the crisis

In his book *What Did Jesus Drive: Crisis PR in cars, computers and Christianity*, Jason Vines tells of his first week working in PR for Chrysler.[8] One of Chrysler's lawyers came to his office and handed him the first draft of a press release announcing a product recall for a Dodge Dakota pickup. The release said that a 'failure to fix the vehicle could lead to a thermal event'. Vines asked what that meant. 'The vehicle could catch fire.'

Hiding behind language like this seems ridiculous on the face of it. But in a crisis, it feels protective, less exposed than the truth. After all, companies hide behind marketing jargon all the time. It's often a sign of uncertainty. A few years ago, my then-business partner and I had a meeting with a large technology company. We'd looked through its website and all its marketing brochures, and still neither of us had a clue what it did. So in the meeting, I asked: 'What do you do for your customers?' No one could answer me. I heard vague words like 'solutions', 'project management', 'innovation', 'consultancy', but nothing I could actually pin down. If I was going to help them communicate, I needed to know what the company did. 'Can you give me some examples?' The response was: 'That's the job of the marketing team.'

Evasive language like this makes a company seem slippery, the truth always just out of reach. In a crisis situation, it's damaging. Even 'paltering' – a relatively new word that means lying by telling a different truth – can damage a company's reputation (saying 'there is no evidence to suggest a link between this product and cancer' might be true, but it isn't quite the same as saying 'this product doesn't cause cancer'). It's probably why politicians are one of the least trusted groups of people in the world.

In these days of social media, lies, or omission of truth, will be detected and exposed. As psychologist Gill Green said to me in Chapter 1, 'People who care about these things are into the detail.' They'll research the facts, and expose the lies.

During a crisis, brands come under intense scrutiny. 'Let the crisis breathe,' Brown advises. 'Pause. Let it register.' It's good advice. Although getting information out quickly is important, it has to be the right information. You can't unsay something you've said publicly, too early in the crisis.

That doesn't mean hiding, though. I see so many companies issuing holding statements acknowledging the crisis, and then going completely quiet. The full facts can be frightening, and it's tempting to hide them until forced to disclose them. But never, ever lie. Telling the truth as soon as you have the facts can save you a lot of trouble later on. It gives you some control over the story, and positions you as the trusted source of information through the crisis. If you don't tell the truth, someone else will do it for you. And they may not be on your side.

Most importantly, take action to put right the wrongs. No major crisis is solved through communications alone. Do the right thing, and be seen to do it. If you have a data breach, what are you doing to stop it happening again? If there is a threat against your business premises, are you doing enough to ensure your people are safe? As Brown says: 'Be totally transparent. Over-communicate. If there's a video of something terrible happening that's your fault, put out your own footage of an army of your people putting it right.'

Summary of actions: Telling the truth during a crisis

1 Foster a culture of truth telling, right the way through the business. That should start at the top of the organization and should be reflected in every part of your communications.

2 Put in place a structure that encourages people to talk about their concerns, and listen to what you're told. Take business action, quickly, and be seen to be doing it. It might be hard at the time, but it'll avoid a much bigger issue in the future.

3 Hold people to account. Clear responsibilities will make it much easier to deal with the source of the crisis, and to put it right.

4 Your language and tone of voice should be clear and easy to understand. Don't hide behind jargon during a crisis (or ever). Explain what's happening, and why. And what you're doing about it.

5 Don't just talk about what you're doing to right the crisis. Let people see you take action.

Notes

1 Lee, K (2013) *Little Liars: Development of verbal deception in children*, University of Toronto, 2 November. https://pdfs.semanticscholar.org/ce2e/96fc8ad2d1c56002d32f738cbbfcf1fc1bd9.pdf.

2 Fu, G, Evans, A D, Wang, L and Lee, K (2008) Lying in the name of the collective good: A developmental study, *Developmental Science*, 11, pp 495–503.

3 Bok, S (1999) *Lying: Moral choice in public and private life*, Vintage Books.

4 Smith, J A (2017) How the science of 'blue lies' may explain Trump's support, Scientific American, 24 March. https://blogs.scientificamerican.com/guest-blog/how-the-science-of-blue-lies-may-explain-trumps-support.

5 Cowley, S (2016) At Wells Fargo, complaints about fraudulent accounts since 2005, *New York Times*, 11 October. www.nytimes.com/2016/10/12/business/dealbook/at-wells-fargo-complaints-about-fraudulent-accounts-since-2005.html?_r=0.

6 Department for Business, Innovation and Skills (2016) Whistleblowing guidance for employers. https://assets.publishing.service.gov.uk/government/uploads/system/uploads/attachment_data/file/415175/bis-15-200-whistleblowing-guidance-for-employers-and-code-of-practice.pdf.

7 Whiteley, P (2011) Are Britons becoming more dishonest? Essex Centre for the Study of Integrity, University of Essex. www1.essex.ac.uk/news/event.aspx?e_id=3879.

8 Vines, J (2014) *What Did Jesus Drive: Crisis PR in cars, computers and Christianity*, Waldorf Publishing.

Withstanding the attack 13

The importance of resilience in your communications teams

Under extreme pressure, you have to be able to rely on people to do their jobs. You have to trust people around you. That means letting go of being the only leader or decision maker.

BRIAN WOOD MC

Learning about resilience from the armed forces

Brian Wood MC is a former soldier with the British Army's Princess of Wales's Royal Regiment. In 2004, aged just 23, he was awarded a Military Cross for bravery – one of the highest awards for gallantry in combat in the UK – for his role in what became known as the Battle of Danny Boy during the Iraq War.

The Battle of Danny Boy – named after a nearby vehicle checkpoint – was the first time since the Falklands War, 26 years earlier, that British soldiers had fixed bayonets to their rifles before going into close combat. On 14 May 2004, Wood's unit was ambushed near Majar Al-Kabir in Southern Iraq by Iraqi insurgents. Wood led his men, outgunned and outnumbered, into enemy fire during a short but brutal battle. Twenty-eight Mahdi Army insurgents were killed. Wood and all his fellow soldiers emerged with no serious injuries.

I met Wood entirely by chance, in a cafe near my office. He left the Army in 2014, and now runs leadership workshops for companies, who could learn a thing or two from the lessons he learned during his 16-year military career (he joined up just before his seventeenth birthday), which spanned operations in the Balkans, Iraq and Afghanistan. As his website says,

'There is no greater leadership challenge than motivating men to put their lives on the line.' He agreed to speak to me about what his experience had taught him about resilience, and the importance of a strong team.

If anyone knows about resilience, it's Wood. The same battle that saw him awarded a Military Cross was subject to a long and expensive legal inquiry, after allegations against the Ministry of Defence of a breach of duty towards Iraqi prisoners. A British law firm, Public Interest Lawyers, claimed that a number of prisoners had been tortured and murdered immediately after the battle. In 2013, Public Interest Lawyers withdrew its allegations, and in 2014 a public inquiry found that the claims of murder and torture were 'deliberate lies'. (The lawyer at the centre of the claims, Phil Shiner, was struck off, having admitted to nine counts of acting without integrity.)[1]

It was a tough time for Wood. The Battle of Danny Boy had left him suffering from post-traumatic stress disorder (PTSD) and the inquiry felt like a betrayal. In his words, he had to 'dig deep' to get through it. 'Sometimes, testing your resilience means going to some dark places,' he says. He now spends a lot of time campaigning for better mental health support in the workplace, and he believes the Army is streets ahead of most corporates in this way.

'The Army is all about belonging. You understand what its values are, which is a big thing when you're young. Whoever you are, whatever your rank and your background, you're part of this one thing that unites you. You're a close-knit team. You all have the same values. You have a purpose.' Purpose is really important in every walk of life, he tells me. 'It doesn't matter what it is. It could be having a dog, or playing a sport, or your family, or your work. But you have to have a purpose. Otherwise...' He doesn't need to go on. Leaving the forces is hard; I know this from my own family (my father and two of my brothers were soldiers). You leave a place where the purpose and values were clear, and it can be a struggle to find the same sense of belonging in civilian life. Most soldiers I know see those they served with as family. I get the sense that Wood's purpose now is to tell his story, to raise awareness and support for people struggling with mental health issues, whatever their environment. He still pushes his own boundaries and limits. After leaving the Army, he cycled 3,000 miles across the United States, from Washington DC to Santa Monica Pier in California, in just 14 days with a group of people with physical or mental injuries, to raise money and awareness for mental health. (When I tell him I feel I'm pushing myself by doing 30 minutes on an exercise bike every morning, he says, entirely genuinely, 'That's a great thing to do. It's all about doing something regularly.')

Wood is an extraordinary man. I feel almost embarrassed asking about how important resilience is in corporate life, when resilience in the context of what he's been through is literally the difference between life and death. But he's passionate about how companies can support their people, and believes that a large part of building resilience in teams is about looking after their mental health, before, during and after the crisis event.

It's a lesson Wood learned the hard way. He didn't talk about his experience of trauma for years afterwards. 'On my first tour of Iraq, I was overwhelmed by what I had to deal with. You see constant trauma happening to people you care about. But you have to deal with it and get back out there the next day.' Talking about it helps, but Wood says it's particularly hard for men to talk. They still feel a pressure to show strength, and needing help can be perceived as weakness. Even to someone who has been awarded a Military Cross. 'If you don't talk about it, you take it out on the people who are closest to you,' he says. 'You get irritated and unreasonable, and lash out. Some people drink. Luckily I realized that I had to get help. I should have done it sooner.' I ask him why he didn't. 'I thought I might lose my job,' he says, simply. 'Of course, I didn't lose my job; that was in my head. The Army is really good at supporting you.' But when you sign up to a set of values that are all about strength, and honour, and being the best, and you're not feeling strong, that must be tough.

Wood says when you're part of a team, those around you will often pick up signals that something's wrong. 'If you're usually really good at something, and your standards slip, it could be a sign of something else going on,' he says. 'The people closest to you will see that first.' So resilience is a team thing? 'When you operate as a unit, you're stronger. You're supported. You can't be on your own in a dangerous situation. When you're coming under attack every day, and you can't get out of your compound, and someone gets injured or killed, you get through it as a team.'

Part of building that strength means looking out for each other in unexpected ways. 'I found out that one lad I was with came from a tough upbringing. He'd been bounced from orphanage to orphanage. He had no family. He didn't even have a next of kin. That meant no messages from home, no mail, no packages. When you're on operations, getting mail is really important to maintain morale. It keeps you going. He needed looking after. I said to him, the Army's your family. And I got on the satellite phone and called my wife, and I asked her to sort out a parcel for him. That had an amazing effect. He was included as part of the group when the next drop came in.'

That really interests me. In corporate life, I say, you're discouraged from asking about people's personal lives, in case it's intrusive, or seen as potentially discriminatory. I have a friend who was shocked when an interviewer asked her if she was married, for example. Wood looks surprised. 'But if you don't know about someone, you won't know how they might react to a situation,' he says. 'Of course you have to be inclusive. You can't discriminate based on that information. But it's important to know the big things in people's lives. If someone has a newborn child, for example, they might be sleep deprived, they might need more support for a while. You invest in understanding what makes them tick. It doesn't mean they can't do the job.'

(It's a sentiment echoed in John Browne's book *The Glass Closet*.[2] Browne – more formally, Lord Browne of Madingley – was CEO of BP from 1995 to 2007, and is credited with transforming the company into a world leader. He concealed his sexual orientation – he is gay – from his business colleagues and the public for nearly four decades, believing it would damage his career. He was outed after a former partner sold his story to the *Mail on Sunday* in 2007, which eventually led to Browne's resignation from BP. He believes that the double life he had to lead in order to hide sexuality from his work colleagues and from the media was ultimately damaging. Colleagues couldn't get close to him. He was distant, aloof. He couldn't open up to those around him, which meant they couldn't open up to him. Perhaps we should open up about our personal lives more, not less, in the workplace.)

I wonder if the corporate world suffers from an ingrained mistrust, something that the armed forces simply can't afford. 'Under extreme pressure, you have to be able to rely on people to do their jobs,' says Brian Wood. 'You have to trust people around you. That means letting go of being the only leader or decision maker.' He tells me that everyone, even the most junior soldiers, now know the mission of an operation, and understand the roles of everyone around them. They can see the bigger picture. And why not? As Wood says, 'If they're the ones with the metal detector in a minefield, they have the most serious job of all. Rank doesn't matter.' You have to know how everyone works together, and trust them to do their job. Sometimes, that means letting go of power. 'If you invest in bringing someone onto the team and then you don't trust them to do their job, that's just bad management,' says Wood. 'If you don't trust them, you'll end up micromanaging them. If you do that, no one will volunteer upwards. They start just doing their job, and not going above and beyond.' That could spell disaster in a crisis situation.

The importance of shared values

Hearing Wood talking about the Army's values, and what it's like to fall short of them, made me think about my own company's values, and whether they are inclusive enough. I think now it's something every company should consider. We used to have a value of 'be positive'. But in an industry that's struggling with mental health (nearly 60 per cent of PR professionals have experience mental health problems, according to a 2017 PRCA/PR Week report),[3] and as a result of talking to Wood we've changed that to 'try to find the positive'. Not everyone can be positive all the time. You're setting up your team to fail.

Wood suggests that 'mutual support' would be a strong value for a company. I think that's a great idea. He says this is where the military excels. You're never alone, never isolated, physically or mentally.

Almost every company has a vision, a mission, a set of values. Every person in that company should be able to articulate them, and live by them. In a crisis situation, though, you have to make decisions, quickly. If you know what your values are, and how they translate into real situations, you know how to behave. You have the confidence to make those decisions. You have what Wood calls 'moral courage'. So when you set your company values, imagine what they'd look like (and sound like) in a crisis situation. It's a powerful way to test them.

Planning resilience

Resilience is 'continuity plus risk management'

Dee Youngs is Business Resilience Manager for the British Government's Joint Forces Command, an organization established in 2012 to organize and manage military capabilities (such as training and education, intelligence, cyber and medical services) that span all three of the UK's defence forces – the Army, the Royal Navy and the Royal Air Force. Part of Youngs' role is to create policies and processes to build resilience, all of which helps to ensure that the nation's critical assets are protected.

She defines resilience as 'continuity, plus risk management'. This is important: many organizations confuse resilience with business continuity. They're different. Resilience helps you withstand your walls being battered. Continuity is what you do when the walls have come down. 'Business continuity is being able to function through the crisis. It's about reacting,' she tells me.

Figure 13.1 Business continuity is being able to continue to operate after the attack

SOURCE Illustration by Patrick Miller, used with permission

Figure 13.2 Resilience is withstanding the attack

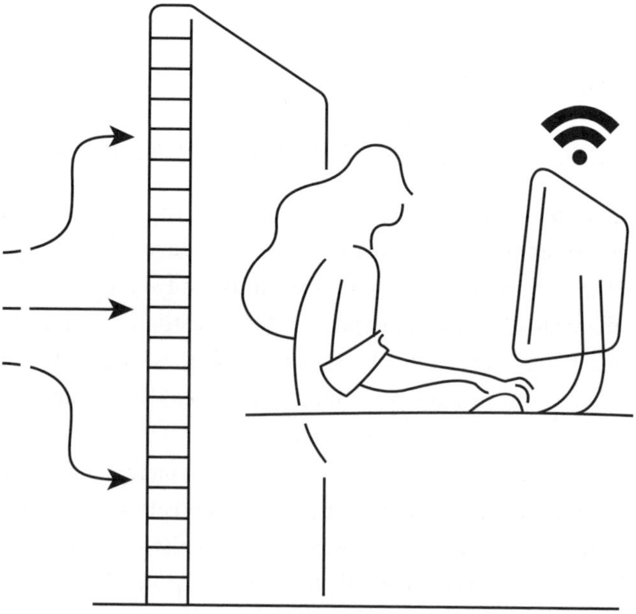

SOURCE Illustration by Patrick Miller, used with permission

'Resilience is being able to withstand the crisis. It's about planning.' She echoes what Brian Wood said to me about bringing the whole business together. 'Resilience matters to all areas of the business – infrastructure, HR, finance, third party contractors. It means the whole organization is fit to go forward.'

Building resilience takes time. It means spotting the flaws in the business, and fixing them. Youngs describes it as 'shoring up your defences'. If you do that, she says, you know exactly what to do as part of your continuity plan.

How to get back to normal

First, of course, you have to define what normal looks like, and who are the critical personnel to get you there. 'You can't decide that in the middle of a crisis,' she says.

For the armed forces, normal looks pretty different than for a company – but the principle is the same. Normal for a company might be your pre-crisis share price, or net promoter score, or sales levels. There could be other indicators of normal: complaints dipping under a certain level, satisfaction scores, retention figures, revenue per customer, or staff turnover.

There are three major parts to resilience:

Table 13.1 The three parts of resilience

1. Physical resilience	Are your buildings resilient? Will they withstand a hurricane or flooding? This leads to business continuity: where will your people work if they can't get into the office? How will your team function?
2. Business resilience	Are you prepared for change? Assess trends based on what's happened in the past, and what you predict will happen in the future. Where do you invest to prepare for climate change, for example?
3. Personnel resilience	Are your people equipped to deal with the threats you've predicted? How will they cope in a crisis? This isn't something just for the board, but for every level of the company.

Supporting mental health at work

Managing stress within the organization is critical to building resilience, Youngs says, and not just during the crisis. Building resilience in an organization means building personal resilience for its members. The Army is looking at areas like flexible working for some personnel (fairly obviously not for those on active service), which surprises me. But unless we're in a state of war, why not? 'We'll look at all ways to deal with residual stress from an active situation,' says Youngs. If the Army can do it, surely commercial organizations can, too. That flexibility might just give someone the space to recover from a traumatic or stressful experience, or keep them at their peak so they are better prepared to manage a crisis situation when it comes.

Youngs talks about focusing on well-being overall, and giving people the support they need across different areas of their life. One element of this is 'white space' coaching, a term for giving people a safe space in which to talk to someone about anything at all, whether it's a work issue or a home issue, and helping them come up with the solutions they need. It's a process that empowers them to manage their mental health, and reduce anxiety. Youngs supports what Brian Wood told me: that resilience means having a total view of what's happening in someone's world, not just one slice of it. In the forces, the importance of family welfare is widely recognized; the potential impact for a soldier's family members, for example, is obvious, and the forces understand they're asking a lot not just of their serving soldiers, but also of their families. Every camp has a family welfare centre, for example. Again, I think business could learn from this. As our work and home lives become more connected, we must support our teams to help them withstand the pressures not just of working life, but of home life, too. If you have a job that takes you away on regular trips abroad, that will have an impact on your home life. It would be helpful for an employer to recognize that and give you practical support in managing that impact.

The forces have always been ahead of other organizations in recognizing the importance of mental health (although there is always work still to be done), recognizing and offering support for conditions like PTSD. Of course, when you're in a life or death situation, no one questions the need for people to be at their peak fitness both physically and mentally. But in my experience, businesses don't necessarily make the connection between mental health and resilience in preparing for a crisis.

The forces also recognize that you can't sustain high levels of pressure indefinitely. Periods of leave follow active service (rest and recuperation – R&R – was first a military term before it entered common language). In a crisis situation in business, you can apply the same principles. Give someone a break to recover after they've been exposed to a period of stress. They'll come back stronger for it.

Brian Wood believes that mental health should be much more of a focus in business, and should be a priority right from the top leaders. 'No one really looks at the stress that work brings. It can be overwhelming. Where do you turn if you need help?' He says every organization should have a support structure in place. That could be a physical place that people can go, or a culture of open doors and communication. 'We support kids in school with their mental health,' he says. 'But we forget that when young people enter the workplace.'

All this takes a shift in culture, and a willingness for business to take some responsibility for its employees' mental health. Building a supportive culture means being clear about how people are to behave as soon as they enter the organization. If you have a culture of constant pressure, presenteeism, and in-fighting, that will slowly break down the organization's resilience. But if, as Wood says, your whole team is working together to achieve a single goal, there's a culture of trust that everyone will step up and do their job well, and everyone in the organization supports each other, then you are effectively building resilience into the business. The whole becomes greater than the sum of its parts.

Build a resilience plan, action it, communicate it and measure it

Resilience is something you can, and should, document and plan. 'It's a series of processes,' says Youngs. She recommends refreshing and updating a resilience plan every three years, or whatever makes the most sense for your business cycle. (Updating it too often means you'll never get anything done.) Include activity plans against the three areas of resilience training above (physical, business and personnel). What are the threats in each section? And what are the actions you can take in order not to be taken down by those threats? That might include looking at culture, security, monitoring and social listening, communications practices (including social media), induction processes, training, managing mental health, well-being initiatives and incentives.

Great planning and initiatives are irrelevant if no one knows about them. 'Shout about it!' says Youngs. Put your plans on the intranet, do regular training, and talk about it in inductions. And, importantly, communicate them to your contractors – you're only as resilient as your weakest link.

How do you measure resilience (before it's too late)? Youngs says you can look at progression. 'What are you doing now that you weren't doing a year ago? Does everyone know the risks and have a resilience and continuity plan?' But first, you need to have SMART (specific, measurable, attainable, realistic and time-bound) objectives. 'At what point are you prepared to say, "We're resilient"?' She stresses the need to run regular exercises, in order to learn lessons in a controlled environment. 'What are the lessons learned from exercises? Does everyone know what they should do in a crisis? These are all things you can test.'

Summary of actions: Building resilience

1. Have a clear vision that everyone in the business is working toward.
2. Communicate clear values that are inclusive.
3. Build a culture of resilience: trust, collaboration, communication.
4. Support mental health and physical health for your teams.
5. Create your resilience plan around three areas: physical, business and personnel.
6. Have SMART objectives that you can measure.
7. Exercise the plan regularly (more on this in Chapter 18).

Notes

1. BBC (2017) Iraq lawyer Phil Shiner struck off over misconduct, BBC News online, 2 February. www.bbc.co.uk/news/uk-38841544.
2. Browne, J (2014) *The Glass Closet: Why coming out is good for business*, W H Allen.
3. Griggs, I (2017) Majority of respondents to industry survey say they have experienced mental ill health, PR Week/PRCA 11 May. www.prweek.com/article/1433196/majority-respondents-industry-survey-say-experienced-mental-ill-health.

PART THREE
Building your crisis communication strategy and response

The brain's response to a crisis and training your team to cope

14

Part of our job is to be able to handle whatever happens, no matter how unexpected or unanticipated it is.

CAPTAIN CHESLEY SULLENBERGER

On a cold afternoon in January 2009, Captain Chesley Sullenberger (known as 'Sully') safely landed US Airways Flight 1549 on the Hudson River, saving all its 155 passengers and crew. The Airbus A320, a minute into its routine flight from New York's LaGuardia Airport to Charlotte, North Carolina, had been hit by a flock of geese and both its engines had lost power. It had effectively become a glider. Sullenberger had to make a fast and critical decision: risk turning the plane round and attempt to get it back to LaGuardia; glide it to a small airport in Teterboro, New Jersey; or find somewhere else to land. The wrong choice would have been catastrophic, as Sullenberger said later. He opted to 'ditch' the aircraft (the aviation term for landing on water) in the Hudson River, and managed to land the plane straight and slowly enough to avoid it breaking up. Recordings from the flight show that Sullenberger and his crew – who between them had more than 100 years of experience in the air – remained calm, despite their fear. Sullenberger told Air Traffic Control: 'We may end up in the Hudson,' and later the more definite: 'We're gonna be in the Hudson.' Afterwards, he said that he had been shocked, but felt 'very focused' during the landing, although in the following days many of the crew suffered from sleeplessness, flashbacks and elements of post-traumatic stress. The crew reported that most passengers in the front of the cabin remained calm (the back hit the water first and with greater impact, so was more chaotic). They adopted the brace position, some made phone calls, others remained quiet in the moments before the landing.

Sullenberger was a former US Air Force pilot and an aviation instructor, as well as one of the industry's most experienced commercial pilots. His background meant he had extensive experience in flying not just powered aircraft, but gliders – something that must have been useful when he had to glide Flight 1549 into the Hudson. Like all airline pilots, he had gone through regular flight training, simulator exercises and classroom training to equip him to handle the unexpected. While you can't train someone for every emergency, you can give them the tools to make decisions and apply lessons to different situations. His experience and training saved 155 lives that day. Sullenberger told CBS News: 'One way of looking at this might be that, for 42 years, I've been making small regular deposits in this bank of experience: education and training, and on January 15, the balance was sufficient so that I could make a very large withdrawal.'[1]

Pilots train for a wide range of different scenarios, including engine failures; and airlines run regular simulator training for pilots. But in an interview on *The Late Show* in 2016, Sullenberger said that he had never done simulation training to land on water, as the flight simulators 'weren't programmed for it'. Double engine failure followed by ditching isn't something that pilots are expected to have to deal with, much less do successfully. But Sullenberger's training, aptitude and experience came into play on that wintry afternoon. He was able to put theory into practice: 'We had to dig deep, adapt what we did know and apply it to solve a problem we'd never seen before.'

The brain's response to a crisis

Fight or flight

When we're faced with a threat, we do one of three things: fight, flee or – if neither of these are possible – freeze. All three can save us. When we spot a threat, our eyes or ears send an instant signal to our brain (to the amygdala), before we've consciously registered it. The amygdala sends a distress message to the hypothalamus, the control room of our brain. That activates a physical response: adrenaline pumps through our bodies, our heart rate and blood pressure goes up, our flow of blood to the muscles increases, and our pupils dilate. Our airways open up to release more oxygen to the brain, and our senses become sharper. We release blood sugar to give us a rush of energy. If the threat continues, we release cortisol, which keeps us alert. Our brain is doing something it learned from our ancient ancestors – it is preparing our body to fight off a predator, or to run from it. It happens so quickly that it can help us jump out of the way of a speeding car, without really thinking about what we're doing (often, people won't remember the precise details of what happened). It kicks in without us having to make a conscious decision – *should I jump left, or right?* It's instinct – or rather a complex set of chemical responses.

If we can't fight the threat, or run from it, we'll do the next best thing to protect ourselves. We'll freeze. A predator may not see us if we stand stock-still. Our best chance of survival could be to play dead, or shut down completely. During times of extreme trauma, we may disassociate from what's happening to us. Our heart rate slows and blood pressure reduces, and our body releases endorphins, which act as a kind of painkiller. Our brain gives us what protection it can to cope with the trauma, when there is no other alternative but to live through it. During the event, or afterwards, this kind of dissociation may mean we can't hear or remember what happened, or what we're told. We 'go blank' or feel numb. We may find it hard to make decisions.

Faced with an immediate threat, we don't have the time to activate our rational, System 2 brain, which considers a decision carefully and looks at all the potential consequences of an action. Everything is geared to help us survive the short-term. It's an incredibly clever system when you're faced with real and immediate danger. But it's not so useful when you need to deploy rational thinking to deal with something that has a longer-term impact, like corporate reputation. During a crisis, you want a team around you who are calm, have clarity of vision and who can make a decision. You do not want people who will fight, run or freeze. That's a challenge when you consider how what our brains are telling our bodies to do.

We saw in Chapter 10 how importance resilience is within a team. But, in my experience, resilience training, if it's done at all, rarely includes crisis communications teams. And yet they will come under extreme and sustained pressure during a crisis, dealing with the public on social media, with journalists, analysts, investors, stakeholders. Resilience to cope with that can, in part, be learned.

When I run crisis simulations for brands' crisis communications teams who have never run a crisis exercise before, I see how quickly a team becomes tired, irritable and snappy when under pressure. There's a clear pattern. For the first hour or two of the exercise, the team members work well together. They communicate well with each other. They're alert, and ready to deal with whatever the crisis throws at them. But by hour three, the cracks start to appear. Their energy is running low. They may not have taken a screen break, or drunk enough water to keep hydrated. They're stiff from sitting too long. Small mistakes creep in: typos, slight contradictions, bypassing processes. After a half-day, they're fractious with each other and with the people they're communicating with – journalists, members of the public, politicians, stakeholders. By hours five and six, they doubt their own ability, so they find it harder to make decisions. Their messages are confused. They're starting to lose control of the crisis. Their ability to cope as the pressure increases might look like this:

Figure 14.1 Ability to cope versus rising stress levels in a crisis

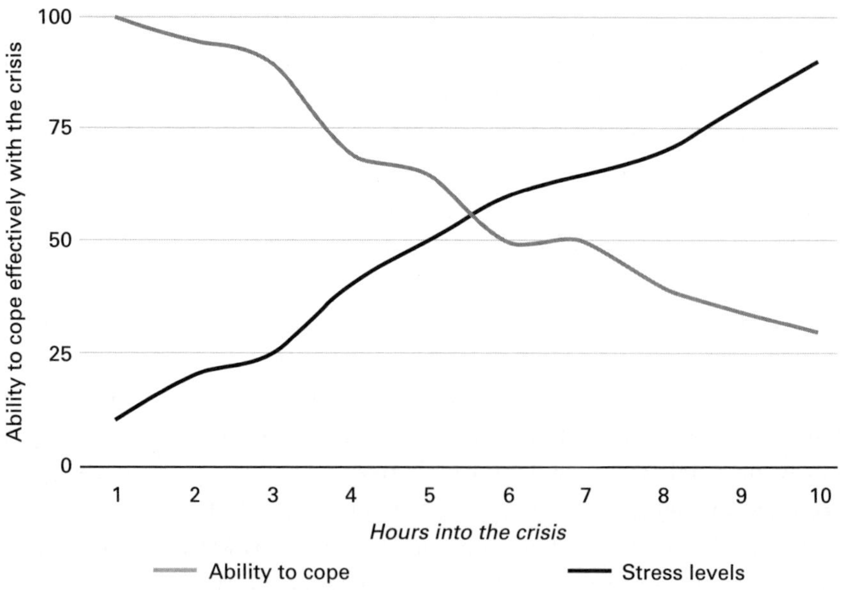

But if you switched out your team every four hours, when their ability to cope is waning, it would look like this:

Figure 14.2 Switching out your teams increases your effectiveness in a crisis

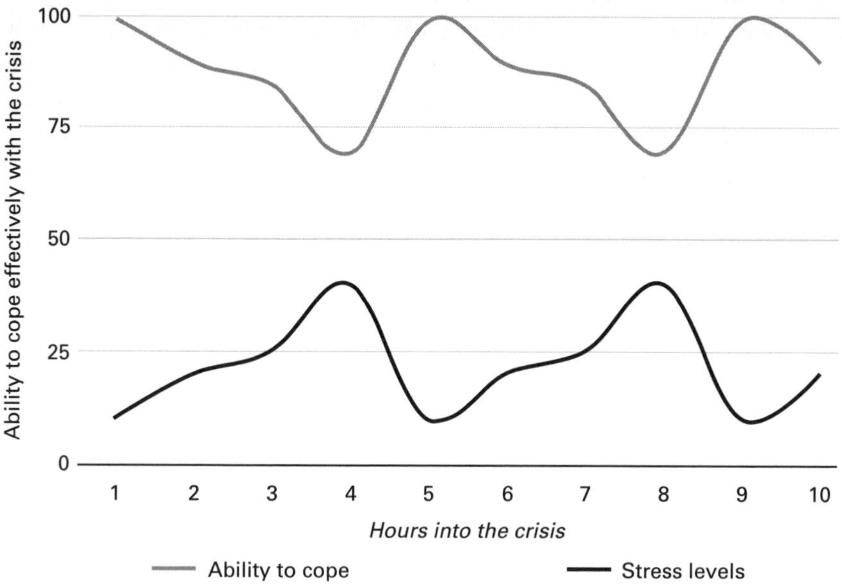

Preparing your team

Building personal resilience

Resilience is sometimes seen as an inherent character trait. And there may be people who are naturally more resilient than others. But you can give people an environment where resilience is built in.

Rachel Boothroyd is a communication and performance coach with a background in law, business and science. In her thirties, she was a senior partner in a global top 20 City law firm in London, the most senior woman in the London office. At 37, she was diagnosed with serious heart disease. She had no known risk factors and didn't fit any of the profiles for someone with heart disease – she was young, slim, fit and had a healthy diet. It was a diagnosis that led her to change her life. She changed her career path, became an ambassador for the British Heart Foundation, and she now runs her own training and coaching firm, The Performance Lift, working with executives and senior teams on all aspects of communication, performance and development, including resilience.

Boothroyd believes her heart disease was triggered by the stress of her working life and resulting isolation (corporate lawyers notoriously do long hours with little time for a healthy social life outside of work). This theory is supported by two major pieces of research. In 2018, the *Journal of the American Heart Association* published research showing a link between isolation and risk of death or hospitalisation from heart disease.[2] In 2016, an observational study by the University of York showed a link between social isolation and loneliness and heart disease.[3]

This is relevant for people dealing with a crisis situation. If you're under attack, you tend to go into isolation. 'The most important thing you can do is to stay connected,' Boothroyd tells me. 'Find connections who understand what you're going through, or who are going through the same thing. You'll become far stronger as a team. If you go into isolation, your resilience wears down. Your ability to withstand pressure is worn away.' (Brian Wood, who talked to me in Chapter 13 about his experience of resilience, says these connections are why Army friendships last for so long; there are tight bonds between people who've gone through something big together.) Boothroyd emphasises that there is a paradox here: 'Your instinct will be telling you to drive ahead alone, it will feel right to isolate and push forwards.' For this reason, she says, resilience training needs to redirect established thought patterns, providing pathways to override unhelpful instincts.

There are cultural shifts that business can make to train and support their teams to become more resilient. Boothroyd talks about focusing first on 'humanness', something she said businesses often don't really think about. 'Who's the ideal worker, from a business point of view? It's someone who is never ill, who has no family issues, whose children are never ill, who gets to work on time, never needs to leave early, plans their holidays or any absences well in advance. Where's the humanness in that? This (western) model of the ideal worker simply doesn't exist.'

So instead of planning around the non-existent ideal worker, businesses should factor in the slightly messier reality. 'That's the biggest change in business,' says Boothroyd. 'We're starting to accept that we're human. We have flaws.'

Part of that is putting a structure in place to support mental health. 'Build a process that means you can recognize the signs that someone's about to go off the rails. If someone is quicker than usual to fly off the handle, they're feeling too much pressure, their brain chemistry is starting to change their responses,' says Boothroyd.

The process I have in my own agency (after doing training with Boothroyd) is to have a two-minute mental health check call with the team every morning. We talk in terms of brain chemistry rather than 'mental health', 'stress' or 'coping'. We find it gives people permission to be open about how they're feeling – we feel more freedom, perhaps less judgement, when we share with each other in this way. That's useful to me, because if one person is under pressure, but another is feeling ready to take on the world, we can play to people's strengths that day, avoiding potential issues. We can also spot trends that could indicate longer-term problems within the team. It encourages us all to open up and support each other, as well as taking charge of our own mental health. As a result, I believe we function better as a team.

Boothroyd encourages businesses to build mindfulness into their training. 'People need head space. They can't sustain long periods without a break. Change your physical environment. Take a walk in nature. Pause. Breathe. This is fundamentally nurturing, and its necessary for our mental health. This has now been scientifically proven with mindfulness often described as a "reboot" for the stress chemicals released in the brain.' Excessive rumination can be damaging, too, she says, and stops us focusing on the task at hand. 'Good resilience training will give you techniques to avoid catastrophic thinking, which creates pressure. If you're thinking about the worst scenario, then you experience it physiologically. Mindfulness training can help you deal with this, and focus on one thing at a time.'

She advises giving yourself a resilience test. 'Ask yourself, "How am I doing this week?" There are behavioural signs of stress hormone overload in the brain (such as unusually quick temper, loss of short-term memory, eating unhealthily) that you can build into a simple personal check-in. Self-cure, so pressure doesn't pile up. If it does, you can end up breaking the relationships that you need to sustain you. That leads to isolation, which leads to more pressure. It's self-perpetuating.'

Creating pauses in your schedule is something that Brian Wood recommends, too. He calls it the 'cigar moment' – the time you take to breath, reconfigure, regroup. Businesses can build these moments into their crisis plans, and train people to stop, breathe, think, talk, and only then react. 'If you're on a battlefield, you need that time out so you can analyse what's happening.' In a business context, that means pausing before sending that email or message. 'Get a coffee first. Take 10 minutes out to think about your response,' says Wood. 'Analyse, think, then execute.'

Building in longer breaks for teams can build resilience, too. You need rest and recuperation after a crisis, otherwise you risk chronic burnout. Encourage people to take their full holiday: ideally two weeks together, which is a good recovery time, according to Wood. Rotate your team, giving people proper time away to recuperate, and never let anyone face the flak alone. 'A fixed target will go down,' says Wood. 'At some point you'll break if you're on your own.' He suggests sending a team away to bond. Footballers do this – they have a break with their teams. They're away from the day-to-day pressure, the media. The come back refreshed, recharged and focused. They've spent time with people who share the same experience.

Teaching optimism

Martin EP Seligman is Director of the Positive Psychology Centre at the University of Pennsylvania. He is known as the 'father of positive psychology', and is one of the team behind the Penn Resiliency Program, a programme of resilience training that is used by organizations across the world, including the US Army. In the late 1960s and early 1970s he was part of a team running an experiment on what he terms 'learned helplessness', which found that people who experience something mildly painful, over which they have no control, will accept it without trying to change their situation. The experiment subjected two groups of people to loud noise. One group could stop it by pushing a button; the second couldn't. A third, control, group, heard nothing at all. Later, all three groups were subjected to a different situation involving noise. All they have to do to switch off the noise is to move their hands. The first and third groups did this; the second didn't. They had learned from the previous experiment that they had no control – they had become passive. But his subsequent research showed that around a third of people who experience 'inescapable shocks' don't become helpless. He discovered that these people showed optimism, and he set out to teach the characteristics of optimism as a way of countering learned helplessness and building resilience. This is the basis of the Penn programme.[4]

Seligman describes the building blocks of resilience and growth as PERMA: positive emotion, engagement, relationships, meaning and accomplishment. The Penn programme focuses on six areas of training:

1. Self-awareness: The ability to pay attention to your thoughts, emotions, behaviours and psychological reactions.
2. Self-regulation: The ability to change your thoughts, emotions, behaviours and physiology in the service of the desired outcome.
3. Mental agility: The ability to look at situations from multiple perspectives and to think creatively and flexibly.

4 Strengths of character: The ability to use your top strengths to engage authentically, overcome challenges and create a life aligned with one's values.

5 Connection: The ability to build and maintain strong, trusting relationships.

6 Optimism: The ability to notice and expect the positive, to focus on what you can control and to take purposeful action.

These are all areas that every business can use to develop resilience in their teams, equip them to handle a crisis and recover from it.

The building blocks of resilience and growth, according to Seligman, are:

- positive emotion;
- engagement;
- relationships;
- meaning;
- accomplishment.

Training one up

Wood talks about 'training one up' in preparation for a crisis. This is a principle used in the Army of training to be able to do the job of the person above you. 'If your next in command is shot, you need to be able to take over their kit and do their job. That could be critical in a combat situation,' he says.

While most businesses won't encounter a situation that extreme, the principle is sound. If the person a level above is taken out of the business for any reason, it should never leave a hole that can't be filled. To train one up, you have to know the intent of the people above you, the broader vision for the whole team and the specifics of their roles. Key to all this, of course, is good communication. Wood suggests asking your finance team what the marketing team does, and encouraging different teams to learn about what they all do. 'Get everyone together to talk to them about what the broader vision and issues are. They'll understand their role in the bigger picture.' You could even try role shadowing, or switching roles for a short period.

Simulation training

Cognitive scientist and Barnard College President Sian Leah Beilock says that one of the reasons we 'choke' or fail to perform under pressure is because we pay too much attention to what we're doing.[5] Her research team worked with football teams, asking them to focus on one detail of their performance – which side of their feet were touching the ball during set moves in practice. They had to concentrate on a detail that usually they would have done unconsciously. The result was that their performance dropped. They were slower.

Beilock says that there are some things best left to autopilot, outside of our conscious awareness. If we focus on too many things at once, we fail. But under pressure, we try to control things we shouldn't – so we mess up. Too much control, as with her footballers, leads to failure.

We get anxious ahead of a situation we think of as stressful, and that anxiety is contagious. Beilock's research shows that, for example, when adults are worried about maths, children around them worry too (she finds this is more in girls and women than boys and men). She observed adults helping their children to do maths homework, and found that the children of parents who believed they couldn't do maths were less likely to do well in maths, too. But when they turned maths into fun activities and problem solving to do with their children, the children's attitudes (and performance) changed. The environment under which you learn matters.

To deal with this anxiety and pressure, Beilock says, we should practise under the conditions we're going to perform under. This helps us get used to the pressure and learn to trust our unconscious ability to perform.

This is why simulation training is so important. In a crisis simulation, your teams get first-hand experience of what it would be like to manage a live crisis. Plans and processes are great, but nothing compares to the pressure of dealing with a real situation. As Sullenberger and other airline pilots have discovered, simulation training creates a realistic environment to help you prepare for the worst case scenario. This stress tests a crisis plan, finds any gaps in process, and identifies potential break points in the teams.

During a crisis, we need to be calm, clear and creative in our problem solving. But our brain's response to the crisis makes that challenging. We need to override our fight or flight instincts. So an experimental, realistic simulation learning and training model is our best chance of success. The key is to reduce the perception of likelihood of failure (unlearning 'learned helplessness' behaviour), and the perceived threat. Boothroyd says you do this by:

1 Associative learning. This is the most powerful way to create lasting learned behaviour. The combination of learning with emotion creates what Boothroyd calls 'a sort of "epigenetic lock"' to the learning. Emotion is a great memory aid: it's said that everyone remembers where they were when Kennedy was shot. The details become unforgettable, locked in by the emotion.

2 Rehearsal. Neuroplasticity is the ability of the brain to create enduring connections when we physically rehearse certain steps or processes. This means that if we practise something, we can programme our brains not to forget it. If you stall a car, you 'automatically' put it right, despite being under pressure.

3 Building team confidence. Working together as a team is vital, as we've seen. But you need confidence in yourself and in those around you. Rehearsing as a team develops cohesion in the team, and confidence in each other.

My father, when he was a soldier in his twenties, used to parachute jump in the army. This was in the days of round canopies and no safety chutes. He learned to perfect a parachute landing fall, or parachute roll – elbows tight to the body, knees bent and together, roll to the side – to protect the body from the impact of landing. Fast forward 60-odd years, and he tripped going down a flight of concrete steps at the back of his house. Most people would instinctively put their arms out to break their fall. Not dad. He went straight into a parachute roll, and landed without so much as a bruise. His instincts, learned from training many decades earlier, had kicked in.

Summary of actions: Equipping your team to cope

1 Develop a personal resilience training model for your crisis team, to equip them to deal with an oncoming crisis.

2 Plan to build in 'recovery' breaks and rotate your teams during a crisis, and prepare to switch out your teams after four hours in the crisis.

3 Develop mental health support processes and awareness in your teams.

4 Focus on 'humanness' and remember the ideal employee doesn't exist. Plan and train accordingly.

5 Train one up, so you can cope with any team changes.

6 Don't micromanage every part of the crisis.

7 Run realistic crisis simulations to lock in learning and override 'fight or flight' instincts.

Notes

1 Couric, K (2009) Capt. Sully worried about the airline industry, CBS News, 10 February. www.cbsnews.com/news/capt-sully-worried-about-airline-industry.

2 Manemann, S, et al (2018) Perceived social isolation and outcomes in patients with heart failure, *Journal of the American Heart Association*, 23 May. www.ahajournals.org/doi/10.1161/JAHA.117.008069.

3 Valtorta, NK, Kanaan, M, Gilbody, S, et al (2016) Loneliness and social isolation as risk factors for coronary heart disease and stroke: Systematic review and meta-analysis of longitudinal observational studies, *British Medical Journal Heart*, 102, pp 1009–16. https://heart.bmj.com/content/102/13/1009.info.

4 Seligman, MEP (1975) *Helplessness: On depression, development, and death*, W H Freeman/Times Books/ Henry Holt & Co. More information on this research and the Penn Programme available at: https://positivepsychologyprogram.com/learned-helplessness-seligman-theory-depression-cure/#seligman-learned-helplessness.

5 Beilock, SL (2010) *Choke: What the secrets of the brain reveal about getting it right when you have to*, Free Press.

Insights from crisis communication influencers on managing the threats facing brands

15

Insight interview 1: Duncan Gallagher, Head of Issues and Crisis EMEA, Edelman

Context is critical

The most important thing in a crisis is to put it into context. Understand exactly what issue you're facing. It's not always as clear as it seems. The issue you end up managing isn't necessarily the one you started with.

Your focus should be on how to protect the brand's licence to operate. If you have a contaminated product, the issue you manage initially will be the product recall. But what really matters is getting the product restocked on the retailer's shelves after the crisis is over. Dealing with the recall is relatively easy. It's what happens next that's more complex. You need to still be trading at the end of the crisis.

Get your team right

I look for three things in a crisis team:

1. A 'benign dictator' leading the team. You need someone who listens, who lets people have their voice but ultimately who makes a decision. You can't make a collective decision.
2. People who are on the team because of their expertise, not their job titles. Don't have the head of IT fronting a data breach crisis just because of their title, if their number two is the expert on cybersecurity.
3. The person heading up your team should be the least impacted by the issue. You don't want the head of IT leading your cyber breach crisis team. He or she won't have the headspace, they'll be focusing on their world. You need someone who can make a business decision. Airlines are good at this. The CEO usually doesn't lead the crisis, as they'll have to do media briefings, meetings with COBRA (the UK government's emergency response team) and so on. So they can't be the one to make a decision to ground planes.

Use PACE or RACI with your crisis team

Use either the PACE or the RACI model for your team. It will save you vital time during the crisis. Work smart, not hard. Don't have a war room that you sit in for 12 hours a day. Working smarter comes from preparing for a crisis. Most companies will know what crises they could face. Do your risk assessments, have a practical plan, know who's in charge, who has what role. Have a process. That could save you 24 hours in a crisis, and it will help take the emotion out of the situation.

Use either PACE or RACI to identify roles and responsibilities

The PACE model:

P: Process owner. The person who leads the team through the crisis.

A: Approver. The person who makes the decisions through the crisis.

C: Contributors. Those who input information or opinions to the crisis.

E: Executors. Those who carry out the work required.

The RACI model (sometimes known as RASCI):

R: Responsible. Someone who ultimately owns the issue.

A: Accountable. The person to whom the 'R' is accountable. This is the person who is ultimately accountable in the crisis, and who will sign off actions.

(S: Supportive. Someone who can provide support during the crisis.)

C: Consulted. Someone who has information or resource that will be useful during the crisis.

I: Informed. The person who needs to be informed and updated through the crisis, but does not need to be consulted.

Always close off an issue

One of the biggest changes I've seen in the last few years is that you have to close an issue off, even if it means reigniting it temporarily. If you don't, it could become the thing that defines you. It will certainly have an impact on your next issue. It's tempting, if people have stopped talking about what's happened, to say, 'It's gone quiet, let's leave it alone now.' But you need to get something on public record that the crisis has ended, or that the allegations aren't true.

Media are not your most important stakeholders

Beware of over-focusing on external audiences. Look at multiple stakeholders, including your internal audiences, not just media. You have to do a detailed stakeholder analysis. What are the concerns and expectations of each group, and are there gaps between those expectations and what you can deliver?

Of course, media are important, but your issue shouldn't be defined by the media agenda. There will be other groups that have much more of a direct impact on your ability to operate – your customers, partners, suppliers, even your landlord in some cases.

A Q&A document will not solve your crisis.

Don't believe that a Q&A document and statement will solve your crisis. Instead, think about the narrative of how you're managing the issue. Get all your facts and talking points down into a coherent story. Forget the Q&A. In the world we live in now, you need content. That might be a series of pieces to camera, or visual content that tells the story of how you're managing the issue.

Leading the crisis doesn't make you the spokesperson

Firstly, ask the question: do you want to put up a spokesperson in the first place? Whoever's up in front of media will always be associated with that issue. If the CEO is not sincere, they shouldn't front the crisis.

Ask the tough questions. Who is the right person to have in front of media? An external consultant can give the tough advice, such as telling a CEO that they're not the right person to be the spokesperson.

You may not want to put the CEO in front of media straight away, depending on the seriousness of the crisis. Leave yourself somewhere to go. If it's an operational issue it might be that the operational head is a better person to front the crisis. Don't overreact and start the process by cancelling Christmas, if you don't need to.

Speed isn't as important as you think

Speed is not the most important thing in a crisis. Don't allow a vacuum to form, but I see so many mistakes made by people rushing to get information out. This is why you have to have strong processes. If you have a model and a structure and an agenda, you can react efficiently. In the aviation industry, if a plane crashes, all airlines have a minute-by-minute process that tells them how to respond in the first 30 minutes. But if you say something that's not right, you'll have to backtrack and dig yourself out of a hole. Crises these days have a long tail.

Be honest

People expect you to have all the answers, but it's better to be honest and say you don't have an answer, than to fudge it. The same principles apply now as they've always done: be transparent, build trust, be heard. Do what you say you'll do.

Crisis communications can't solve bad business decisions

It takes more than communications to manage a crisis. It is possible to protect the share price and the company's licence to operate, and to make tough decisions that protect the long-term reputation of the company. But none of those will be achieved by communications decisions alone. You have to take tough business decisions. A good crisis consultant will push back to companies, and say 'To get out of this you need to change your business practices.'

Insight interview 2: James Dunny, Director and EMEA Head of Crisis and Issues Management, Fleishmanhillard

Chemistry is the most overlooked part of a crisis team

In a crisis, people need to react quickly, and the chemistry of the team is so important. When you walk into a boardroom there are a number of different dynamics at play. The CEO may be stressed because he might lose his job, the Chief Financial Officer may see the crisis as an opportunity to further their career. People bring different agendas to the process. You like to think that the team is working together to solve the problem, but the truth is they don't always.

Look at the relationships between the people on your crisis team and how they communicate with each other. All too often, the person who shouts the loudest gets their way. The Chief Science Officer might be shy and unable to have their voice heard so their opinion gets overlooked. A great leader will listen to everyone, not just the loudest. They'll know the personalities of their team and how they mix.

You see what people are really like in a crisis. The dynamics are fascinating. It takes a good team to get through a messy crisis. They have to work well together. If they don't, it will all come apart very quickly.

Your leader is the conductor of the team.

Too often people expect their leader to be the best and most knowledgeable person in the room. But they're not necessarily. They have the skill to bring in the best people, and let them do their job. The leader is a conductor, and a decision maker.

External consultants can tell it how it is

External consultants are more able to give the tough advice. If you're outside the organization, you bring a different perspective to what is happening around the crisis boardroom table. You may not know the culture inside out, or the fact that there's a merger happening in three weeks, or that the person who caused the crisis is the brother of the head of IT – but you can say to the CEO 'you need to take that person out of the room'. An external consultant can provide good objective advice when required where an in-house communications expert may struggle. A good leader will listen to advice, even if it's hard to hear, as ultimately it is their neck on the line.

Communication is the message received, not the message delivered

We deal with absolutes now, with people who are so sure they're right. They want their time on social media to pass judgement, without knowing the full story. That's very difficult in a crisis situation where some people don't want to hear the truth if it doesn't suit their agenda. The public can be fed misinformation by a self-serving politician, or by a commentator who doesn't have the facts. Think about who benefits – and who doesn't – from the truth being available.

In many crisis situations the role of third party advocates and confidants is crucial By already having established third party relationships a company can brief the necessary people, such as media or politicians, who can then themselves ask the right questions. This can be very successful in helping to influence the direction of a crisis. It can be far more effective than releasing a statement that no one wants to hear.

Legal and communications should work together

Communications and legal advisers naturally have a diametric position. Our job as communications advisers is to make sure the company reputation is still intact tomorrow. Legal's job is to win a case in a number of months or years' time. Legal deals in absolutes; it looks at the crisis through a single lens: this is the law. Communications deals in uncertainty and experience.

We each need to understand the other's role, and work together to serve both interests.

Have a single crisis plan

So many companies have separate plan for crisis communications and business continuity plans (BCPs). But communications is a key part of business continuity, so the two must be combined. Just having a BCP, without integrating communications, is dangerous and can lead to misplaced confidence in a company's crisis response plans.

Admit your mistakes

People are willing to forgive a mistake, but they're not willing to forgive the mismanagement of that mistake. If you handle it well, you can turn it into an opportunity.

It's easier for strong leaders and personality-driven companies to admit their mistakes. But in a big corporate it is rare that individuals will put their head above the parapet. So often, the most successfully managed crises are driven by leaders – a face for the business. Sometimes, people just want someone to say sorry. It might cost you (in compensation for example), but you'll still have your company at the end of it.

Tell people what to expect

Tell people what you're doing to solve the crisis, and how long it's going to take. Never underestimate the turnaround time. If you say 'It'll take 10 days', and then it takes seven, you look on top of the situation. If you say 'It'll take five days', and it takes seven, you look out of control. It's taken the same amount of time, but the perception is completely different.

Invest in preparation, training and drills

My son does karate. He keeps training, keeps doing his moves. He's developing muscle memory. He can react without thinking. It's the same in a crisis. You don't have time to read a manual from scratch. You need corporate muscle memory – a team that knows exactly what's expected of them, and how to work together.

During a crisis, you can purchase legal and communications support, customer service backup and so on. But you can't buy time. That's why you invest in preparation, training and drills. It reduces the time it takes you to act.

Verify the facts

Verify where all your information is coming from. Have a central repository of information to make sure all communications are consistent and fact-checked. Inconsistency creates doubt and uncertainty.

Nature abhors a vacuum

If you wait until you have all the facts, you'll never say anything. Of course, you don't want to go out and say something too quickly that could be wrong. But acknowledging the crisis and saying 'We're looking into it and we'll update you' tells people that this company knows about the problem and is taking it seriously. Be first with the right information. Or someone else will put out information that may not be correct.

Understand what's driving people's responses

What's the incentive for people to respond in a certain way to your crisis? If you have a whistleblower, for example, are they motivated by the promise of financial reward (as part of the US whistleblower programmes)?

Good forensic social media monitoring is very valuable so you can understand what people are saying about you, and what's driving the public agenda.

Insight interview 3: Adrian Wheeler, author of the PRCA'S practice guide 'Crisis communications management'

The most important thing is to do something

There is a huge temptation to do nothing. A crisis is a shock; CEOs who are not used to surprises often react by calling meetings and waiting to see how things develop. This is fatal. Once the initiative is lost it can never be regained.

The initial statement is all-important. It must be quick, calm, concerned, dynamic and human.

Avoid the most common pitfalls: delay, formality and legalism

Delay. There is no time to consult and seek consensus. In other words, crisis response follows rules that are the exact opposite of the way most organizations are managed in normal times.

Formality. The language used in crisis statements must show empathy. This is hard for most CEOs, whose natural mode of expression is formal, corporate and risk-averse.

Legalism. Some lawyers understand the importance of reputation protection in a crisis, but most are concerned with liability. Legalese doesn't work in a crisis. The CEO must come across as someone who cares. Legal language doesn't work.

First actions for leaders

Get to the scene. Take action to look after the people who have been affected. Make an initial statement expressing sympathy and promising to put things right. Handle all media interviews personally.

The qualities of a great team

They are a real team – they know each other and work well together. They can work under extreme pressure and provocation, keeping their nerve. They are calm, collected and professional when all around is chaos and panic. They have stamina. A crisis can last for days.

Advice for a crisis team when a crisis strikes

1 Take the initiative. Issue the CEO's initial statement within an hour.

2 Keep the initiative with media and stakeholder communications from start to finish.

3 Manage the CEO's activities. He or she is the central figure.

You have an hour

The 'Golden Hour' is a cliché but it's true. We have an hour, and we need an hour: we have to verify (is it real?) and then compose our initial statement. This takes skill and time: the language and tone must be exactly right – we won't get a second chance.

The 'Golden Hour' applies to all media, whether social, online or traditional.

The CEO should be available 24/7

The vital factor is the CEO's availability 24/7. The team should expect deputies to be in place to take over after they have been working for 10 hours. This won't happen unless someone has made plans.

Afterwards, the team should expect a thorough review. What worked? What didn't? What did we learn? How can we do it better next time?

You can't control a crisis

But you can and should control how the organization *responds*. It's all about doing and saying the right thing in the heat of a crisis. That sounds easy but isn't.

Reputational damage is almost always the result of how an organization is seen to communicate – rarely, if ever, as a consequence of the facts of the crisis.

Organizations that react quickly, calmly and humanly often see their reputational assets increase in the wake of a crisis.

Few of us know or care about the details of a crisis, but we all admire a CEO who faces the music bravely and seems to care about the people whose lives or welfare have been affected.

The role of leadership in a crisis and preparing your crisis team

16

You ask, what is our aim? I can answer in one word. It is victory; victory at all costs; victory in spite of all terror; victory, however long and hard the road may be, for without victory there is no survival... But I take up my task with buoyancy and hope. I feel sure that our cause will not be suffered to fail among men. At this time I feel entitled to claim the aid of all, and I say, 'Come then, let us go forward together with our united strength.'

WINSTON CHURCHILL'S FIRST SPEECH TO THE HOUSE OF COMMONS ON BECOMING PRIME MINISTER, 13 MAY 1940[1]

Setting the strategic intent

The role of a leader in a crisis is to make difficult decisions (often without all the facts); to bring clarity to chaos; to set the course for recovery; and to set the standards and the example to the rest of the organization.

But, before all that, the leader must define what crisis expert and Managing Director of crisis management consultancy Insignia, Jonathan Hemus, calls the 'strategic intent' of the business in managing the situation. This is the outcome you want to achieve, through the actions you take in response to the crisis.

That's easier said than done, says Hemus. 'One of the most common mistakes for a leader in the early stage of a crisis is starting to do things without thinking first,' he tells me. 'The pressure of a crisis situation means you're facing the biggest challenge of your business career. You're in a confusing and unclear situation. You have limited time to act, a lack of information, and an acute awareness that everything is at stake – your job, your organization's future, its value, its reputation, its employees. This could be the single most important day of your business life, and the event that defines your career. So you start doing things before you really think them through.'

I ask him how a leader should come up with the strategic intent for the crisis response. 'Imagine you're six months into the future. What would you want your stakeholders to say about what happened, and how you responded? Write down, in a clear, simple sentence, what you want the outcome to be. That intent will focus your efforts and your team's efforts. It will make decision-making easier, because you can evaluate all your decisions against that single intent. Your team will know what to do, because they know what the business wants to achieve.' This creates the 'united strength' that Churchill spoke of, going forward together to achieve a single aim.

If you are a restaurant owner, and your restaurant is closed because of a flood, for example, your strategic intent might be to maintain the loyalty and business of your customers in the medium to long term. To do everything you can, not to lose them to a competitive restaurant down the street. Every action through the crisis is designed to retain the loyalty of those customers. One way to do that might be to reopen the restaurant as quickly as possible – but that in itself is not the strategic intent. It's a means to achieving it, of course – but the intent is customer loyalty. That means you have a customer base once the restaurant reopens.

Acting on strategic intent

I ask Hemus about the crisis that hit the food chain Pret A Manger in 2018, and whether its strategic intent in handling the crisis was clear. Pret hit the headlines after it was revealed that a teenager, Natasha Ednan-Laperouse, had died in 2016 after she had suffered a severe reaction to eating a Pret baguette that contained sesame. The baguette did not carry an allergen warning. Pret had not broken the law – a strange quirk in UK food labelling regulations meant that food made on site didn't have to carry allergen information. Then, another death came to light, this time a woman named Celia Marsh, who collapsed and died in December 2017 after eating a Pret flatbread sold as dairy-free, but which was found to contain milk protein.

(Pret attributed the blame for this to a supplier of dairy-free products, CoYo; CoYo said its claims were unfounded.)

Pret has since changed the labelling on its foods, but the thing that interests me about this case is why it took two years for Pret to do something that it could have done immediately after Ednan-Laperouse's death. It must have known that this case would come to light once the inquest into her death was held.

'Pret did some of the right things, but it did them too late,' says Hemus. 'We don't know what its strategic intent was at the time of Ednan-Laperouse's death, but it clearly didn't lead Pret to change its labelling policies to prevent another tragedy.' Had Pret's strategic intent been to protect its customers and prevent anything like this happening again, perhaps it would have changed its labelling policies more quickly.

Pret has worked hard to build a reputation for doing the right thing, and its values – at least prior to this crisis – were clear. The company may have thought this was a tragic one-off, and would not happen again. That was a mistake, says Hemus. 'When you suffer a major crisis, you are significantly more vulnerable to a second crisis than at any normal time,' says Hemus. 'If you have, or are perceived to have done something wrong, you become a target, for all the wrong reasons. You must take all possible steps to avoid something similar happening again, and take them quickly. People will forgive an organization for a single incident as long as it doesn't reveal an ingrained corporate failure, and so long as they respond appropriately, and with empathy.'

When Pret's CEO, Clive Schlee, wrote to Natasha Ednan-Laperouse's parents in August, it was described by them as 'too little, too late'.[2] It was nearly a year after their daughter had died.

Hemus and I talk about the contrasting response of Nick Varney, CEO of Merlin Entertainments (the company that owns the UK theme park Alton Towers). In 2015, a roller coaster called Smiler crashed at Alton Towers, injuring 16 people, and leaving two teenage girls needing leg amputations. In 2016, Merlin was fined £5 million for what was described as a 'catalogue of errors' by Paul Paxton, representing the families.[3] Right from the start of the crisis, Varney addressed the issue personally, speaking with compassion and regret. He apologized to those injured, and took responsibility for the crash, stating that 'It is something we will never forget and it is something we are utterly determined will never be repeated.' Notably, he did not wait for the findings of an inquiry to say sorry, nor to take responsibility.

Is this the fault of lawyers that some companies don't take responsibility for their actions? Hemus says it is up to leaders whether they take the advice they are given by their legal teams: 'A leader in a crisis will receive advice from all sorts of specialists – lawyers, communications experts, risk specialist, accountants. They'll all come at it from different viewpoints. A lawyer will give their best legal advice based on risk. But that's just one part of the decision. Reputation is another. A leader earns their salary by making the decision based on that counsel. Advisers advise: leaders decide.'

Making decisions in a crisis

Mark Fritz is an author, coach and speaker on leadership. I first met him when I attended a workshop he ran on leadership and accountability, called 'Why you never wash a rental car'. I asked him how a leader should move quickly to decisive action.

'The key is to develop options as quickly as possible,' he says. 'It gives leaders confidence that they are choosing a good option and thus making a good decision.' I think about that. I wonder whether Pret's leadership had options presented to them, and, if so, what they would have looked like. As Fritz says: 'Good is only good by comparison.' If only one option is given to you, it will look like the best one.

The challenge, says Fritz, is coming up with those quality options right away. Doing that means getting the right people together. 'The more you involve the key people who are going to be part of the execution plan, the more they're invested in delivering a good outcome. A leader needs people who are close to the customer and the market and bring outside perspective to the issue.' This is critical to being able to move quickly, he says. 'If you want to move quickly, get the right people involved, fast. Success is all about the quality of the people you bring into the room.'

He says the best leaders will ask the right questions, and pitch those questions at the right level – something he calls 'entering the right door at the right floor.' A good leader will control a conversation by how they ask questions. They'll have the ability to dig deeper into the important issues, and keep the conversation high level to avoid getting stuck in the less important detail. They'll get to the nub of the issue quickly. 'A leader will ask: "What is the picture I need to see in order to make the right decision?" If the picture is 80 per cent complete, they'll be confident enough that they can see the rest.' (I think of something Hemus said in our conversation, too:

'A leader's job in a crisis is to make decisions without all the facts. If they had all the facts, there wouldn't be a decision to make.')

Once you have the right people in the room, they need managing to create that environment where they can communicate clearly in order to make good decisions. Fritz says part of that is ensuring no one plays the blame game, which can waste critical time. 'Don't spend too much time on what's happened, but on what you're all going to do. If you qualify that up front, you set a positive tone.' He talks to me about the importance of keeping a clear focus – that strategic intent that Hemus talks about – and not letting anyone distract you from that. 'Prep two or three questions you need to get answers to. You have to know what you want to achieve. That helps you keep focused.'

It's easy to be derailed in a crisis situation, where there is likely to be a lot of emotion in the room. Fritz recommends staging meetings with the team, to have the best chance of staying focused. He advises leaders to set the tone of a meeting by seeding the first couple of comments, and asking the individuals who are the most effective to talk first. The leader's role is like that of an orchestra conductor, he says: 'You've got to make good music. Don't start with the worst player in the room.' He gives advice that I find fascinating: 'If we're all at a table, I might stand behind the person who I know will derail the conversation. That immediately neutralises them because they can't see me, so they're less likely to open the discussion. You can't do it for long, but it's an effective way of ensuring they don't set the path for the conversation. Position yourself strategically.'

Learning to cope with the pressure

As we saw in Chapters 13 and 14, when under pressure, cracks appear quickly in even the best teams. Part of a leader's role is to keep that team functioning. An important part of that is providing the right environment, says Fritz. 'As a leader, you have to force your team to take breaks. Be aware of their time. Make your conversations productive – people's frustrations rise when they see a lot of talk with no results. Be rigid with timekeeping.'

To keep the team functioning, the leader has to function, too. That means finding space to think – and sometimes to stop thinking about the problem. 'A quiet mind is able to hear its own inspiration and ideas,' says Fritz. 'Learn how to quiet your mind.'

Techniques to do that include meditation and breathing exercises, and taking regular breaks. 'If you have even a small break it can help you listen to your instinct,' he says. He talks of the positive impact of 'recovery habits' – regular meditation, or hobbies outside of work – on a leader: 'Overall, leaders who are self-aware, and have good recovery habits are those who can keep perspective in a crisis. They need that space to break the cycle we can all have, of magnifying a problem in our heads. You need to act, but unless you quiet the chatter in your brain, you can't get there.' He says that constantly worrying at a problem in your head can do more damage than good: 'What you repeat in your head, you magnify, so you might be giving the wrong question to your subconscious to work on. Top athletes have a quiet place they can go to in their heads. The easiest way to do that is through deep breathing exercises. It stops the chatter.'

It helps, too, if the leader has been exposed to conflict in the past. 'If leaders have developed the skills to handle conflict, they'll be better equipped to handle a crisis,' says Fritz. 'Resilience is not something build up in a hurry, but over time. Stretch your comfort zone.'

Listening, empathy and action

As we will see in Chapter 17, empathy is probably the word I hear bandied about in crisis rehearsals more than any other. And, while it should be blindingly obvious, empathy is actually surprisingly hard to communicate in a way that is trusted. That's usually because it is meaningless unless it's backed up with action. And that action is down to leaders in a crisis situation.

I ask Fritz about empathy and leadership. Is empathy something leaders naturally have, or can they learn it? And does it help in a crisis situation, or can it hinder decision making? 'Empathy improves a leader's ability to listen, not just to the words, but to the meaning and feeling behind the words,' he says. 'Empathy helps you to ask better questions. It makes people feel you're moving to their side of the table and understanding what they're going through. But ultimately, the proof of listening is in what you do. It's in what you play back to people, or the action you take. The more you listen, the more you have to take action. If you don't want to take action, don't ask the question.'

He believes that, like any leadership skill, you can learn to be better at empathy. 'Some people are naturally empathetic, and other too much so. You need empathy, but not so much that you take all the burden on yourself as a leader. You can't take on all the problems of your team, or it will slow you down.' Fritz warns against empathy with no action: 'It's important to listen, but be careful what you commit to doing. You need to build credibility and trust. If you don't do what you've committed to, that trust will go.'

Listening can be harder than it seems, too. 'Leadership style is generally one of control,' says Fritz. 'Leaders generally don't like to hear from people in the field too much, because they give them headaches. So they'd rather talk to the people who'll say yes to them.' He advises what he calls 'walk-around leadership': 'I advocate a "nose in, hands out" approach. Put your nose in and talk to people in the field. The more you do that, the more your team will do the same, and stay close to the issues.'

I ask him about the approach I see a number of global companies take in a crisis, which is to remove control from local teams back to the centre as soon as a crisis hits. I understand the principle, but I can't help feeling it shows a lack of trust. Fritz's view is that an organization's performance is only as good as the people at the bottom want it to be. That means giving people responsibility and accountability. Taking away that responsibility can disengage them, make them less interested in solving the issue. Fritz quotes Colin Powell: 'The commander in the field is always right and the rear echelon is wrong, unless proved otherwise.'[4] It is, after all, those 'in the field' who are closest to what their customers think. And it is they who should be responsible for providing consistent messages to customers and the market.

Taking action

- Ask the right questions to the right people.
- Be empathetic, and listen 'between the lines'.
- Agree a common goal or outcome.
- Only commit to what's realistic.
- State what you'll do and then do it.
- Be seen to be doing it, and report on actions regularly.
- Don't take it all on yourself – give responsibility to your team.
- Follow up with your team on what needs to be done by when.
- Have regular check-in calls with your team to hold everyone accountable.

A crisis will reinforce the values of leadership

Etymologists say that the word crisis has two origins: the Greek word *krino*, which means separate, judge or decide (from it comes the word *krites*, which means judge, and *kriterion*, a standard to judge by); and the related word *krisis*, which means a decisive moment, or turning point (in the Greek New Testament, the Day of Judgement is *hemera kriseos*).[5] In English, we talk about something 'reaching crisis point', meaning a point at which a decision must be made, and action taken. It's a point of no return.

Can that bring a positive outcome? A day of judgement, or a turning point has two outcomes, one positive and one negative, after all. Or is that just a nice linguistic analogy?

'A crisis can be an opportunity for a leader to reinforce the focus of the company and its values,' says Fritz. And, of course, the strategic intent of the business is never more obvious than during a crisis.

In 2018, I ran two crisis workshops, for two very different brands, in different sectors. Both sell via retailers to consumers. Both companies had a large number of people taking part in the workshop, divided into separate teams. Their approaches couldn't have been further apart.

The (entirely fictional) scenario for both was a variation of a product recall, the result of a defective product that was detrimental to public health. Initially, the root cause of the problem was not clear – whether it was a problem with the manufacturer, its supply chain, or misuse by the consumer. But the health impact was severe, and wherever fault lay, the products were causing significant damage. Their responses spoke volumes about their senior leadership style.

Company A

Company A did not know how its values would come into play in this scenario, and did not have a clearly stated strategic intent for managing the crisis.

The leader of one group ignored the concerns of his team, and ordered the communications team to state unequivocally that the product was safe. Until he saw it with his own eyes, he said, he would not take action; the financial cost of a recall would be too high. The team had an argument about how to proceed, but eventually the leader got his way. The rest of the team became disengaged – they didn't believe they were doing the right thing. The crisis escalated. Fault was proven, and the arguments broke out again – they had made the wrong decision, the communications team was coming under fire for statements that were woolly and seen to be dodging blame, and public judgement was against them.

The leader of another team behaved differently. She trusted the views of her team, and they decided together that the most important thing to do was to ensure public safety, and worry about blame later. They put their customers first, whatever the short-term cost; the long-term benefits were more important. While managing and communicating through the crisis was tough, they had a far less rocky road than the first team.

What was interesting to me was that two groups of people from the same company, working in the same department (albeit in different regions), could hold opposing views. The teams didn't know the values of their company, or how they should act. They relied instead on their own instincts – which led them in opposite directions.

Company B

Company B also had separate teams to tackle the crisis scenario. I was fascinated to watch them all at work – the leader of each group took exactly the same position, entirely separately, and got agreement from their teams: the most important thing was to ensure safety. The crisis undermined the values of the company. Every group could articulate those values and, more importantly, knew how to put them into action. They understood, without conferring, what the company would expect of them. IT behaved consistently through the crisis, in keeping with its values, and although communicating with people affected by the crisis was not easy, the teams didn't create unnecessary obstacles for themselves.

So leadership within the crisis is important – but so is the reinforcement of values and culture ahead of the crisis. As Mark Fritz says: 'A leader's role is driving direction (strategic intent) and pace (values and culture). In a crisis situation, actions by the leader will reinforce intent by deciding what to do, and also values and culture, but how they do it.' He advises leaders to have to hand powerful stories and examples to refer to that provide guidance on how to act: 'Stories bring life to words. They give consistency and real examples of how to behave. Trust doesn't mean the same to everyone, for example. Nor does what's fair.' But real examples give people a benchmark to work from.

Summary of actions: Leadership in a crisis

1. Define the strategic intent of the crisis. This will set the framework for decision-making and communications.
2. Remember that if you have a crisis, you become significantly more vulnerable to a second crisis.
3. Create the right environment to make good decisions. Stage meetings and set the tone. Get the right people together, and keep the conversation high-level. Don't let one person derail discussions.
4. Get as full a picture as possible before you make a decision. Like a jigsaw, if you can see 80 per cent of the picture, you can fill in the gaps.
5. Quiet your mind before you make decisions. Take time out and create good recovery habits to build resilience.
6. Listen (to the right people) and show empathy. But don't take on all the burden of your team, or it will slow you down.
7. Act on what you hear, and report regularly on that action. It will build trust.
8. 'The commander in the field is always right and the rear echelon is wrong, unless proved otherwise' (Colin Powell).
9. See a crisis as an opportunity to reinforce your company values, and your leadership values.

Notes

1. Churchill, W (1940) Blood, toil, tears, sweat, 13 May. www.historyplace.com/speeches/churchill.htm.
2. Topping, A (2018) Pret A Manger: From high street darling to industry bogeyman, *Guardian*, 12 October. www.theguardian.com/business/2018/oct/12/pret-a-manger-from-high-street-darling-to-industry-bogeyman.
3. BBC (2016) Smiler crash: Alton Towers operator Merlin fined £5m, BBC News Online, 27 September. www.bbc.co.uk/news/uk-england-stoke-staffordshire-37481825.
4. Harari, O (2003) *The Leadership Secrets of Colin Powell*, McGraw-Hill Education.
5. Timpson, T (2015) The vocabularist, BBC News Online, 15 September. www.bbc.co.uk/news/blogs-magazine-monitor-34154767.

Showing humanity and empathy in a crisis

17

When it counts and when it's empty

What is empathy?

Empathy – the ability to understand what someone is feeling from their point of view – is probably the most-used word in crisis communications. Almost every crisis team I've worked with has talked about the importance of empathy in a crisis statement.

It's actually pretty hard to do. Not long ago, I worked with the communications team of a large company as they simulated a crisis that included a fatal industrial accident, with strong public feeling against the company as a result. The team members were some of the nicest, most empathic people I've ever met – but they struggled to show it in their communications.

One of their tasks as part of the simulation was to inform the public that five people had died as a result of the accident. Their company's corporate values included a commitment to protecting the safety of employees and the public. The team decided that their statement should reinforce this value – it was important to them that the public realized they didn't take the deaths lightly, and that this was an extraordinary event. They agreed that the statement had to convey information about the deaths in a way that showed empathy, confirm their corporate values, and be short enough to be shareable on social media.

After many drafts and much discussion, the proposed statement read: 'We are deeply sorry to have to confirm that five people have died and 10 have

Figure 17.1 Empathy

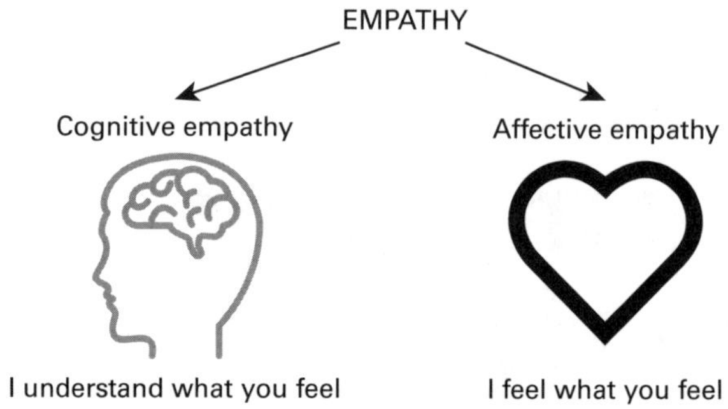

been injured as a result of the accident at [location]. Safety is our number one priority here at [company name]. We are in contact with the families of those affected.'

How would you feel if you were a relative of one of those hurt or killed in an accident, reading that statement? First, the safety message is irrelevant – safety measures didn't work in this case. Second, the company doesn't sound as though it understands how people feel about the accident. While it conveys sympathy ('we are deeply sorry'), there is no empathy. It creates disconnection, not connection.

Broadly, there are two types of empathy. Affective empathy is the ability to feel emotion based on another's experience. We feel as though we're going through what they are. It can mean we mirror what they feel, feeling anxious when they feel anxious, or even crying when they cry. Cognitive empathy is less visceral, but it means the ability to identify with and understand what someone is going through. This can be put to good use during a crisis: it will help you to do the right thing and behave with compassion and humanity. As Atticus Finch says in Harper Lee's novel *To Kill a Mockingbird*, 'You never really understand another person until you consider things from his point of view – until you climb inside of his skin and walk around in it.'

Developing empathy

Professor Theresa Wiseman is Clinical Professor of Applied Health Research in Cancer Care at the University of Southampton and The Royal Marsden NHS Foundation Trust. In her 1996 research paper 'A concept analysis of empathy' she examines what empathy means in a nursing context, and lists four defining attributes:

- See the world as others see it.
- Understand another's current feelings.
- Be non-judgemental.
- Communicate the understanding.[1]

This is a good framework for empathy in a crisis situation, and could be used as a filter for statements. Does your communication demonstrate that you see the crisis from the point of view of those who have been affected, that you understand the depth of public feeling, that you do not judge that feeling? If so, then it has empathy.

But there is a fundamental difficulty, here. How does a faceless, non-human organization show it understands feelings? True empathy comes from humans, not corporations. Another reason to put your CEO up to front the crisis communication. They may need help communicating empathy, as we saw in Chapter 11 in the case of United Airlines' CEO, Oscar Munoz.

There's another major consideration, too. To *show* empathy, you have to *have* empathy. As crisis expert Jonathan Hemus says to me: 'Empathy is absolutely essential in a crisis. Not just expressing empathy, but actually having empathy. If you can't see a situation from someone else's point of view, you're likely to fail in managing that crisis. It's one of the absolute fundamentals of successful crisis management.' A common pitfall, he says, is for an organization to say how much the crisis is affecting it: 'You hear crisis communicators say, "We the organization are hurting, it's costing us so much." It's entirely the wrong premise from which to successfully manage the crisis.'

I ask Hemus what happens to organizations that just don't have empathy. 'Even if you don't have innate empathy, you need to develop it, or find someone else who can look at the crisis from the outside in,' he says. 'Among leaders we see a range of personality types and varying degrees of empathy. Leaders need to be driven and focused, which may mean they are less empathic. If you do have a leader who lacks empathy, but understands that it's important, then they need a trusted advisor who they listen to, who will provide that empathic view. Someone who can tell them some home truths. An enlightened leader will listen.'

Sometimes, developing empathy means making yourself vulnerable at a time when your instinct is to steel yourself. But you have to know how others feel. Empathy starts with listening. You must identify with the situation of others. Then you have to open up to the possibility of feeling their emotions – which can be draining. You have to set aside your own baggage in order to be non-judgemental. Too much affective empathy could cloud your ability to make rational decisions.

But, ultimately, if you don't have empathy, you can't communicate effectively in a crisis. And you're unlikely to behave with compassion.

Empathy comes easier to some than to others, but you can learn to develop it. That might be more necessary than you think: research in the United Kingdom shows that empathy may be in decline, with 51 per cent of the UK population believing we have less empathy than we did even one year ago, according to a 2018 survey by YouGov for the Scouts Association.[2] If that indicates a wider trend, then it will lead to more division and polarization in society.

There are simple ways to develop your empathy. Practise 'radical listening' – really listening to someone telling you how they feel, while being fully present, without interrupting or judging them. It's harder than it sounds. Try to actively identify unspoken emotion in others by listening to their tone of voice, or watching their facial expressions. Be curious about people you come into contact with, their stories and their lives; imagine yourself in their shoes. Have a conversation with someone you wouldn't normally talk to. These things will help you to create connections with people, and develop your ability to be empathic. It's a useful skill as a communicator.

Expressing empathy and behaving with compassion

I ask Hemus who should be the face of the crisis if your leader doesn't have natural empathy. 'There are no hard and fast rules, but there are guidelines,' he says. 'You want to communicate care, compassion and empathy for the people who have been affected. That means you should put someone forward to speak to media who is naturally empathic. If your CEO is not, it can be someone else, depending on the severity of the crisis. If you've had a major service outage, and your customer services director is empathic, it may be appropriate for him to speak to media. But if you're a rail company and there have been deaths following a major accident, your CEO has to speak, and your job as an advisor is to help them express empathy and behave in the right way.'

We talk, inevitably, about BP and the Gulf of Mexico disaster. 'Tony Haywood should have visited the site early on, had a day with media, and then appointed Bob Dudley to take operational charge, reporting directly to him, and providing media with regular updates,' says Hemus. 'He didn't have to be the face of BP throughout the whole situation. He wasn't a comfortable spokesperson and ultimately he made the crisis worse.'

In 2006, two young children, Christianne and Robert Sheppard, died of carbon monoxide poisoning from a defective boiler in a hotel in Corfu, while they were on a family holiday. Their holiday company, Thomas Cook, was roundly criticized for its response, which showed little empathy and no compassion. It did not apologize to the family of the children at the time, and initially refused to help with the family's legal fees, despite having accepted £3 million from the owner of the hotel. (It later donated £1.5 million of that money to Unicef.) The company's share price dropped 3 per cent after the crisis, arguably costing far more than apologizing and accepting liability would have done.

Justin King, the former Chief Executive of Sainsbury's, led an independent inquiry into the deaths nearly a decade later, in 2015. He found that the company had 'a tendency to protect cost rather than maximise the customer experience,' and that 'legal rather than the human considerations dominated the landscape'. His report noted that while the company had contacted the family over the nine years, those contacts were 'sometimes ill-timed and often ill-judged.'[3]

Peter Fankhauser, Chief Executive of Thomas Cook, told the 2015 inquest into the children's deaths: 'I feel so thoroughly, from the deepest of my heart, sorry, but there's no need to apologize because there was no wrongdoing by Thomas Cook.' The statement smacks of legal pressure to avoid saying sorry; there's just no genuine humanity or empathy in it at all. It was a defensive response.

Francis Ingham, commenting on the story in the *Independent* (2015), said at the time: 'When companies go into defence mode, they stop being human. The fundamental fact is that they [Thomas Cook] were not human. They needed to show they understood some of the pain caused.'[4]

Being human

Rod Cartwright is a corporate PR and crisis communications expert who works with some of the biggest organizations in the world. He has played global and European leadership roles at agencies such as Ketchum and Archetype (formerly Text 100). In his role as Regional Director for Europe, the Middle East and Africa at Archetype, he played a leading role in developing 'Think Human' – a platform designed to help brands to think, talk and act in a way that speaks to people's core human wants, needs and values. The worst crises are those that strike at people's core values (Cartwright has said to me before that the very worst crises involve the three Ps: people, the planet and pets – the things that we hold closest), so I talk to him about how 'Think Human' could be applied in a crisis situation.

'The world has changed since the crash of 2008,' he says. 'It's got more complicated. In the US and Europe we have the rise of populism and the mass disillusionment of those who have felt largely forgotten. Trust is at an all time low. Add to that mix the presence of technology and the march of artificial intelligence (AI) in every area of our lives. It may be advancing humanity and doing amazing things for good, but still it brings with it the very real threat of alienation for many people. Humans are more than data sets that can be dealt with purely by algorithms or robots. We crave human connection, we want to speak to real people, who talk like we do, or we end up feeling isolated.'

Cartwright believes that technology can enhance the human experience; it does not fundamentally change it. Storytelling existed before Instagram, after all, and the concept of friendship predates Facebook. Technology gives us the ability to scale and facilitate those connections. Robots might replace some of those transactional or functional communications – asking a retailer to track an order, for example – which can be answered more quickly and efficiently by robots, but they're unlikely to become our close friends. (Although there is some interesting research that shows AI-powered visual virtual assistants can mirror expressions to give the impression of empathy and calm a difficult situation – but it's very early days, and that's a whole other book.)

Technology enhances the human experience, and yet some organizations are completely robotic in the way they communicate. There's an obvious irony here – we develop robots to be as human as possible, while our humans are becoming more like bots. 'They are not wired to communicate in a way that is human,' he says. 'Brands should put everything they do through a prism of how they think, act, speak and look, and how those actions engage with people's core human needs, wants and values. That will determine how you engage with people and make you more human, more relatable, more trustworthy.' Above all, he says, be decent: 'Measure everything you do against basic human decency.' He cites the brilliantly human response by Mars to Donald Trump Jr, who compared refugees to Skittles: 'Skittles are candy; refugees are people.'

'Think Human' encourages business to follow these principles:

- 'Think human' in your corporate ethos and strategy. What human problem do you solve, or what human experience do you facilitate?
- 'Act human' in your corporate behaviour (both inside and outside the business); make sure there is no gap between what you claim to do and what you actually deliver.
- 'Speak human' in your language and tone of voice, avoiding jargon and corporate language. Do you speak the way your audience speaks?
- 'Look human' by using visual storytelling, which can be more powerful than words alone.

There are brands that 'think human' supremely well in a crisis situation. I've talked about fast-food chain KFC elsewhere, but it warrants a mention here, too. When a supply chain issue meant its restaurants ran out of chicken, the company did the unthinkable – it apologized. The headline of a print ad said: 'We're sorry.' Underneath were the very human words: 'A chicken restaurant without any chicken. It's not ideal. Huge apologies to our customers, especially those who travelled out of their way to find out we were closed.' The language is clear, plain and human.

Being imperfect and saying sorry

Every company will make a mistake at some point. Cartwright believes that people accept imperfection from an organization if it's handled well, and if the organization tells it straight. 'Bad news will always get out,' he says. 'Who would you rather deliver and control the message – you or someone else who may not value the truth?' In a former role as Director of Global Corporate Practice at Ketchum, Cartwright oversaw annual, global research into the relationship between leadership and communication, including asking people about the leadership qualities they value in a leader. The ability to admit mistakes and demonstrate empathy consistently scored highly. But just as important in a crisis was the ability to take specific action to fix the problem. 'Organizations and the human beings within them make mistakes. So admit it, show you care, and then do something about it.' He calls this 'operationalizing empathy'. 'Unless you act on it, empathy is just words. It fulfils the human need to know you care, but on its own that's not enough.'

His next sentence surprises me: 'Tyra Banks uses a great term. She talks about being "flawsome".' It's not often we use supermodels as role models for crisis communications, but why not. It's a great term. 'Admit your failings. Be vulnerable. It's what makes you human. The Pope starts every speech and sermon by saying "Pray for me." It's an admission of imperfection, even from those at the top. Communicators are always striving for perfection, but people are imperfect.'

What about saying sorry? This is such a contentious issue in crisis management that we call it 'the S word' – most companies avoid it at all costs, often on the advice of their legal team. 'Lawyers are wired to be cautious,' says Cartwright. 'But there's a big difference between expressing genuine sorrow that something has happened, and saying sorry that you caused it (taking liability). Saying sorry is a very human thing and can be a critical tool in the crisis communications toolkit.'

Now, I'm not a lawyer, but I believe you can be genuinely sorry without admitting liability. Here's an example. I'm talking to John Brown, founder of Don't Cry Wolf, about the S word. During the conversation, I tell him that my home was damaged by a fire in 2016. It's an old building and the fire spread quickly. (Thankfully no one was hurt.) John says, instinctively: 'I'm so sorry, that's awful.' We both stop, and laugh. It was such a human reaction for him to say sorry. 'I can say to you I'm sorry your flat burned down. That doesn't mean it was my fault – I didn't start the fire – but I'm genuinely sorry it happened.' Like Cartwright, he talks about 'doing the right thing' rather than focusing on the possibility of liability. 'Imagine you've been delayed on a flight, with three children. What if the airline just said: "We'll get you home. We'll worry about the details later." Is that admitting they're in the wrong? Of course not. It's saying "I have the capability to ease your pain. I don't have to. But I can make things better, and so I will. I'm a decent human being. And I have faith that you're a decent human being too. My priority isn't who's at fault. It's getting you and your family home." Don't address a crisis from a communications perspective – address it from a human perspective. You're a human, with the ability to help someone in a bad situation.'

Sometimes, saying sorry is just the right thing to do, even if it does mean admitting liability. Wahaca is a Mexican restaurant chain founded by Mark Selby and Masterchef winner Thomasina Miers. In 2016, more than 400 of its customers and staff were affected by a norovirus outbreak. It hit the business hard. Eighteen restaurants out of its 25 were closed temporarily and sales dropped 45 per cent. Wahaca reported a £4.8 million loss for the year to June 2017, compared to a £640,000 profit the previous year, in part because of the crisis.

According to *The Times* in 2018, Selby was advised not to apologize. In an interview with the paper he said, 'Even if it was a risk, we just had to go out and apologize... If we weren't humane about it, we wouldn't have had a business anyway.'[5] Selby and Miers hand-wrote letters to those people who'd been affected, and even apologized in person in one case, where a wedding party had become ill. Being human is sometimes simply a judgement call by leadership.

Summary of actions: Developing empathy and being human

1. Build an 'empathy framework' for your crisis communications, using Wiseman's four attributes: see the world as others see it; understand another's current feelings; be non-judgemental; and communicate the understanding.
2. Actively develop empathy skills. Practise 'radical listening'; identify unspoken emotion in others; be curious about people; have face-to-face conversations with strangers.
3. 'Think Human', to use Cartwright's phrase: think human, act human, speak human and look human.
4. Admit your imperfections and tell the facts how they are.
5. Say sorry.
6. Behave with compassion and do the right thing for people affected by a crisis. Sometimes that means going against legal advice.

Notes

1 Wiseman, T (1996) A concept analysis of empathy, *Journal of Advanced Nursing*, 23, pp 1162–67.

2 YouGov and The Scouts Association (2018) Scouts calls for action to end UK's 'crisis of empathy', 2 October. https://scouts.org.uknews/2018/10/scouts-calls-for-action-to-end-uks-crisis-of-empathy/#_ftn2.

3 Bourke, J (2015) Thomas Cook: From a tragedy to a corporate disaster, *Independent*, 19 May. www.independent.co.uk/news/business/analysis-and-features/carbon-monoxide-deaths-from-a-tragedy-to-a-corporate-disaster-for-thomas-cook-10259735.html.

4 *Ibid.*

5 Kelly, L (2018) What to do when you're hit by a crisis, *The Times*, 14 October. https://www.thetimes.co.uk/article/what-to-do-when-youre-hit-by-a-crisis-p37w0f33s.

What do I do first? 18

Getting your priorities right in a crisis

Primum non nocere. (First, do no harm.)

MISATTRIBUTED TO HIPPOCRATES

When I run crisis simulation exercises, the first thing most participants do is to consider how the media will respond to the crisis. They craft their media statement, anticipating the questions journalists will ask.

But the role of a crisis adviser has gone far beyond managing the media; and media may not be your most critical audience, at least initially. As Duncan Gallagher said in Chapter 15, don't let your crisis response be defined solely by the media agenda.

There's no doubt that the media have a huge influence in a crisis. And we know, they can influence government and regulators as well as the general public. But the people directly impacted by the crisis should be your first concern, closely followed by your employees, your customers, your investors, shareholders and stakeholders, all of whom may have a greater influence on your survival. They will also be the people that the media approach during the crisis, so make sure they have the information and the support they need.

The critical first hour

We talk about the 'Golden Hour' in crisis management – that critical first hour of the crisis, when you're establishing the facts, agreeing a strategy and action plan, and preparing your first response. Social media means there is great pressure on you to respond more quickly (Facebook recommends responding to all queries within 15 minutes). Unless you have planned for this issue and have everything in place ahead of time, resist this pressure. It's far better to take the full hour and get it right. Your first response will be what is remembered (as Kate Adie said, Chapter 8).

The time you have to activate your plan depends on the nature of the crisis. Broadly, there are two types of crisis. There are those that are unexpected and immediately visible externally, like a terrorist incident, an oil spill or a plane crash. Then there are those where you have some ability to control the timing of public awareness and communications. If you know there's a public inquiry coming up, for example, you can prepare for the findings. If you have a data breach, you may know about it before the general public finds out.

When planning for a crisis, consider two types:

1. A crisis that is unexpected and immediately visible, such as:
   - **a** a natural disaster;
   - **b** a public health issue;
   - **c** an industrial or transportation accident;
   - **d** contamination, either accidental or malicious;
   - **e** a corporate scandal;
   - **f** a terrorist attack;
   - **g** hacking;
   - **h** technology failure.
2. A crisis that is expected and not immediately visible, such as:
   - **a** a public enquiry;
   - **b** a data breach or theft;
   - **c** a regulatory, financial or taxation issue;
   - **d** an internal issue.

Assemble your team

You should, as part of your crisis planning, have your team already organized into defined roles, and trained to know exactly what their role entails during a crisis. Alert them to the crisis. You do not want to be scrambling a crisis team once the crisis has broken, nor do you want to be contacting human resources to find the out-of-hours contact details for them. Remind each member of the team of their role in the crisis. Clarity is critical. (See Chapter 21 for more detail on preparing your team for a crisis.)

Get to the facts

Don't assume that the first thing you hear is the truth of the crisis. Get to the scene of the crisis, find out the facts for yourself. Hear from more than one source, and remember that some people will have an agenda behind what they tell you (particularly if they, or their department, are culpable). When you communicate, you must know that what you're saying is undisputed fact.

Continually update the facts as they unfold. You should have a single repository of facts that the crisis team can access (there are various technologies that will help you automatically push out new information as you have it, overriding old documents so there's no confusion with version control).

Check and recheck the facts as they come in. Once something's on record, especially on social media, it's very hard to correct it.

Assess the severity of the crisis

In 1943, a Canadian psychiatrist, JT MacCurdy, published his book *The Structure of Morale*.[1] In it, he examines the impact of fear on morale. During the Second World War, he says, people in Britain were prepared for the impact of being bombed, mostly by propaganda or by war films. Both focused on the most devastating effect a direct hit by a bomb could have – loss of life, destruction of property, the end of a way of life. In a film, every bomb hits its target. The only way to survive would be to be out of the area, or deep in a shelter.

MacCurdy says that as the first sirens were heard in 1940 in London, people scurried to their bomb shelters not really knowing if they would emerge. He quotes a friend of his saying: 'When the first siren sounded I took my children to our dug-out in the garden and I was quite certain we were all going to be killed. Then the all-clear went without anything having happened. Ever since we came out of the dug-out I have felt sure nothing would ever hurt us.' MacCurdy says this reaction is typical. When the sirens became more commonplace, and where bombs weren't dropped, people got bored, not afraid. Many stopped taking shelter altogether. They had started to believe they wouldn't be hit.

His research shows that when a bomb explodes in a congested area, it divides people into three broad groups:

1 **Those who are killed.** MacCurdy says: 'The morale of the community depends on the reaction of the survivors... corpses do not run about spreading panic.'

2 **Near misses.** These are the people who are in the area where the bomb explodes. They witness the devastation and horror, and are deeply affected by it.

3 **Remote misses.** These are people who hear the sirens, and they hear the bomb drop, but are not in the immediate vicinity. They are safe. They feel excitement and relief. And they feel something else that is very important: they feel invulnerable. (This may be why the bombings of London by the Luftwaffe, designed to bring the city to its knees, actually did the opposite in terms of morale, bonding people in the famous 'Blitz spirit', determined not to be defeated. It made those who had survived, braver.)

A company that has been through a crisis but survived (the 'near misses') may reel from the shock. They will be affected; they will change their behaviour to avoid the crisis in the future. But companies that fall into the 'remote misses' group – those who may have seen others in their sector go through a crisis, but haven't experienced it themselves – may have that same feeling of invulnerability as Londoners who escaped the bombing. *We survived the crash; the rumour didn't get out; the data breach wasn't made public.*

It's a dangerous place to be. A belief that a crisis won't happen to you can make you underestimate its severity when it does hit. If you can categorize the crisis objectively against a list of predefined criteria – without relying on your instinct about how serious it may or may not be – you will be more realistic about whether the threat is serious or not. Just because you've dodged a bullet in the past doesn't mean you will dodge it again.

Criteria for defining the severity of a crisis

1 Current impact:

- a How many people are affected?
- b To what extent and how seriously are they affected?
- c What is the current financial implication?
- d What is the current reputational implication?

2 Potential impact:

 a How many people could be affected in the future (and over what time period)?

 b To what extent and how seriously could they be affected?

 c What could the future financial implication be?

 d What could the future reputational implication be?

Define or reapprove the strategic intent for the crisis

One of the very first things to do is to establish the strategic intent of the crisis, as defined by the organization's leadership (as Jonathan Hemus talks about in Chapter 16). This is the job of senior leadership, not just of communications. It is the first priority because it will define every decision that comes later.

'If you have done your preparation work, and you understand your risk landscape, you will have defined your top threats and can prepare your strategic intent in advance,' Hemus says. 'It's helpful to have that ready and it will save you valuable time. But always test, verify and reapprove it when the crisis breaks.'

This strategic intent focuses the crisis team on the long-term, Hemus says, rather than taking the easiest – but potentially detrimental – course of action for survival in the short term. 'People tend to focus on the short term because of the pressure they're under during a crisis,' he says. 'It's easy to deal with the most obvious threat to the organization first, but that may not necessarily be the most important priority.'

The most serious crises will have serious and significant financial implications for the business – loss of sales, the cost of stopping production, fines or compensation packages. It's tempting to focus on the bottom line now, rather than in the long term. That's why the strategic intent is so important, Hemus says. 'Every action and decision during the crisis will be defined by the strategic intent, which is in the best long-term interest of the company. It provides an antidote to a short-term view, that might save money now, but that has the potential to cost the business billions in the long term.'

Hemus gives this example: if you're a manufacturer, and you find a single contaminated product, what do you do? You suspect it's an isolated case, and you know the cost of shutting down the production line is significant. The temptation is not to take the financial hit until you're sure of where and how the contamination happened. But if your strategic intent is to protect the health of your customers the decision to cease production becomes much easier.

In 1982, Johnson & Johnson stopped production and advertising of Tylenol capsules, initiated a nationwide product recall, alerted consumers and pulled all the products off the shelf. Seven people died after taking the capsules, which had been laced with potassium cyanide. Tylenol was the victim of a deliberate contamination plot.

James Burke, the company's Chairman, decided immediately that the company should put safety ahead of profit. It was a decision that cost millions of dollars in the short term, but in the long term won back the trust of consumers, and saved the brand's reputation.[2]

The company was open and transparent about what was happening. It acted fast to initiate the recall, and issued a warning to hospitals, pharmacies, stores and the general public about the risk. It took action to ensure the tampering couldn't be repeated, designing and producing new, tamper-proof containers – which prompted other drug manufacturers to follow suit. It even put up a reward to find the person or people behind the contamination (no one was ever prosecuted for the murders).

Its action saved the company. Tylenol recovered its market share and survived the crisis.

Pause and think

If you don't want to react with emotion, force a pause, no matter how uncomfortable it makes you feel. It will give your brain time to catch up and you'll make better decisions.

Making decisions that are in the long-term interest of the company require a clear head and time to think – two things that are hard to find in a crisis.

'Far too few crisis management teams spend sufficient time considering the situation and planning before they act,' says Hemus. 'People feel that the last thing they should be doing is thinking: in fact, they should be doing! Under pressure, you often see senior leaders being very tactical, when they should be stepping back and thinking strategically. If all they do is give the team a clear strategic intent and priority areas on which to focus, they'll add far more value than by getting involved in writing statements, or reverting to the tasks associated with a job they were doing 15 years ago.'

That's not just true for leaders. Taking a breath before you issue a statement or make a decision about how to respond can be the difference between success and failure.

Activate your communications response

While leadership is defining or reapproving the strategic intent, the communications team can be agreeing their initial response. 'Those two things can happen in parallel,' says Hemus. 'Your first statement will be light on specifics, but will say you're aware of the situation, you're investigating, and will provide more information as you have it. It should position you as being on top of the situation, concerned, and acting on the information you have.'

It should not over-promise. It is easy to say, under pressure, that you'll take personal responsibility for the crisis, to guarantee that no one will be out of pocket, that the technology will be fixed, that the problem will never happen again. If you're going to make promises like that, you'd better be able to deliver on them, or your credibility will be severely damaged. At a time when you need to build trust, honesty now, however unpalatable, is better than a broken promise two weeks later.

In the background you should immediately activate social listening and media monitoring, to keep on top of consumer reaction to the crisis. You could consider ongoing polling or more detailed research to measure consumer opinion and track reaction to the crisis (more on that in Chapter 20).

And remember, don't fall into the trap of saying you'll update your audiences and then not doing so. Provide regular updates, even if you don't have much to say. It will position you as being ahead of the situation, reduce the number of queries you get from people who want to know what's going on, and minimize the risk of rumours spreading from other sources.

Don't just focus on the media. It's important, but not your only communications channel. While you core message will be the same across all audiences, adapt it for different channels. The words you use to respond to people on Twitter will not be exactly the same as what you say to media.

Think about the channels you're communicating over. Where are your stakeholders most likely to see or hear your response? Adapt your response for different channels and remember that they have global audiences. If you're a global company, and you have a product recall that only affects the United Kingdom, make sure that's clear in every communication. Always give context to your response.

Take action

As Adrian Wheeler says (Chapter 15), 'Do something.' In a crisis, you will be judged on what you do, not what you say. Create a plan that focuses on two things:

1 Taking care of the people who have been affected by the crisis.

2 Putting right the underlying cause of the crisis.

Tell your audiences what you are doing on both counts.

Remember your employees

It's easy to forget about employees in a crisis, focusing instead on external audiences. But your employees will be at the front line of the crisis, answering questions from stakeholders, often fielding questions from media, and talking to friends and family about the situation outside of work. They will be the people who either support you through the crisis and defend your reputation, or damage it.

They should be among the first people you inform in a crisis, before you talk to the media. There's nothing worse than your employees hearing from the media about an issue that affects the company they work at. Keep them updated as things change and evolve. Brief them face-to-face where possible, and encourage a senior member of the leadership team to answer questions, however difficult they are. Listen to what they have to say – there may be people who can offer valuable insight into your crisis and communications strategy, and how it is being received.

Remind employees, contractors and freelancers of their duties to the company in a crisis. They should have guidelines on what they can and cannot say about the company, particularly on social media. It's very easy in a strange situation, where people are unnerved by what's happened, to do or say the wrong thing to the wrong people. In the most serious incidents, they may well be targeted by journalists who want the inside scoop on the story, from someone who hasn't been media trained. I once worked for a company that had extremely thorough crisis plans, but on the day a crisis broke the regular receptionist was sick and the company had hired in a temporary replacement. She was the person that a national newspaper journalist spoke to first about a serious incident. She hadn't been briefed on what had happened, and she spoke freely about the rumours she'd heard (which were inaccurate). It took a lot of unnecessary firefighting to put that right.

Review all your planned marketing activities

In 2012, the stage for a Radiohead concert in Ontario collapsed, killing one person and injuring many others. The organizers, Live Nation, sent out a tweet announcing the concert had been cancelled. Shortly afterwards, a scheduled tweet was sent from the LiveNation Twitter account. It said: 'Help us create a photo album from the show! Share your Instagram photos from the show tonight…'[3]

Always review your planned marketing activity for appropriateness in light of the crisis.

Behave according to your company values

A crisis is not a time to spout your company messages, but it is a time to demonstrate company values. I have written elsewhere in this book about the importance of transparency and telling the truth in a crisis, and the key steps to starting to rebuild trust: be honest, take responsibility, say sorry.

After the crisis is over, you will be remembered by what you did to put it right. This will define how you are perceived by people in the years to come.

Summary of actions: The golden hour

1. Assemble your team.
2. Get to the facts.
3. Assess the severity of the crisis against predefined criteria, to make you more objective.
4. Define or reapprove the strategic intent of the crisis.
5. Activate your initial communications response.
6. Set up social listening and crisis monitoring to assess the mood of your audiences; review this information regularly.
7. Communicate beyond media: remember your employees, partners, suppliers, stakeholders and public audiences.
8. Communicate on all relevant channels; don't rely solely on media to convey your message.
9. Take direct action: create a plan to care for those affected; put right the underlying wrong.
10. Provide regular updates on what you're doing to fix the problem.
11. Review your planned marketing activity.
12. Behave according to your company values. You'll be judged by them.

Notes

1 MacCurdy, JT (1943) *The Structure of Morale*, Cambridge University Press.
2 Caesar-Gordon, A (2015) The perfect crisis response, 28 October. www.prweek.com/article/1357203/perfect-crisis-response.
3 Stratten, S (2010) Worst scheduled tweet timing. Ever. 16 June. www.unmarketing.com/2012/06/16/worst-scheduled-tweet-timing-ever.

Harnessing the crowd

19

Using influencers and advocates to calm the crisis: An interview with Scott Guthrie

If influencers are associated with your brand, they will be asked questions about you. They are part of your crisis plan whether you want them to be or not.

SCOTT GUTHRIE

In Chapter 3 I spoke to the influencer marketing consultant, writer and commentator, Scott Guthrie, to help me define influencer marketing. For this chapter, I asked him to talk to me about whether brands might work with influencers in a crisis situation and, if so, what best practice might look like. (As in previous chapters, I take influencers to mean people who genuinely have the ability to change opinion and behaviours, not just people with a large social media following.)

He advises companies to 'make friends when you don't need them, not just when you do'. In a crisis situation, you might need people around you who understand your brand, and can help get a message out quickly. All too often, influencers are forgotten in a crisis. But, as Guthrie says, if they're associated with your brand, they'll be asked questions about you. Make sure they have the information they need, in order to respond to the people they influence.

I asked Guthrie seven broad questions:

1. How can brands work with influencers in a crisis situation?
2. When are influencers useful and when are they a hindrance during a crisis?
3. How should brands communicate in a crisis situation via their influencers? Should they only use those they already have a relationship with, or is there a role for new influencers in a crisis situation?

4 How important is it for brands to keep their influencers informed about the crisis, as part of the crisis plan?
5 Can and should a brand try to control what an influencer says in a crisis situation? Is there any consequence to that?
6 How can brands build trust by working with influencers during the crisis, and after the crisis as part of a recovery plan?
7 Is there a difference in how you communicate during a crisis via influencers and brand advocates (and should there be)?

His answers are below.

How can brands work with influencers in a crisis situation?

It may be nuanced, but in order to create the best results from a working relationship between a brand and an influencer, the relationship should be long-term and be based on mutual benefit. Yes, brands can benefit from working with influencers in times of crisis – on the proviso they already have established positive working relationships with them.

Scott Guthrie says that social media influencers can play a role in four key areas during a crisis:

1 Humanising the brand.
2 Communicating in an authentic voice.
3 Social listening – providing an online focus group about what the brand's audience is saying about the crisis.
4 Earning trust for the brand. Communicating via a relatable, third-party channel assists the brand in transparent communication.

Social media influencers are influential because they consistently create compelling content that chimes with their audience and moves them to do something. Creators know what their audiences like and what they don't care for. They listen to feedback from their followers, and they interact with their audience by responding to comments. They analyse the data on past posts, creating more of what their audience wants.

The term 'influencer' is often used interchangeably with the term 'brand advocate'. But influence is neutral. Influencers are change agents who may hurt just as much as they may help a communicator's cause. Advocates are supporters, people – often customers – who talk favourably about a brand or product. They do not necessarily hold power to influence. So, in times of business-as-usual brands will be looking to work with influencers who have an affinity with their company and products.

Like it or not, if an influencer already has an association with a brand they are already part of the crisis management programme. Their followers (and anyone online with an interest, positive or otherwise) are likely to ask questions or comment on the crisis situation.

This is also true of subject matter experts with influence, whether they were previously a paid-for advocate of a brand or not. The chances are that people will turn to them for their take on the current situation – whether that's a positive or negative point of view.

When are influencers useful and when are they a hindrance during a crisis?

Influencers are useful when the brand has a crisis management response programme in place. When the brand appreciates that the influencer is an advocate for the brand but is not an employee of that brand. These creators have their own brand to support. Brands should work with influencers to communicate quickly and authentically with the target audience, to ensure they're aware of how you're working to resolve the situation and encourage them to use their own authentic voice when addressing any crisis-related messaging.

They are most useful when there is an existing, trusted, relationship in place with the brand. The essence of crisis management is speed. It would be a hindrance to attempt to identify, select and recruit new influencers and then brief them on how to carry key messages to their audience. After all, you don't learn how to swim only once you're drowning.

However, remember that influence is neutral. Influencers are change agents. They form or change opinions. They alter behaviours. As such, they may hurt just as much as they may help a communicator's cause.

In a crisis situation, it is as important to neutralise negative sentiment from subject matter experts and other influencers online. This necessitates knowing who is talking about your brand and the sentiment of the content they are publishing around your brand during a crisis situation, then providing them with facts about the situation and your roadmap, including a timeline, for rectifying the situation.

How should brands communicate in a crisis situation via their influencers? Should they only use those they already have a relationship with, or is there a role for new influencers in a crisis situation?

It takes considerable time to identify, select, vet and recruit the most appropriate influencers for your brand. Recruitment is a combination of quantitative measures based on audience size, the rate at which their content resonates with their audience, the overlap between their audience and the brand's target audience, and of subjective measures. Do they share the same values as your brand? Is their tone of voice commensurate with yours? Do they share an affinity with your products? Do they always turn up on time or produce content to the deadline? For these reasons, you should work with influencers that you already have a relationship with.

There's the age-old adage: have friends before you need friends. Former Australian Prime Minister, John Howard, put it another way when he said, 'You can't fatten a pig on market day.' This is another reason why building long-term, mutually beneficial relationships between brand and influencer are so important. It's important to have those strong influencer relationships in place before a crisis hits. Avoid bringing in a wave of new influencers only as a response to a negative situation. Instead, leverage existing relationships to focus on strong communication goals and community engagement.

That said, you should also be listening to all conversations happening online mentioning your brand. You need to identify the dissenters who have an impact. And aim to neutralise their negative sentiment by providing them with timely, accurate facts about the situation, along with the brand's intended solutions to rectify the situation.

No comment or direct message should go unanswered by the influencer. Communicators need a well-considered response plan in place. The basic responses can be handled by the influencer. More complicated responses might be given via a URL link to a brand-owned 'frequently asked questions' landing page. For negative, angry posts or complicated questions, take the conversation offline.

How important is it for brands to keep their influencers informed about the crisis, as part of the crisis plan?

Like it or not, if an influencer already has an association with a brand they are already part of the crisis management programme. Their followers (and the online community in general) are likely to ask questions and comment via direct message or the comment section in their news feeds.

Brands absolutely need to keep their influencers fully informed. Ensure they're aware of how you're working to resolve the situation and encourage them to use their own authentic voice when addressing any crisis-related messaging.

Give them a rundown of what happened, what you are planning in order to rectify the situation, and the timeline for this to take place. Be as transparent as you can. Gain the influencer's trust and they will, in turn, gain the consumers' trust.

Keep the influencers involved at all stages. Their audience will want to feel assured that the brand is placing its customers first every step of the way.

The essence of effective crisis management is speed. Brands need to have ready access to their influencers' contact details. This might make it advantageous to nurture influencer relationships in-house rather than at arm's length via agencies.

Can and should a brand try to control what an influencer says in a crisis situation? Is there any consequence to that?

It is vital for an influencer to 'translate' the brand's crisis messaging into their own tone of voice. The value that influencers bring to both brands and their audience is that they can humanise the brand and provide an added layer of authenticity and transparency to the situation.

Figure 19.1 The skill of the influencer is to translate a brand's key messages into creative content that resonates with the influencer's audience, who are then compelled to act

Remember, influencers are brand partners, not employees. Use a creative brief that outlines the key messages that should be conveyed – rather than a script that needs to be regurgitated.

How can brands build trust by working with influencers during the crisis, and after the crisis as part of a recovery plan?

In our post-truth era, as consumers, we are sceptical. We have lost faith in journalism, in politicians, in big brands. We do, however, trust people like us. We think of social media influencers as people like us. We relate to them. And we trust them, too. This makes them powerful voices during times of crisis. We are more likely to turn to these people like us for advice before we consider listening to a brand's official spokesperson.

Having messaging come directly from real people instead of from a corporate-sounding spokesperson makes it feel more authentic. This feeling of authenticity means that it will have a better chance of resonating with your audience.

Post-crisis influencer blog posts, YouTube uploads and Instagram posts help you populate search engine results with relevant, current and positive brand content. Compare this with a digital advertisement. If a communicator buys an advertisement, that ad is removed as soon the media spend has been expended. Influencers' content usually stays online in perpetuity and resurfaces in search results accordingly.

Is there a difference in how you communicate during a crisis via influencers and brand advocates (and should there be)?

As I have mentioned above, the terms 'social media influencers' and 'brand advocates' should not be used interchangeably. In times of business as usual, brands should look to work with social media influencers who are brand advocates, those with an affinity for their brand. This makes for more authentic content and they will always pass the 'smell test' with their audience. In other words, an influencer's audience will know instantly if the brand fit isn't right for them. Get it wrong and the influencer will be branded a sell-out. Their followers will vote with their feet and unfollow. Lose your audience and you've lost your influence.

Figure 19.2 In order to hit the sweet spot content should be authentic, chime with the audience and satisfy brand requirements

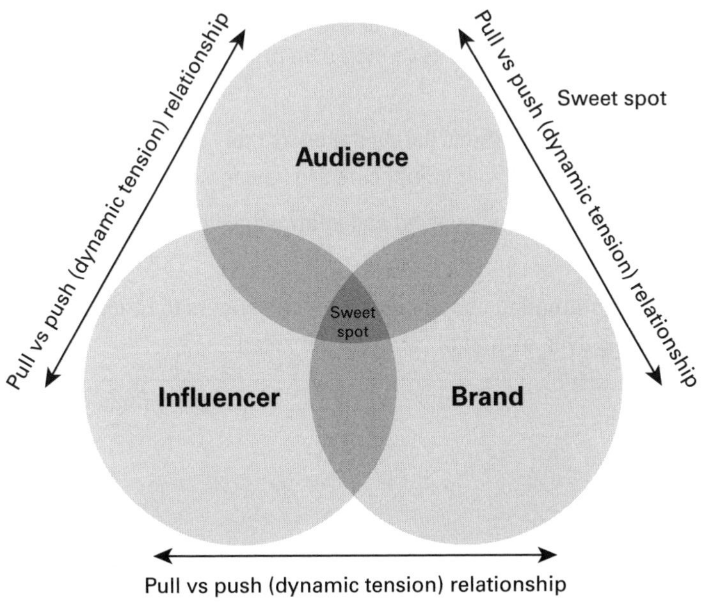

In times of crisis, brands should work with their existing network of brand advocate influencers to endeavour to get facts to their key audience quickly, and authentically. However, brands also need to identify anyone with influence online who is actively talking about the crisis situation and seek to neutralise any negative sentiment by providing them with facts and the route to a solution.

The need for quick content turnaround might mean less polished content production. The type of messaging will be different, too – a move from selling products to answering questions and helping to restore trust.

Summary of actions: Working with influencers during the crisis

1. Influencers can help a brand during a crisis by: humanising the brand; helping the brand to communicate in an authentic voice; social listening; and earning trust.
2. Include your influencers in your crisis planning process.
3. Think of the impact of a crisis on each influencer, and what the risk might be.
4. During a crisis, only work with influencers that you have an established relationship with.
5. Work with your influencers during a crisis; don't expect them simply to be your mouthpiece (they have their own brand and audiences to consider).
6. Listen to all conversations during the crisis that relate to your brand, including those that your influencers are having with their fans.
7. Keep your influencers involved and informed all the way through the crisis.
8. Consider co-creating content with your influencers to rebuild trust after the crisis is over, as part of your recovery plan.

The role of technology in crisis management

20

Using predictive analysis, social listening, search data and insights

Predicting a crisis

On 5 February 62 AD, an earthquake rocked Campania in southern Italy. Its epicentre was in Pompeii, a wealthy tourist city on the Bay of Naples, where it destroyed most of the city's houses, made from timber, brick and stone. Pompeii was a popular town for the rich to build holiday villas – its pleasant climate, fertile soil and fine wines made it an idyllic getaway. But the earthquake unnerved its elite inhabitants. Those who could afford to, left the town for good. Over the next 15 or so years, Pompeii was rebuilt by a new wave of people who came to live in the city, mostly merchants, drawn by a booming economy and trading routes through the bay. Life carried on much as before.

On 22 August 79, Pliny the Elder, who was Head of the Roman Fleet based in Miseno, across the bay from Pompeii, noticed the wine in his glass moving. He assumed it was a small ground tremor, nothing unusual – there had been several that summer. Soon afterwards, he heard that the water supply to the region had been cut off. A major aqueduct had failed, and people nearby reported an unusual smell of sulphur. That heralded three days of unimaginable devastation and chaos. The eruption of Mount Vesuvius first poured two and a half metres of pumice on Pompeii and Herculaneum.

Many were killed from falling rock but others managed to escape in the darkness. Vesuvius paused; some Pompeians returned to the city to collect valuables and see if their houses remained standing.

Then came the relentless pyroclastic surge, a fast-moving mixture of poisonous gas, ash and rock that destroyed everything in its path. It's estimated that 2000 people were killed, buried by the volcano.

The Romans didn't know the connection between earthquakes and volcanic eruptions, although many who were rich enough to leave had been worried enough by the quakes to do so after the destruction in 62 AD. There had been other signs, too: writing a century after the eruption, the historian Cassius Dio reported portentous sightings ahead of the eruption of giants roaming the land, who were seen as a prediction of a volcanic eruption (sightings that could have been caused by gas escaping from vents in Vesuvius).

Predicting or tracking disaster

Our portents today are a bit more scientific than spotting roaming giants, but the principle remains that if you can spot the early signs, you might avert (or at least reduce the impact of) the issue.

Artificial intelligence is used by governments and corporations to identify data patterns and predict risks of events such as environmental disasters, climate change or population growth-related issues. Insights from this data can influence policies and budgets, and be used to spot and avoid hazards.

In medicine, data mined from social media, search and mobile phone records are used to predict the spread of disease. In 2014, data collected from social media and local news reports by HealthMap (a health data mapping tool) showed a new 'haemorrhagic fever' was spreading. Nine days later, Ebola was officially recognized by the World Health Organization.[1]

Health organizations use big data – including data from social media – to spot and analyse threats to public health from flu outbreaks to food poisoning. According to *Government Technology* magazine (2015) the Chicago Department of Public Health uses Twitter to identify cases of food poisoning, so they can inspect the relevant restaurants and take action before the issue spreads. Similarly, the New York City Department of Health and Mental Hygiene uses Yelp reviews to identify instances of food poisoning.[2]

This information can track shifts in the public mood, too. John Brownstein, the co-founder of HealthMap and Associate Professor of Paediatrics at Harvard Medical School, says that using data collected from social media, blogs, news sites and forums gives an aggregate picture of what's happening and can also be useful in creating what he calls 'situational awareness' – the impact of an event on public opinion. 'There's value in understanding the public perception and communication and how government can refine its communications based on the response of the population. Using social media to understand people's attitudes and beliefs in that way is extraordinarily powerful,' he told Government Technology in January 2015.[3]

Predicting human behaviour

This data-driven insight into human attitudes and behaviour can be useful to spot an emerging issue and intervene early. In 2013, Eric Horvitz, a technical fellow and directors at Microsoft Research, analysed data from social and online media to seek patterns of language and behaviour that could help identify mothers at risk of postpartum depression, something that could be used to intervene and bring help to those who need it.[4]

Facebook uses analysis of what we post, how regularly, and the language we use, to identify when we are about to start a relationship, when we fall in love and when we break up.[5] (In the days before the relationship goes public, the research says, lovers post to each others' walls more frequently; posting drops dramatically in the early days of the relationship, although the posts that are made are more positive than usual. On the day of a breakup, there's a massive spike in posts, followed by a 50 to 75 per cent increase in the number of interactions in the period following the breakup.)

Information like this is gold dust to marketers, of course. Predictive analytics is the practice of using past data to forecast a future outcome. It is commonly used in business to predict events such as machine failure in manufacturing, business models (for example, credit models in financial services), resourcing (policing based on crime data), customer value and, of course, to drive marketing decisions. At its most simple, the practice of predictive analytics in marketing is Amazon recommending you buy something based on what others like you have done. Using the Facebook example above, it can predict not just what (or whom) you might like, but how you are likely to behave. In marketing, that means the ability to approach you with product information at the optimum time and in the optimum way. In a crisis situation, it could mean anticipating and averting risk, or understanding how people are likely to respond to a difficult situation. This could let you deliver the right message at the right time, over the right channel – using direct contact, paid social media, paid or organic search as part of your communications mix.

As with everything, predictive analysis is only as good as the data – and data modelling assumptions – it uses. Thomas Davenport, a Professor of Management and IT, writing for the *Harvard Business Review* in 2014, points out that invalid predictive models failed to foresee the financial crash of 2008–09 because the underlying assumption in the model was that house prices would keep rising, and people with mortgages would continue to be able to repay them.[6] Google's own predictive flu tracker, Google Flu Trends, was abandoned in 2015 after it failed to predict major flu outbreaks between 2011 and 2013 (the idea behind it was to take search data relating to flu to forecast accurately the prevalence of flu).

But if the underlying assumptions are sound, predictive analytics can be used to detect risks by analysing patterns of behaviour and the relationships between factors in that behaviour. To avert a crisis, you have to see it coming. Data from social media listening, sentiment analysis, news monitoring, insight into the emotional intent of customers, and spikes in search patterns can all be used to spot unusual activity that could signal an issue looming on the horizon. Combine this with predictive analysis to forecast the likely outcome of that issue and how people will react to it, and you have a powerful crisis mitigation tool. And it might not be your own data that predicts the problem. If a competitor experiences a backlash against a new marketing campaign, for example, that data could be invaluable in predicting how your own customers will respond to you in a similar situation. Forewarned is forearmed.

Using AI for crisis planning and risk mitigation

Stephen Waddington is a communications consultant, author, lecturer and UK MD for Metia, a marketing and communications agency. He also worked with the Chartered Institute of Public Relations (an organization of which he was president in 2014) to start the #AIinPR project, a crowdsourced initiative to encourage the PR industry to adopt and embrace AI in planning, managing and analysing the impact of PR campaigns.

I ask him what role technology and AI play in a crisis, and what the potential is for brands to use AI to mitigate risk. 'There's a lot of hype that robots are going to take over our jobs,' he says. 'But they're going to help us do our jobs better. They'll give us the data to understand audience behaviours, and they're smarter warning devices.'

We talk about the use of predictive analytics in understanding the public mood, and monitoring to spot an issue early on. 'There's some really interesting developments in areas like geofencing and location-based data,' he says. 'Newsrooms are using tools to create heatmaps of online chatter. A flurry of posts will tell a journalist where something is happening, and they can investigate.' If the organization at the centre of an issue isn't doing the same, that's going to give newsrooms the advantage. If journalists can see where a story is breaking in real time, they could well get there before the organization is even aware of it.

The key to good data is looking at different sources, Waddington says. 'We get obsessed with Twitter, and it's a good source of information, but it needs to be correlated with other data. Look at information you're getting back from the field in an organization. If you have a product issue, the first place you're likely to really hear about it is from customer service. Look at your internal sources first.'

During the crisis: Understanding the public response

Continual monitoring and analysis

During a crisis, continual monitoring lets you understand what the public view is of the crisis. But don't rely on a single channel to give you a true picture. 'There might be lots of chatter on Twitter about an issue, and it appears to be damaging for a brand just because of the volume of noise,' says Waddington. 'Of course, from a PR point of view, the amount of noise has an impact. But what we can do now thanks to social and search data is look more broadly at the nuances of how people discuss an issue.'

He recommends combining data from social media, search and customer service data, and segmenting that data to understand what's really going on. 'You can work out what people really think about a subject, and then look at its subsets,' he says. 'Take immigration as an example. It's a nuanced issue. It might appear on the face of it that the country has an anti-immigration stance. But if you look deeper into the conversations that are happening in communities around skills, or the National Health Service, they tell you something different. Business intelligence tools can help brands make sense of conversations at scale, and cluster conversations, mapping the key stakeholders, individuals or organizations that are influencing them. Brands can use this to understand what the people that matter to them are saying.

They can decide what they care about, what they need to respond to, and what they can ignore.'

Polling and analysis

In the aftermath of Hurricane Katrina in August 2005, a poll by USA Today and Gallup found that the majority of Americans disapproved of the federal response to the disaster. Sixty-five per cent thought the response of President Bush was 'too slow', and 70 per cent thought FEMA's response was not adequate.[7]

Polling during a crisis can be an effective way to gauge the public mood and reaction to your handling of the crisis, and it can be a useful benchmark against which to compare what you're hearing on social media. Is the social media reaction giving you a true picture of how people feel? How do your customers feel? Polling can measure how your messages and tone of voice are being received, how well your spokesperson is connecting with your audiences, and whether the public believes that you care about the issue. Done in real time, that intelligence means you can refine your response.

Social listening

Monitor keywords or hashtags to identify a potential issue. Don't just monitor your own brand name – a crisis may not start with you, but could come from a competitor, supplier, partner, advocate or influencer doing something or talking about an issue that will have a negative impact on your industry.

Track:

- An increase in chatter online that could signal an issue breaking.
- Sentiment and public mood. If you have more negative comment than usual on your own pages, look into why that is. During and after the crisis, you can track how the public is reacting to the crisis, and to your response.
- All channels, not just news and social media. A crisis can break anywhere. Track your customer channels, forums, blogs, changes in search data – anywhere you might spot early warning signs.
- Influencers – who is influencing the public conversation about an issue that could damage your organization? They might be members of the public, journalists, advocates or other commentators.

Summary of actions: Using technology in crisis management

1. Use social listening, search analysis and customer service data insights to spot a breaking issue early, and use predictive analysis to forecast the likely outcome of the crisis.
2. Combine data from social media, customer service, news, search and any other channels available to you, to track the public response during the crisis.
3. Segment data to understand nuanced conversations happening in difference communities.
4. Continually analyse that data during and after the crisis and use it to refine your response.
5. Use regular polling as a tool to understand how your crisis response is resonating with key audiences.

Notes

1 Gilpin, L (2014) How an algorithm detected the Ebola outbreak a week early, and what it could do next, Tech Republic, 26 August. www.techrepublic.com/article/how-an-algorithm-detected-the-ebola-outbreak-a-week-early-and-what-it-could-do-next.
2 Brown, J (2015) Using social media data to identify outbreaks and control disease, Government Technology, 8 January. www.govtech.com/em/health/Social-Media-Data-Identify-Outbreaks.html.
3 Brown, J (2015) Using social media data to identify outbreaks and control disease, Government Technology, 8 January. www.govtech.com/em/health/Social-Media-Data-Identify-Outbreaks.html.
4 De Choudhury, M, Counts, S and Horvitz, E (2013), Predicting postpartum changes in emotion and behavior via social media, Microsoft Research, April. www.microsoft.com/en-us/research/wp-content/uploads/2016/11/predicting_postpartum_changes_chi_2013.pdf.

5 Morris, I (2016) Facebook knows when you fall in love, and that's pretty creepy, *Forbes*, 31 December. www.forbes.com/sites/ianmorris/2016/12/31/facebook-knows-when-you-fall-in-love-and-thats-pretty-creepy/#7dbb36356f52.
6 Davenport, TH (2014) A predictive analytics primer, *Harvard Business Review*, 2 September. https://hbr.org/2014/09/a-predictive-analytics-primer.
7 Roberts, J (2005) Poll: Katrina response inadequate, CBS News, 5 September. www.cbsnews.com/news/poll-katrina-response-inadequate.

21 Practical steps to prepare, execute and analyse a crisis response (and avoid common pitfalls)

'Greater investment in preparation and rehearsal, and in risk monitoring, such that management is better informed, earlier, is no longer a luxury and will bring rewards when crisis strikes,' says Dr Deborah Pretty, founding director of Pentland Analytics. In 2018, she wrote the third in her research report series on the impact of a crisis on company value: *Reputation Risks in the Cyber Age*, in conjunction with the insurance company, Aon.[1] (She had previously conducted the same research in 1993 and 2000.) Her 2018 research found that, on average, a company loses 5 per cent of its shareholder value over one year following a major crisis event. But, the report says, that figure 'masks significant differences across firms in their ability to recover value following a reputation crisis'.

Pretty's research shows that companies divide into two distinct groups following a crisis, which she categories as 'winners' and 'losers'. The winners outperform pre-crisis expectations and gain an average of 20 per cent in value one year after the crisis. The losers drop, on average, close to 30 per cent of their value.

Figure 21.1 Crisis phases

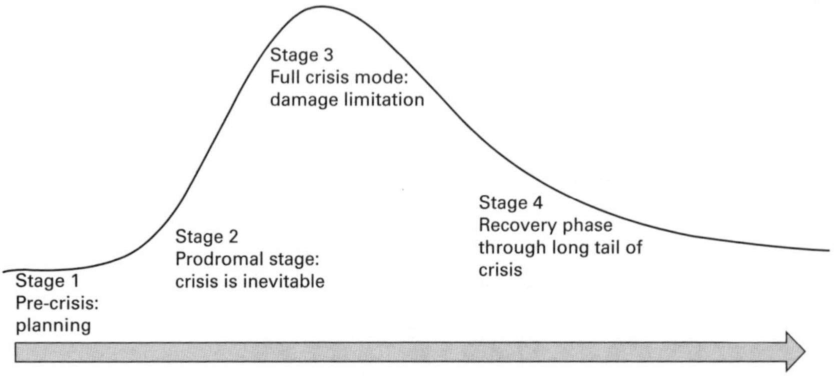

It's worth noting that these values are roughly double what they were in the year 2000 – the result of what Pretty calls a 'post-social media world'. This shift, her report says, 'can be attributed to the power of social media, technology and contemporary culture,' focusing on two areas:

1 Crisis communications must be 'not just swift, but instant and global'. As Pretty says: 'Social media is unforgiving.'
2 A shift in cultural expectations. Companies are expected to 'atone for their mistakes and do so conspicuously', says Pretty.

You can picture a crisis in four clear stages:

1 Pre-crisis planning.
2 The 'prodromal' stage (the moment at which a crisis is inevitable and inescapable).
3 Full crisis mode, where you focus on damage limitation.
4 The recovery phase.

In the following sections, I will look at the steps you can take to prepare, execute and analyse a crisis response.

1 Pre-crisis planning

Crisis planning can seem like a mammoth task, but it really doesn't have to be. The most important thing is to have a clear structure, detailed plans and a solid escalation and decision-making hierarchy.

Step 1: Agree the wider crisis team

The first step is to agree your wider crisis team. This may already be defined as part of your operational crisis management plan, or your business continuity plan. It should include representatives from across the business, including the leadership team, HR, legal, compliance and risk, internal communications, PR and communications, marketing, technology and IT, social media, customer service – and anyone else who will be responsible for managing the crisis and communicating to internal and external audiences. Be absolutely clear what the roles are for each, who is authorized to activate a crisis plan, and who is ultimately responsible for decision making; you do not want decision by committee. (Duncan Gallagher in Chapter 15 recommends using the RACI or PACE models to determine roles during a crisis.)

The team can be refined for each crisis, depending on where the issue falls within the organization. Appoint decision makers for each function. Later, you can agree who the crisis lead will be in different types of situation (a data breach, a corporate scandal, an industrial accident, etc), once you've completed Step 2, scenario planning.

Step 2: Scenario planning

With your crisis team, come up with every possible scenario you can think of that could negatively impact the reputation of your company. Again, much of this work may have been done as part of the operational crisis plan, or the business continuity plan. In my experience, there is always more to be offered by the communications team, who tend to think in terms of long-term reputation risk based on the perception of the brand and consumer behaviour, rather than functional issues (service outages and so on) that might damage the business in the short term.

Categorize these scenarios first by type, and then by level of threat to the reputation of the company. Focus more on the threat level, and don't worry too much about having clean lines between types of issue. There will be crossover. A data breach that impacts a few people and does not put any financial information at risk will be a very different threat to one that exposes the personal and financial data of thousands of customers.

Companies do this in lots of different ways. Some collaborate on shared documents; others hold workshops with their wider crisis team that can be replicated across markets. I prefer the workshop approach – it can be messy, but you have everyone's full attention for a few hours to get the job done.

Always leave some leeway for a crisis that comes completely out of the blue, something you haven't planned for. If your crisis plan focuses more on what damage an event can do than what category it's in, your plan will be more flexible. As you spot the new crisis event, you can assess the potential damage it could do, slot it into your crisis plan at the appropriate threat level, and act accordingly.

> You might structure your scenario plan like this:
>
> **Threat level: 4 (highest level)**
>
> - Damage potential: an event that has the potential to damage the organization's ability to operate in the long term.
> - Example scenarios:
>   - catastrophic data breach;
>   - issue affecting public health;
>   - accident involving loss of life;
>   - global service outage.
>
> And so on, through your different levels.

Step 3: Advise on what crises could be avoided by business action

Assess these scenarios and see what business action you could take to minimize their impact, or even avoid them altogether. Something that the National Health Service could have learned in 2017, when it felt the full devastating impact of the Wannacry attack.

On 12 May 2017, the UK's Department of Health and Social Care got a message saying that four NHS trusts had fallen victim to a ransomware attack. Their IT systems – affecting hospitals and medical clinics – had been taken down by hackers who demanded money to restore the system. That afternoon, the attack had spread to 16 trusts, and it was declared a major cybersecurity incident. Within a week more than 600 NHS or affiliated organizations and 80 hospital trusts had been affected. Thousands of people had medical appointments cancelled.

It could have been prevented, according to a report by the National Audit Office.[2] The NHS was not sufficiently prepared for the crisis, which could have been prevented simply by maintaining IT systems, patching and updating security software.

Learn from similar crises, either that you've faced, or that others in your industry have faced. Shore up your systems to avoid going through it again. According to reports, one year on from the Wannacry attack, the security of the NHS – although much improved – was still vulnerable to cyber attacks.

Step 4: Agree action for each level of crisis

If you jump in to activate your crisis plan a level up, or – worse – before you're actually in a crisis (it's more common than you think), you could make the situation a whole lot worse than it needs to be. Define what normal looks like, as Lisa Barnett talked to me about in Chapter 9, what an issue looks like, and what a full crisis looks like. Then define the appropriate level of action for each level. That might include guidance on when to take no action, too, but keep a watchful eye on an issue to monitor when it escalates.

Step 5: Develop your crisis communication plan

A business continuity plan will take into account how the business will function. But how will it communicate? Integrate your communications plan into the business continuity and operational crisis plans.

At its most basic, your plan should include:

- **The contact details of all your crisis team, including backups in case one or more of the team is out of reach.** I've seen more than one crisis plan which only has office-hours telephone numbers and work emails listed as a way to contact the executive team.
- **Clearly defined authority and a chain of command**, including individual roles and responsibilities, and deputies for each role who can step up if needed.
- **A clear activation plan and escalation process.** Every employee should know how to spot a potential threat, and whom it should be reported to. The words that send chills down a crisis team's spine are, 'I thought that was a bit odd, but I didn't think to do anything about it.' Within your team, have a team of people who are authorized to activate the crisis plan. They should be part of the wider crisis team, and should be accessible

through a line management structure to anyone who might spot a crisis. Activation can be as simple as a telephone call to the crisis leader who can send a (secure) message to the crisis team: 'We are in crisis level 2, plan activated.' That process should include who can make the decision to wake the Chief Executive on holiday at three in the morning. Not everyone will feel comfortable doing it; if it's in your plan, it's a much easier decision to make.

- **A defined decision-making process**, including one person who ultimately has responsibility for making a decision (the leader).
- **All the relevant access information that you need out of normal working hours** – to buildings, social media accounts, websites and so on.
- **A detailed action plan** for the first 24 hours of a major crisis.
- **Approval processes** (see below).
- **Approved templates for statements**, to speed up approvals. Include here guidance on how to personalize statements when you're responding publicly to people on social media. Your corporate media statement may not travel well on Facebook.
- **Strategic intent statements and company values.** These make decisions much easier to make.
- **Tone of voice guidelines.** It's so common to see a company veer from its usual tone of voice during a crisis. Where it has worked hard to be open, engaging and transparent with its public (particularly on social media), suddenly it closes off, becomes overly corporate and legal-sounding. It can be damaging. Give examples of the kind of words and phrases you can use publicly, so not every message on Twitter has to be approved through a lawyer. You won't have the time.
- **Facts and figures.** Have all the facts and figures about the business to hand. You'll need to know things like the number of employees at each location, where you operate in the world, your fleet size, and so on. Don't leave this until the crisis hits. You'll have enough to do establishing the facts of the crisis without worrying about how many employees you have.
- **Instructions.** How to activate your crisis monitoring and social listening, how to contact your external agencies, how to access your website and social media accounts – all the practical information you'll need during the crisis.
- **Access to key external contacts**, who's responsible for contacting each of them and at what stage of the crisis. They will include customers, investors,

shareholders, employees, partners, suppliers, agencies, contractors, media, influencers.

- **A checklists** of what should be done by when. This means managing a crisis becomes following a process as much as possible, which takes significant stress off the crisis team.

All this information should be securely held, and comply with relevant data regulation.

Step 6: Streamline your approval process.

A lawyer I worked with once told me that she had got to draft 97 of a two-line crisis holding statement. The approval process took nearly two days and the statement was issued far too late to do any good. It's an extreme example, but it's not as unusual as you might think. Keep everyone who needs to approve a statement close – and ideally, get as much as you can pre-approved.

Step 7: Train your team, and simulate a crisis to rehearse them

A crisis plan is all very well but if your team doesn't know how to use it, it's useless. Hold regular training sessions on your plan (this has the added advantage of making you review the plan and spot any gaps in it).

Hold realistic simulations to rehearse a crisis, testing your plans and processes, and building muscle memory in your teams, so they're better prepared to cope (as we discussed in Chapters 13 and 14). Most crisis organizations recommend rehearsing twice a year to build that muscle memory and override the 'fight, flight or freeze' reflexes.

Step 8: Revise and update your plans regularly

A plan is only as good as its updates. If it has old information in it, it won't be much help to you. Review it regularly (at least annually).

Considerations

Think about your back-up plans. What happens if a member of your core team is ill, or called away? Or the crisis breaks while they're on a plane?

How will you communicate if all your systems are down? Have a communications system that is accessible off the corporate network. But – and this might sound obvious – make sure it's secure. I'm sure there will be people reading who will laugh and say, 'Of course my crisis plan is secure!' And that's great. But I met a lovely and extremely skilled woman who worked for a household name company, at a crisis communications conference. She told me that in the event of a disaster, she could contact any member of her team, and could run the entire crisis from her mobile phone. I was impressed. I asked her about the secure system she used to access all this. She pulled out her wallet from her handbag. In it, was a fold-out card that had the personal phone numbers, email addresses and home contact details of every member of her crisis team; details of how to access the company's social media accounts and website; and a summary of the company's crisis plans. A hacker's dream. Sometimes your crisis plan itself can be a crisis in the making.

Common pitfalls to avoid: Preparing for a crisis

- Not listening to public sentiment early enough. Listening to the public can help you catch some issues early enough that you avoid the crisis altogether.
- Making the crisis plan so complicated that it's not usable when you need it. A one-page document of plain language and clear instructions is more valuable than 100 pages of jargon and complicated structures.
- Not being able to access (let alone activate) your plan securely outside of office hours. You need to be able to access your plan and contact your crisis team 24/7.
- Not training teams on how to act on the crisis plan. Imagine putting on a play and not doing a rehearsal. Test your crisis plan – and your team – by running realistic crisis simulations.
- Not coordinating your teams. I have worked with more than one brand where marketing owns Facebook, PR owns Twitter, and the two have no way of communicating during a crisis.

2 The prodromal stage

The 'prodromal' stage is where you see the early symptoms of the crisis, which signal that a crisis is very likely, if not inevitable. (*Prodromal* is a word used in medicine that means the early symptoms of disease; you don't always get the benefit of this time in a crisis. When you do, use it wisely.)

This is the time to breathe before the crisis hits, to flex your muscle memory and activate your crisis plan, focusing on the priorities as outlined in Chapter 16. To recap:

- Pause. Breathe. Think about your course of action.
- Assemble your core team, and remind them of their roles and responsibilities.
- Get to the facts of the crisis, quickly.
- Define or reapprove the strategic intent of the crisis.
- Assess the likely severity of the crisis and map against your crisis plan. Prepare for the crisis to move up the severity level as it develops further.
- Get your initial communications response ready.
- Brief everyone who needs to know. Consider pre-briefing media so you get ahead of the story.
- Plan your communications strategy and crisis narrative.
- Set up social listening and monitoring, and review the public mood regularly.
- Keep reassessing the movement of the crisis, so you know when to activate your full plan.

Common pitfalls to avoid: The prodromal stage

- Ignoring a brewing crisis. If you know the crisis is coming, get ahead of it. It's always better for you to tell your story than for someone else to.
- Removing control from teams who have the best knowledge of their audiences and stakeholders. This is particularly common in listed companies where a central team will whip away all control from local teams at the first sign of a breaking crisis. That can mean the crisis is being managed in the wrong time zone, the wrong language, and by people who are not close to those affected. I understand that a central

team from the global headquarters will want to manage shareholder relations, coordinate the global response and ultimately take responsibility. It is right to involve your central teams to set the strategy, guide the response and support local teams, but you should trust your people on the ground to play their part.

- Not listening early on to public concerns. Your crisis might shift focus, and good social listening or polling could help you get ahead of a changing issue.

3 Full crisis mode: Damage limitation

This is the toughest time of the crisis, with all hands on deck, but in many ways it could be the simplest. It's where you reap the rewards of good planning. It's not when you want to be rewriting the crisis plan you never finished because other things took priority (we've all been there). Key actions to remember:

- Activate your full crisis plan.
- Regroup the core crisis team regularly (checkins every hour or so for the worst crises – this should be documented in your crisis plan) to review actions, the public mood, your communications strategy. Tweak and refine.
- Listen to what's being said about you, and empathise. Understand what those affected are going through. You're not just dealing with facts: you're dealing with fear, frustration, betrayal, grief, outrage. View your corporate statements through that lens.
- Read your statements out loud. Imagine you're talking directly to one of the people affected. How will they feel when they hear your words?
- Coordinate your response with agencies, suppliers, partners – anyone who might be approached for comment, or who is involved in the crisis.
- Keep your response consistent. Don't be pushed into saying something you don't mean.
- Stay calm. You'll be under pressure. Take regular time out. Look after yourself and your team. If you can, switch out the teams regularly, particularly those dealing directly with the public on social media. It can be incredibly draining to deal with a mass outpouring of emotion.

Regularly swapping over the team can keep your team refreshed and better able to cope.

- Talk to people on the channels they want to engage on. Most teams will try to take the response offline, but it can be more effective (and efficient) to answer questions on the channels chosen by your consumers or stakeholders. Why respond on Twitter asking someone to call a helpline, unless you have to? That creates two points of engagement when you could have answered their query there and then.
- Work together. Even when you're under pressure, it's worth taking a few minutes to bring the full team together to share their experiences, support each other and refine the strategy.
- Respond to misinformation and rumour. Always correct the facts.

Common pitfalls to avoid: Full crisis response

- Siloing the crisis response, focusing on business continuity now, rather than on your company reputation that will allow you to trade in six months.
- Responding to pressure to do something you're not comfortable with, making a promise you can't keep, responding in anger.
- Using an over-corporate, uncaring tone of voice.
- Using language most people don't understand. No one knows (or cares) what your industry certification standard means. Speak in plain language that someone outside your organization understands.
- Focusing only on media, not other external channels (including social media).
- Not adapting statements to your audience or channel. All that work you've done to create positive engagement on social media can be wiped out during a crisis with a series of corporate statements that lack empathy.
- Only responding to those questions that are easy. Some questions will be tough. But if you only respond to those that praise you, for example, you'll be seen as ducking the issue.
- Getting into debates that you can't win. This is usually because the team is tired, and not making great decisions.

- Not giving context to a statement (time, location, date). It's easy and common for people to take a screenshot of your tweet, and use it for months to come.
- Not responding to misinformation and rumour.
- Refusing to talk to people on their chosen channels. This can create twice as much traffic for your teams to deal with. And sometimes it benefits you if you're seen to be responding publicly.
- Not closing off the crisis. Tell people when the issue is resolved, even if it seems to have gone quiet.

4 The recovery stage

Most crises will have a long tail. You may not get back to normal for months, or even years. But you will need to keep operating. Don't assume you can jump straight back to how things were before the crisis hit (Chapter 9).

Hold an honest analysis of how the crisis developed, how your crisis teams performed and how your processes stood up. Was it, overall, successfully handled? What are the lessons learned? Could it have been avoided? Could it happen again? Don't wait for the next crisis to remember what went wrong in this one.

During the recovery stage, focus your marketing efforts on rebuilding trust. Make amends for what's happened. In the worst crises (eg Tylenol, Chapter 18), you will be forever associated with the event. But you don't want it to be the only thing that's talked about. Change your behaviour to ensure it doesn't happen again, and the crisis will be seen as a catalyst for positive change, rather than the single event that defines your company's reputation.

Common pitfalls to avoid: Full crisis response

1. Thinking the crisis is over because it's gone quiet. You may be handling queries and comments on social media relating to the crisis for months.
2. Avoiding an honest analysis of how the crisis went. A transparent process for appraising the crisis could help you refine your plan, and avoid a crisis in the future.

Notes

1 Petty, D (2018) *Reputation Risk in the Cyber Age*, Aon and Pentland Analytics, 2018. www.aon.com/getmedia/2882e8b3-2aa0-4726-9efa-005af9176496/Aon-Pentland-Analytics-Reputation-Report-2018-07-18.pdf.

2 Hughes, O (2018) Wannacry one year on: A retrospective look at NHS IT's black-letter day, *Digital Health*, 11 May. www.digitalhealth.net/2018/05/wannacry-one-year-on.

FURTHER READING

Bergstein, R (2017) Should companies comment on politics? Forbes, 1 February. Available from www.forbes.com/sites/rachellebergstein/2017/02/01/should-companies-comment-on-politics-a-branding-expert-weighs-in/#4ec36e952f76.

Bhargava, R (2019) *Non-Obvious 2019: How to predict trends and win the future*, Ideapress Publishing.

Booker, J (2013) Fighting for civil rights at the soda fountain, The Coca Cola Company, 14 January. Available from www.coca-colacompany.com/stories/fighting-for-civil-rights-at-the-soda-fountain.

Dewan, S (2006) Coca-Cola donates land to Civil Rights Museum in Atlanta, *New York Times*, 23 October. Available from www.nytimes.com/2006/10/23/us/24civilcnd.html.

Lavoie, J, Leduc, K, Arruda, C, Crossman, AM and Talwara, V (2016) Developmental profiles of children's spontaneous lie-telling behavior, Science Direct, 11 December. Available from www.sciencedirect.com/science/article/pii/S0885201416302088.

Neatpour (2018) Sips of history: Martin Luther King, Jr and the Coca-Cola Co, 15 January. Available from http://neatpour.com/2018/01/sips-of-history-martin-luther-king-jr-the-coca-cola-co.

Rucker, P and Freed, D (2016) Senators push Wells Fargo CEO on pay clawbacks after bogus accounts, Reuters, 20 September. Available from www.reuters.com/article/us-wells-fargo-accounts-ceo-idUSKCN11Q08U.

Ryan, L (2016) Should companies comment on politics? The Cut, 10 November. Available from www.thecut.com/2016/11/why-some-people-are-burning-their-new-balance-sneakers.html.

Wood, B (2019) *Double Crossed: A code of honour, a complete betrayal*, Virgin Books.

INDEX